EP Math
Algebra 1
Workbook
Answers

Easy Peasy

All-in-One
Homeschool

ISBN: 9798399284361

Note that the worked-out solutions do not restate the problems but rather show the subsequent steps.

LESSON 1

1. $3 \times 3 \times 3 \times 3 = 81$

2. $(-10) \times (-10) \times (-10) = -1000$

3. $5 - 32 + 2 = -27 + 2 = -25$

4. $24 \div 6 - 2 + 7 = 4 - 2 + 7 = 2 + 7 = 9$

5. $15 - 8 \times 5 = 15 - 40 = -25$

6. $3 \times 1 - 2 + 7 = 3 - 2 + 7 = 1 + 7 = 8$

7. $1^4 - 6 \times 1^6 = 1 - 6 \times 1 = 1 - 6 = -5$

8. $5 + 2^5 \div 8 \times (-2)^2 - 3 = 5 + 32 \div 8 \times 4 - 3$
$= 5 + 4 \times 4 - 3 = 5 + 16 - 3 = 21 - 3 = 18$

9. $1 \times 1 \times 1 \times 1 \times 1 \times 1 \times 1 \times 1 = 1$

10. $(-2) \times (-2) \times (-2) \times (-2) \times (-2) = -32$

11. $-(3 \times 3 \times 3) = -27$ 12. $(-9) \times (-9) = 81$

13. $4 + 2 = 6$ 14. $4 \times 2 = 8$

15. $-34 + 15 = -19$ 16. $4 \times 11 = 44$

17. $9 + 6 \times (-7) = 9 - 42 = -33$

18. $8^2 \div (-4)^2 = 64 \div 16 = 4$

19. $9 + 5 \times 1^5 = 9 + 5 \times 1 = 9 + 5 = 14$

20. $4 \div 2^2 \times (-2)^4 = 4 \div 4 \times 16 = 1 \times 16 = 16$

21. $30 - 64 \div 32 - 25 = 30 - 2 - 25 = 28 - 25 = 3$

22. $4 + 3^3 \div 9 \times (-1)^2 = 4 + 27 \div 9 \times 1$
$= 4 + 3 \times 1 = 4 + 3 = 7$

23. $9 + (3 \times 8 - 8 \div 2) - 4^2 = 9 + (24 - 4) - 4^2$
$= 9 + 20 - 4^2 = 9 + 20 - 16 = 29 - 16 = 13$

24. $36 \div (36 - 7 \times 5)^4 + 7 = 36 \div (36 - 35)^4 + 7$
$= 36 \div 1^4 + 7 = 36 \div 1 + 7 = 36 + 7 = 43$

25. $\dfrac{(-4) \times 7 + 3}{9 - 16 \div 4} = \dfrac{-28 + 3}{9 - 4} = \dfrac{-25}{5} = -5$

26. $\dfrac{5 - 4^2 \div 8 \times (-2)^3}{(9 - 7) \times 2 + (-3)^1} = \dfrac{5 - 16 \div 8 \times (-8)}{2 \times 2 + (-3)^1}$

$= \dfrac{5 - 2 \times (-8)}{2 \times 2 + (-3)} = \dfrac{5 - (-16)}{4 - 3} = \dfrac{21}{1} = 21$

LESSON 2

1. $3^2 - 6 \cdot 3 + 9 = 9 - 18 + 9 = 0$

2. $3^3 + 3^2 - 9 \cdot 3 - 5 = 27 + 9 - 27 - 5 = 4$

3. $(5x^2 - 4x^2) + (2x - x) + (3 + 1) = x^2 + x + 4$

4. $9x - 6 + 2x + 8 - 4x$
$= (9x + 2x - 4x) + (-6 + 8) = 7x + 2$

5. $2x - 4y + 5y - 10x$
$= (2x - 10x) + (-4y + 5y) = -8x + y$

6. $2.9g$ 7. Pages read $= 22d$
Pages left $= 168 - 22d$

8. $2 \cdot 4 + 3 = 11$ 9. $(-3) \cdot 8 + 8 = -16$

10. $\dfrac{-3 \cdot 4}{8} = -\dfrac{3}{2}$ 11. $\dfrac{-(-3)}{4^2 - 1} = \dfrac{1}{5}$

12 $(2x + 4x - x) + (4 - 6) = 5x - 2$

13. $4x + 6 + 3x - 15 = (4x + 3x) + (6 - 15) = 7x - 9$

14. $10x + 2 - 7 - 7x = (10x - 7x) + (2 - 7) = 3x - 5$

15. $6x + 12 - 6x + 3 = (6x - 6x) + (12 + 3) = 15$

16. $5x - 4y - 3 + 4y - 4x$
$= (5x - 4x) + (-4y + 4y) - 3 = x - 3$

17. $8x^2 - 14x + 7x - 3x^2$
$= (8x^2 - 3x^2) + (-14x + 7x) = 5x^2 - 7x$

18. $10/p$ 19. $68h$

20. Total cost $= 2.7b$
Change $= 20 - 2.7b$

LESSON 3

1. Subtract 8 from both sides: $x = 1$

2. Add 7 to both sides: $x = 13$

3. Divide both sides by –4: $x = -3$

4. Multiply both sides by 2. $x = 10$

5. Subtract 3 from both sides: $4x = 8$
Divide both sides by 4: $x = 2$

6. Add 8 to both sides: $3x = 21$
Divide both sides by 3: $x = 7$

7. Add 7 to both sides: $-2x = 12$
Divide both sides by –2: $x = -6$

8. Add 2 to both sides.   9. Divide both sides by –9.

10. Subtract 7 from both sides, then divide both sides by 3.   11. Add 4 to both sides, then multiply both sides by 5.

12. Subtract 9 from both sides: $x = 6$

13. Divide both sides by 7: $x = 9$

14. Subtract 7 from both sides: $4x = 4$
Divide both sides by 4: $x = 1$

15. Switch sides: $6x - 2 = -14$
Add 2 to both sides: $6x = -12$
Divide both sides by 6: $x = -2$

16. Subtract 6 from both sides: $-5x = 15$
    Divide both sides by −5: $x = -3$

17. Subtract 34 from both sides: $4x = -24$
    Divide both sides by 4: $x = -6$

18. Multiply both sides by 5: $x = -30$

19. Multiply both sides by 6: $x = 4$

20. Subtract 7 from both sides: $\frac{1}{3}x = -7$
    Multiply both sides by 3: $x = -21$

21. Subtract 15 from both sides: $-\frac{1}{2}x = -4$
    Multiply both sides by −2: $x = 8$

22. Divide both sides by 5: $x = -9$

23. Add 8 to both sides: $x = 24$

24. Subtract 30 from both sides: $6x = -54$
    Divide both sides by 6: $x = -9$

25. Add 14 to both sides: $8x = 88$
    Divide both sides by 8: $x = 11$

26. Add 16 to both sides: $7x = -49$
    Divide both sides by 7: $x = -7$

27. Subtract 19 from both sides: $-2x = 28$
    Divide both sides by −2: $x = -14$

28. Add 5 to both sides: $\frac{1}{9}x = 7$
    Multiply both sides by 9: $x = 63$

29. Add 8 to both sides: $\frac{1}{5}x = 5$
    Multiply both sides by 5: $x = 25$

LESSON 4

1. $6x + 3$

2. $8x - 1$

3. Subtract 2x from both sides: $2x - 8 = 0$
   Add 8 to both sides: $2x = 8$
   Divide both sides by 2: $x = 4$

4. Subtract x from both sides: $-3x = 6$
   Divide both sides by −3: $x = -2$

5. Add 9x to both sides: $16x - 9 = 7$
   Add 9 to both sides: $16x = 16$
   Divide both sides by 16: $x = 1$

6. Simplify each side: $6x - 4 = 2$
   Add 4 to both sides: $6x = 6$
   Divide both sides by 6: $x = 1$

7. Simplify each side: $6x + 5 = 5x - 15$
   Subtract 5x from both sides: $x + 5 = -15$
   Subtract 5 from both sides: $x = -20$

8. Simplify each side: $7x - 26 = 6 - x$
   Add x to both sides: $8x - 26 = 6$
   Add 26 to both sides: $8x = 32$
   Divide both sides by 8: $x = 4$

9. Simplify each side: $4x = 8x + 12$
   Subtract 8x from both sides: $-4x = 12$
   Divide both sides by −4: $x = -3$

10. $2x + 8 = 0$
    $2x = -8$
    $x = -4$

11. $-5x = 40$
    $x = -8$

12. $5x + 5 = 0$
    $5x = -5$
    $x = -1$

13. $7x - 9 = 6$
    $7x = 15$
    $x = 15/7$

14. $20 - 8x = -2$
    $-8x = -22$
    $x = 11/4$

15. $8x - 9 = 7$
    $8x = 16$
    $x = 2$

16. $14x - 53 = 17$
    $14x = 70$
    $x = 5$

17. $-2x + 20 = 7$
    $-2x = -13$
    $x = 13/2$

18. $4x - 12 = 3x + 5$
    $x - 12 = 5$
    $x = 17$

19. $5x = 2 - 2x$
    $7x = 2$
    $x = 2/7$

20. $x - 6 = -x + 6$
    $2x - 6 = 6$
    $2x = 12$
    $x = 6$

21. $6x + 19 = 9x + 18$
    $-3x + 19 = 18$
    $-3x = -1$
    $x = 1/3$

22. $-3x + 8 = -16$
    $-3x = -24$
    $x = 8$

23. $10x - 12 = 8$
    $10x = 20$
    $x = 2$

24. $3x - 8 = -29$
    $3x = -21$
    $x = -7$

25. $-6x + 5 = -13$
    $-6x = -18$
    $x = 3$

26. $9x + 32 = 11$
    $9x = -21$
    $x = -7/3$

27. $18 - 9x = -36$
    $-9x = -54$
    $x = 6$

28. $7x + 4 = 2x - 11$
    $5x + 4 = -11$
    $5x = -15$
    $x = -3$

29. $6x + 9 = -2x - 15$
    $8x + 9 = -15$
    $8x = -24$
    $x = -3$

30. $5x - 5 = 8x + 2$
    $-3x - 5 = 2$
    $-3x = 7$
    $x = -7/3$

31. $-7x + 8 = 2x + 6$
    $-9x + 8 = 6$
    $-9x = -2$
    $x = 2/9$

32. $-\dfrac{1}{3}x + 5 = -2$

$-\dfrac{1}{3}x = -7$

$x = 21$

33. $\dfrac{1}{2}x - \dfrac{1}{4} = \dfrac{1}{4}$

$\dfrac{1}{2}x = \dfrac{1}{2}$

$x = 1$

34. $\dfrac{3}{4} + 4x = 2x + \dfrac{1}{2}$

$\dfrac{3}{4} + 2x = \dfrac{1}{2}$

$2x = -\dfrac{1}{4}$

$x = -1/8$

35. $\dfrac{5}{2}x - \dfrac{1}{5} = \dfrac{1}{2}x + \dfrac{6}{5}$

$2x - \dfrac{1}{5} = \dfrac{6}{5}$

$2x = \dfrac{7}{5}$

$x = 7/10$

LESSON 5 ·······································

1. Multiply both sides by 10: $3x + 5 = 8$
Subtract 5 from both sides: $3x = 3$
Divide both sides by 3: $x = 1$

2. Multiply both sides by 100: $20x - 1 = 4$
Add 1 to both sides: $20x = 5$
Divide both sides by 20: $x = 1/4$

3. Multiply both sides by 100: $140 - 6x = 110$
Subtract 140 from both sides: $-6x = -30$
Divide both sides by –6: $x = 5$

4. Multiply both sides by 4: $3x - 1 = 2$
Add 1 to both sides: $3x = 3$
Divide both sides by 3: $x = 1$

5. Multiply both sides by 12: $10 + 3x = 15x$
Subtract $15x$ from both sides: $10 - 12x = 0$
Subtract 10 from both sides: $-12x = -10$
Divide both sides by –12: $x = 5/6$

6. Multiply both sides by 10: $2x + 7 = x + 6$
Subtract x from both sides: $x + 7 = 6$
Subtract 7 from both sides: $x = -1$

7. Multiply by 10.
$20x + 73 = 59$
$20x = -14$
$x = -7/10$

8. Multiply by 10.
$34 - 14x = -78$
$-14x = -112$
$x = 8$

9. Multiply by 100.
$600x - 61 = 70(2 - x)$
$600x - 61 = 140 - 70x$
$\quad\rightarrow\quad$ $670x - 61 = 140$
$670x = 201$
$x = 3/10$

10. Multiply by 100.
$3x + 15 = -2x - 50$
$5x + 15 = -50$
$\quad\rightarrow\quad$ $5x = -65$
$x = -13$

11. Multiply by 10.
$8x - 5(x + 3) = 2x$
$3x - 15 = 2x$
$\quad\rightarrow\quad$ $x - 15 = 0$
$x = 15$

12. Multiply by 10.
$12(x - 1) = 15(x + 3) - 3$
$12x - 12 = 15x + 42$
$\quad\rightarrow\quad$ $-3x - 12 = 42$
$-3x = 54$
$x = -18$

13. Multiply by 5.
$x + 3 = 10$
$x = 7$

14. Multiply by 8.
$3x + 2 = -4$
$3x = -6$
$x = -2$

15. Multiply by 15.
$9x + 10 = 12$
$9x = 2$
$x = 2/9$

16. Multiply by 12.
$9x + 10 = 15$
$9x = 5$
$x = 5/9$

17. Multiply by 20.
$15 - 8x = -4$
$-8x = -19$
$x = 19/8$

18. Multiply by 10.
$7x + 4 = 5$
$7x = 1$
$x = 1/7$

19. Multiply by 12.
$8x + 3x - 12x = 12$
$-x = 12$
$x = -12$

20. Multiply by 4.
$4x = 2(6x + 1) - 3$
$4x = 12x - 1$
$-8x = -1$
$x = 1/8$

21. Multiply by 100.
$300x - 605 = 895$
$300x = 1500$
$x = 5$

22. Multiply by 100.
$-80x + 95 = 35$
$-80x = -60$
$x = 3/4$

23. Multiply by 10.
$21x - 47 = -57 + 16x$
$5x - 47 = -57$
$\quad\rightarrow\quad$ $5x = -10$
$x = -2$

24. Multiply by 100.
$550 - 200x = 10x + 424$
$550 - 210x = 424$
$\quad\rightarrow\quad$ $-210x = -126$
$x = 3/5$

25. Multiply by 6.
$4x + 5 = 12$
$4x = 7$
$x = 7/4$

26. Multiply by 10.
$x + 2 = 6$
$x = 4$

27. Multiply by 9.
$6 + 7x = -1$
$7x = -7$
$x = -1$

28. Multiply by 20.
$16x - 15 = -11$
$16x = 4$
$x = 1/4$

29. Multiply by 10.
$6x - 5 = 6 - 5x$
$11x - 5 = 6$
$11x = 11$
$x = 1$

30. Multiply by 12.
$3(3x - 1) - 8x = 4$
$x - 3 = 4$
$x = 7$

LESSON 6

1. $5x = 5$ or $5x = -5$
$x = 1$ or $x = -1$

2. $x + 5 = 9$ or
$x + 5 = -9$
$x = 4$ or $x = -14$

3. $|x - 3| = 6$
$x - 3 = 6$ or
$x - 3 = -6$
$x = 9$ or $x = -3$

4. $|4 - 5x| = 4$
$4 - 5x = 4$ or
$4 - 5x = -4$
$-5x = 0$ or $-5x = -8$
$x = 0$ or $x = 8/5$

5. $5|x + 2| = 10$
$|x + 2| = 2$
$x + 2 = 2$ or
$x + 2 = -2$
$x = 0$ or $x = -4$

6. $3|3x + 4| = 15$
$|3x + 4| = 5$
$3x + 4 = 5$ or
$3x + 4 = -5$
$3x = 1$ or $3x = -9$
$x = 1/3$ or $x = -3$

7. $4x = 20$ or $4x = -20$
$x = 5$ or $x = -5$

8. $-x = 11$ or $-x = -11$
$x = -11$ or $x = 11$

9. $x + 4 = 6$ or
$x + 4 = -6$
$x = 2$ or $x = -10$

10. $|8 - x| = 2$
$8 - x = 2$ or
$8 - x = -2$
$x = 6$ or $x = 10$

11. $|6x| = 5$
$6x = 5$ or $6x = -5$
$x = 5/6$ or $x = -5/6$

12. $2|4x| = 4$
$|4x| = 2$
$4x = 2$ or $4x = -2$
$x = 1/2$ or $x = -1/2$

13. $9 - 3x = 12$ or
$9 - 3x = -12$
$-3x = 3$ or $-3x = -21$
$x = -1$ or $x = 7$

14. $2x + 4 = 6$ or
$2x + 4 = -6$
$2x = 2$ or $2x = -10$
$x = 1$ or $x = -5$

15. $|7x - 6| = 1$
$7x - 6 = 1$ or
$7x - 6 = -1$
$7x = 7$ or $7x = 5$
$x = 1$ or $x = 5/7$

16. $|1 - 5x| = 1$
$1 - 5x = 1$ or
$1 - 5x = -1$
$-5x = 0$ or $-5x = -2$
$x = 0$ or $x = 2/5$

17. $4|x + 4| = 4$
$|x + 4| = 1$
$x + 4 = 1$ or
$x + 4 = -1$
$x = -3$ or $x = -5$

18. $-|5x - 3| = -7$
$|5x - 3| = 7$
$5x - 3 = 7$ or
$5x - 3 = -7$
$5x = 10$ or $5x = -4$
$x = 2$ or $x = -4/5$

19. $|x - 7| = 24$
$x - 7 = 24$ or
$x - 7 = -24$
$x = 31$ or $x = -17$

20. $3|5x + 1| = 42$
$|5x + 1| = 14$
$5x + 1 = 14$ or
$5x + 1 = -14$
$5x = 13$ or $5x = -15$
$x = 13/5$ or $x = -3$

21. $9x = 27$ or $9x = -27$
$x = 3$ or $x = -3$

22. $-5x = 3$ or $-5x = -3$
$x = -3/5$ or $x = 3/5$

23. $x - 4 = 9$ or
$x - 4 = -9$
$x = 13$ or $x = -5$

24. $|x + 5| = 6$
$x + 5 = 6$ or
$x + 5 = -6$
$x = 1$ or $x = -11$

25. $|-4x| = 8$
$-4x = 8$ or $-4x = -8$
$x = -2$ or $x = 2$

26. $3|6x| = 18$
$|6x| = 6$
$6x = 6$ or $6x = -6$
$x = 1$ or $x = -1$

27. $-2x + 5 = 9$ or
$-2x + 5 = -9$
$-2x = 4$ or $-2x = -14$
$x = -2$ or $x = 7$

28. $8x + 3 = 3$ or
$8x + 3 = -3$
$8x = 0$ or $8x = -6$
$x = 0$ or $x = -3/4$

29. $|x + 6| = 3$
$x + 6 = 3$ or
$x + 6 = -3$
$x = -3$ or $x = -9$

30. $|2x - 5| = 7$
$2x - 5 = 7$ or
$2x - 5 = -7$
$2x = 12$ or $2x = -2$
$x = 6$ or $x = -1$

31. $-3|x + 2| = -12$
$|x + 2| = 4$
$x + 2 = 4$ or
$x + 2 = -4$
$x = 2$ or $x = -6$

32. $4|5 + 2x| = 4$
$|5 + 2x| = 1$
$5 + 2x = 1$ or
$5 + 2x = -1$
$2x = -4$ or $2x = -6$
$x = -2$ or $x = -3$

33. $|x + 9| = 35$
$x + 9 = 35$ or
$x + 9 = -35$
$x = 26$ or $x = -44$

34. $|x| + 8 = 14$
$|x| = 6$
$x = 6$ or $x = -6$

LESSON 7

1. See Lesson 3.

2. See Lesson 3.

3. See Lesson 4.

4. See Lesson 5.

5. See Lesson 5.

6. See Lesson 6.

7. $x = -12$

8. $x = 3/7$

9. $x = 40$

10. $x = -2/3$

11. $2x = -24$
$x = -12$

12. $5x = 80$
$x = 16$

13. $\dfrac{x}{8} = 2$
$x = 16$

14. $\dfrac{x}{5} = -5$
$x = -25$

15. $2x = -2x + 8$
$4x = 8$
$x = 2$

16. $-6x - 2 = 16$
$-6x = 18$
$x = -3$

17. $4 - 2x = -5x + 7$
$4 + 3x = 7$
$3x = 3$
$x = 1$

18. $7x - 5 = 17 - x$
$8x - 5 = 17$
$8x = 22$
$x = 11/4$

19. Multiply by 100.
$30x + 25 = 145$
$30x = 120$
$x = 4$

20. Multiply by 10.
$77 - 32x = 237$
$-32x = 160$
$x = -5$

21. Multiply by 20.
$12x - 5 = 10$
$12x = 15$
$x = 5/4$

22. Multiply by 12.
$10 - 9x = 16$
$-9x = 6$
$x = -2/3$

23. $4x = 12$ or
$4x = -12$
$x = 3$ or $x = -3$

24. $|4x + 2| = 2$
$4x + 2 = 2$ or
$4x + 2 = -2$
$4x = 0$ or $4x = -4$
$x = 0$ or $x = -1$

25. $3x = -12$
$x = -4$

26. $-7x = 49$
$x = -7$

27. $x - 7 = -x + 6$
$2x - 7 = 6$
$2x = 13$
$x = 13/2$

28. $6x + 8 = 9x - 25$
$-3x + 8 = -25$
$-3x = -33$
$x = 11$

29. Multiply by 100.
$320 - 60x = 374$
$-60x = 54$
$x = -9/10$

30. Multiply by 1000.
$8x + 27 = 75$
$8x = 48$
$x = 6$

31. Multiply by 21.
$14x - 15 = 27$
$14x = 42$
$x = 3$

32. Multiply by 6.
$4x + 15 = 3$
$4x = -12$
$x = -3$

33. Multiply by 8.
$16 - 6x = -5$
$-6x = -21$
$x = 7/2$

34. Multiply by 9.
$3(x - 2) + 4 = x + 6$
$3x - 2 = x + 6$
$2x - 2 = 6$
$2x = 8$
$x = 4$

35. $x + 9 = 8$ or
$x + 9 = -8$
$x = -1$ or $x = -17$

36. $-3|x| = -6$
$|x| = 2$
$x = 2$ or $x = -2$

37. $3x - 12 = 6$ or
$3x - 12 = -6$
$3x = 18$ or $3x = 6$
$x = 6$ or $x = 2$

38. $-5|2x - 6| = -10$
$|2x - 6| = 2$
$2x - 6 = 2$ or
$2x - 6 = -2$
$2x = 8$ or $2x = 4$
$x = 4$ or $x = 2$

LESSON 8

1. $x = -12$

2. $x = -3$

3. $x = 1$

4. $x = 0$ or $x = -1$

5. $0x = 5$
No solution

6. $x - 4 = 7x$
$-6x = 4$
One solution

7. $8 - 2x = -2x + 8$
$0x = 0$
Infinitely many solutions

8. $|2x + 5| = -2 < 0$
No solution

9. $2 - 5x = -5x + 2$
$0x = 0$
Infinitely many solutions

10. $3x + 1 = 6x$
$-3x = -1$
One solution

11. $|x - 3| = 8 > 0$
Two solutions

12. $5|3x + 2| = -5$
$|3x + 2| = -1 < 0$
No solution

13. $4x = 32$
$x = 8$

14. $15 - 6x = 15 - 6x$
$0x = 0$
Infinitely many solutions

15. $x + 11 = 51$
$x = 40$

16. $10x - 10 = 60$
$10x = 70$
$x = 7$

17. $-18x + 17 = 27$
$-18x = 10$
$x = -5/9$

18. $15 - 6x + 6x = -9$
$0x = -24$
No solution

19. $|3x| = 6$
$3x = 6$ or $3x = -6$
$x = 2$ or $x = -2$

20. $5|x| = -20$
$|x| = -4$
No solution

21. Multiply y 3.
$x - 15 = 2$
$x = 17$

22. Multiply by 5.
$2x + 15 = 2x + 15$
$0x = 0$
Infinitely many solutions

23. $7x - 42 = -7$
$7x = 35$
$x = 5$

24. $18x - 10 = -10$
$18x = 0$
$x = 0$

25. $4x + 9 = 4x + 9$
$0x = 0$
Infinitely many solutions

26. $4 + 3x = -7x + 5$
$10x = 1$
$x = 1/10$

27. $12x + 20 = 20 + 12x$
$0x = 0$
Infinitely many solutions

28. $1 + 5x = 5x + 8$
$0x = 7$
No solution

29. $-3|5 - x| = 9$
$|5 - x| = -3$
No solution

30. $2|x + 3| = 12$
$|x + 3| = 6$
$x + 3 = 6$ or $x + 3 = -6$
$x = 3$ or $x = -9$

31. Multiply by 15.

$9x - 5 = 4$

$9x = 9$

$x = 1$

32. Multiply by 4.

$4x + 3 = 8x + 1$

$-4x = -2$

$x = 1/2$

33. Multiply by 12.

$8x + 6 = 9x + 10$

$-x = 4$

$x = -4$

34. Multiply by 6.

$3(x - 3) + 2x = 5x$

$5x - 9 = 5x$

$0x = 9$

No solution

35. $\dfrac{|3x - 5|}{5} = 2$

$|3x - 5| = 10$

$3x - 5 = 10$ or

$3x - 5 = -10$

$x = 5$ or $x = -5/3$

36. $\dfrac{2}{5}|x + 4| = 2$

$2|x + 4| = 10$

$|x + 4| = 5$

$x + 4 = 5$ or $x + 4 = -5$

$x = 1$ or $x = -9$

37. Multiply by 7.

$6|2 - 7x| + 2 = 14$

$6|2 - 7x| = 12$

$|2 - 7x| = 2$

$2 - 7x = 2$ or

$2 - 7x = -2$

$x = 0$ or $x = 4/7$

38. Multiply by 10.

$3|5x - 7| + 8 = 2$

$3|5x - 7| = -6$

$|5x - 7| = -2 < 0$

No solution

LESSON 9

1. Let x = the first even integer

$x + 2$ = the second even integer

The sum is 26, so $x + (x + 2) = 26$.

Solve for x, and you get $x = 12$.

The numbers are 12 and 14.

2. Let x = the first odd integer

$x + 2$ = the second odd integer

The sum is 32, so $x + (x + 2) = 32$.

Solve for x, and you get $x = 15$.

The numbers are 15 and 17.

3. Let x = the first integer

$x + 1$ = the second integer

$x + 2$ = the third integer

The sum is 27, so $x + (x + 1) + (x + 2) = 27$.

Solve for x, and you get $x = 8$.

The numbers are 8, 9, and 10.

4. Let x = the regular price

$0.25x$ = the discount

The sale price = the regular price – the discount, so $x - 0.25x = 43.5$.

Solve for x, and you get $x = 58$.

The regular price was $58.

5. Let x = the regular price

$0.4x$ = the discount

The sale price = the regular price – the discount, so $x - 0.4x = 16.8$.

Solve for x, and you get $x = 28$.

The regular price was $28.

6. Let x = Nicole's age

$x + 5$ = Jamie's age

$x - 2$ = Nicole's age 2 years ago

$(x + 5) - 2$ = Jamie's age 2 years ago

Jamie's age 2 years ago = twice Nicol's age 2 years ago, so $(x + 5) - 2 = 2(x - 2)$.

Solve for x, and you get $x = 7$.

Nicole is 7 years old. Jamie is 12 years old.

7. Let x = Mia's age

$x - 6$ = Mia's age 6 years ago

$42 - 6$ = Mia's father's age 6 years ago

Mia's father's age 6 years ago = 6 times Mia's age 6 years ago, so $42 - 6 = 6(x - 6)$.

Solve for x, and you get $x = 12$.

Mia is 12 years old.

8. Let x = Max's age

$x - 10$ = Ellen's age

$x + 2$ = Max's age in 2 years

$(x - 10) + 2$ = Ellen's age in 2 years

Max's age in 2 years = twice Ellen's age in 2 years, so $x + 2 = 2(x - 10 + 2)$.

Solve for x, and you get $x = 18$.

Max is 18 years old. Ellen is 8 years old.

9. Let x = the width of the rectangle

$3x$ = the length of the rectangle

Perimeter = 2(length + width), so $2(x + 3x) = 40$.

Solve for x, and you get $x = 5$.

The rectangle is 5 feet by 15 feet.

10. Let x = the width of the rectangle

$3x - 5$ = the length of the rectangle

Perimeter = 2(length + width), so $2(x + 3x - 5) = 22$.

Solve for x, and you get $x = 4$.

The rectangle is 4 feet by 7 feet.

11. Let x = the number of nickels

$x + 5$ = the number of dimes

Total value = $(x + 5)$ dimes at $0.10 each + x nickels at $0.05 each, so $0.10(x + 5) + 0.05x = 0.95$.

Solve for x, and you get $x = 3$.

Emma has 8 dimes and 3 nickels.

12. Let x = the number of quarters

$x + 2$ = the number of nickels

Total value = x quarters at $0.25 each + ($x + 2$) nickels at $0.05 each, so $0.25x + 0.05(x + 2) = 1.60$.

Solve for x, and you get $x = 5$.

Joey has 5 quarters and 7 nickels.

13. Let x = the first integer

$2x - 5$ = the second integer

The sum is 25, so $x + (2x - 5) = 25$.

Solve for x, and you get $x = 10$.

The numbers are 10 and 15.

14. Let x = the first odd integer

$x + 2$ = the second odd integer

$x + 4$ = the third odd integer

The sum is 27, so $x + (x + 2) + (x + 4) = 27$.

Solve for x, and you get $x = 7$.

The numbers are 7, 9, and 11.

15. Let x = the previous price

$0.1x$ = the price decrease

The current price = the previous price – the price decrease, so $x - 0.1x = 108$.

Solve for x, and you get $x = 120$.

The previous price was $120.

16. Let x = Anna's age

$3x$ = Joey's age

$x + 5$ = Anna's age in 5 years

$3x + 5$ = Joey's age in 5 years

Joey's age in 5 years = twice Anna's age in 5 years, so $3x + 5 = 2(x + 5)$.

Solve for x, and you get $x = 5$.

Anna is 5 years old. Joey is 15 years old.

17. Let x = the length of the shortest side

$2x$ = the lengths of the other two sides

Perimeter = sum of three sides, so $x + 2x + 2x = 45$.

Solve for x, and you get $x = 9$.

The dimensions are 9, 18, and 18 inches.

18. Let x = the number of ones

$2x$ = the number of fives

$3x$ = the number of tens

Total value = x ones at $1 each + $2x$ fives at $5 each + $3x$ tens at $10 each, so $x + 5(2x) + 10(3x) = 82$.

Solve for x, and you get $x = 2$.

Max has 2 ones, 4 fives, and 6 tens.

LESSON 10

1. Let t = travel time in hours

$D = rt$, so $1600 = 320t$.

Solve for t, and you get $t = 5$.

It will take 5 hours.

2. Let r = speed of the train

$D = rt$, so $720 = r \times 4$.

Solve for r, and you get $r = 180$.

The average speed was 180 miles per hour.

3. Let t = time it will take for the two trains to meet

Total distance traveled in t hours = train 1's distance + train 2's distance, so $110t + 90t = 800$.

Solve for t, and you get $t = 4$.

It will take 4 hours.

4. Let t = time it will take to meet each other

Total distance traveled in t hours = the full circle = Brian's distance + Jamie's distance, so $5t + 7t = 6$.

Solve for t, and you get $t = 0.5$.

It will take 30 minutes.

5. Let r = speed of train 1

$r + 10$ = speed of train 2

Total distance traveled in 4 hours = train 1's distance + train 2's distance, so $4r + 4(r + 10) = 720$.

Solve for r, and you get $r = 85$.

One travels at 85 mph and the other at 95 mph.

6. Let r = speed of plane 1

$r + 150$ = speed of plane 2

Total distance traveled in 3 hours = plane 1's distance + plane 2's distance, so $3r + 3(r + 150) = 2250$.

Solve for r, and you get $r = 300$.

One travels at 300 mph and the other at 450 mph.

7. Let t = time taken to walk the circle the first time

$5 - t$ = time taken to walk the circle the second time

Distance walked the first time = distance walked the second time, so $6t = 4(5 - t)$.

Solve for t, and you get $t = 2$.

It took 2 hours to walk the circle at 6 mph, so the trail is $6 \times 2 = 12$ miles long.

8. Let t = time taken from home to the museum

$1.75 - t$ = time taken from the museum to home

Distance from home to the museum = distance from the museum to home, so $15t = 20(1.75 - t)$.

Solve for t, and you get $t = 1$.

It took 1 hour to ride to the museum at 15 mph, so Thomas lives $15 \times 1 = 15$ miles from the museum.

9. Let t = time it will take bus 2 to overtake bus 1

   $1 + t$ = time bus 1 will travel until bus 2 overtakes it

   Bus 2's distance in t hours = Bus 1's distance in $(1 + t)$ hours, so $70t = 60(1 + t)$.

   Solve for t, and you get $t = 6$.

   It will take 6 hours for bus 2 to overtake bus 1.

10. Let t = time it will take Carol to overtake Josh

    $0.5 + t$ = time Josh will walk until Carol overtakes him

    Carol's distance in t hours = Josh's distance in $(0.5 + t)$ hours, so $5t = 3(0.5 + t)$.

    Solve for t, and you get $t = 0.75$.

    It will take 0.75 hours, or 45 minutes.

11. Let t = travel time in hours

    $D = rt$, so $180 = 72t$.

    Solve for t, and you get $t = 2.5$.

    It will take 2.5 hours, or 2 hours 30 minutes.

12. Let t = time it will take for the two trains to meet

    Total distance traveled in t hours = train 1's distance + train 2's distance, so $85t + 75t = 880$.

    Solve for t, and you get $t = 5.5$.

    It will take 5.5 hours, or 5 hours 30 minutes.

13. Let r = speed of plane 1

    $r + 60$ = speed of plane 2

    Total distance traveled in 5 hours = plane 1's distance + plane 2's distance, so $5r + 5(r + 60) = 4300$.

    Solve for r, and you get $r = 400$.

    One travels at 400 mph and the other at 460 mph.

14. Let t = time taken from home to work

    $1.4 - t$ = time taken from work to home

    Distance from home to work = distance from work to home, so $60t = 45(1.4 - t)$.

    Solve for t, and you get $t = 0.6$.

    It took 0.6 hour to drive from home to work at 60 mph, so Sandra lives $60 \times 0.6 = 36$ miles from work.

15. Let t = time it takes train 2 to overtake train 1

    $2 + t$ = time train 1 will travel until train 2 overtakes it

    Train 2's distance in t hours = Train 1's distance in $(2 + t)$ hours, so $150t = 100(2 + t)$.

    Solve for t, and you get $t = 4$.

    It will take 4 hours.

LESSON 11 ·

1. Substance = salt = 8 g

   Solution = salt + water = 8 + 17 = 25 g

   Concentration = substance/solution = 8/25 = 0.32

   You get a 32% saline solution.

2. Amount of salt = 40% of 45 ounces = $0.4 \times 45 = 18$

   There are 18 ounces of salt in the solution.

3. Let w = amount of water to mix

   Substance = salt = 15 g

   Solution = salt + water = $15 + w$ g

   Concentration = 30% = 0.3

   Concentration × solution = substance, so $0.3(15 + w) = 15$.

   Solve for w, and you get $w = 35$.

   You need to mix 35 g of water.

4. Let w = amount of water to mix

   Substance = acid = 2 milliliters

   Solution = acid + water = $2 + w$ milliliters

   Concentration = 4% = 0.04

   Concentration × solution = substance, so $0.04(2 + w) = 2$.

   Solve for w, and you get $w = 48$.

   You need to mix 48 milliliters of water.

5. Salt in 10% solution = $0.1 \times 9 = 0.9$ g

   Salt in 15% solution = $0.15 \times 6 = 0.9$ g

   Salt in the mixture = $0.9 + 0.9 = 1.8$ g

   Amount of the mixture = 9 + 6 = 15 g

   Concentration of the mixture = 1.8/15 = 0.12

   The mixture is a 12% solution.

6. Salt in 15% solution = $0.15 \times 12 = 1.8$ g

   Salt in 25% solution = $0.25 \times 18 = 4.5$ g

   Salt in the mixture = $1.8 + 4.5 = 6.3$ g

   Amount of the mixture = 12 + 18 = 30 g

   Concentration of the mixture = 6.3/30 = 0.21

   The mixture is a 21% solution.

7. Alcohol in water = 0 liters

   Alcohol in 12% solution = $0.12 \times 30 = 3.6$ liters

   Alcohol in the mixture = 0 + 3.6 = 3.6 liters

   Amount of the mixture = 15 + 30 = 45 liters

   Concentration of the mixture = 3.6/45 = 0.08

   The mixture is an 8% solution.

8. Let x = ounces of 25% solution

   $x + 15$ = ounces of 20% solution

   Acid in 25% solution + acid in 10% solution = acid in 20% solution, so $0.25x + 0.1 \times 15 = 0.2(x + 15)$.

   Solve for x, and you get $x = 30$.

   We need to add 30 ounces of 25% solution.

9. Let x = liters of water

$x + 12$ = liters of 18% solution

Salt in 30% solution = salt in 18% solution, so $0.3 \times 12 = 0.18(x + 12)$.

Solve for x, and you get $x = 8$.

We need to add 8 liters of water.

10. Cost of candy 1 = 6 lbs × $4.50/lb = $27

Cost of candy 2 = 4 lbs × $6.50/lb = $26

Cost of the mixture = 27 + 26 = $53

Amount of the mixture = 6 + 4 = 10 lbs

Unit price = cost/quantity = 53/10 = 5.3.

The mixture costs $5.30 per pound.

11. Let x = pounds of coffee A

$x + 3$ = pounds of the mixture

Cost of coffee A + cost of coffee B = cost of the mixture, so so $9x + 12 \times 3 = 10(x + 3)$.

Solve for x, and you get $x = 6$.

We need to mix 6 pounds of coffee A.

12. Amount of salt = 40% of 50 grams = $0.4 \times 50 = 20$

There are 20 grams of salt in the solution.

13. Let w = amount of water to mix

Substance = salt = 15 ounces

Solution = salt + water = $15 + w$ ounces

Concentration = 30% = 0.3

Concentration × solution = substance, so $0.3(15 + w) = 15$.

Solve for w, and you get $w = 35$.

You need to mix 35 ounces of water.

14. Let x = amount of alcohol to add

Substance = alcohol = x liters

Solution = alcohol + water = $x + 60$ liters

Concentration = 25% = 0.25

Concentration × solution = substance, so $0.25(x + 60) = x$.

Solve for x, and you get $x = 20$.

You need to add 20 liters of alcohol.

15. Let c = concentration of the mixture

Hydrogen chloride in 10% solution = $0.1 \times 5 = 0.5$ cups

Hydrogen chloride in 30% solution = $0.3 \times 15 = 4.5$ cups

Hydrogen chloride in the mixture = 0.5 + 4.5 = 5 cups

Amount of the mixture = 5 + 15 = 20 cups

Concentration = substance/solution, so $c = 5/20 = 0.25$.

The mixture is a 25% solution.

16. Let x = liters of 60% solution

$x + 30$ = liters of 50% solution

Alcohol in 60% solution + alcohol in 20% solution = alcohol in 50% solution, so $0.6x + 0.2 \times 30 = 0.5(x + 30)$.

Solve for x, and you get $x = 90$.

We need to add 90 liters of 60% solution.

17. Let x = unit price of the mixture

Cost of candy 1 = 6 lbs × $5/lb = $30

Cost of candy 2 = 9 lbs × $4/lb = $36

Cost of the mixture = 30 + 36 = $66

Amount of the mixture = 6 + 9 = 15 lbs

Unit price = cost/quantity, so $x = 66/15 = 4.40$.

The mixture costs $4.40 per pound.

18. Let x = pounds of peanuts

$x + 5$ = pounds of the mixture

Cost of peanuts + cost of almonds = cost of the mixture, so $3x + 8 \times 5 = 5(x + 5)$.

Solve for x, and you get $x = 7.5$.

We need to mix 7.5 pounds of peanuts.

LESSON 12

1. Add 4 to both sides.

2. Divide both sides by −3.

3. Subtract 5 from both sides, then divide both sides by 2.

4. Add 3 to both sides, then multiply both sides by 4.

OR multiply both sides by 4, then add 12 to both sides.

5. Add 7 to both sides: $\qquad y = -x + 7$

6. Subtract x from both sides: $\quad -4y = 8x$

Divide both sides by −4: $\qquad y = -2x$

7. Switch sides: $\qquad\qquad -6x + 5y = 4x + 5$

Add $6x$ to both sides: $\qquad 5y = 10x + 5$

Divide both sides by 5: $\qquad y = 2x + 1$

8. Switch sides: $\qquad\qquad rt = D$

Divide both sides by r: $\qquad t = \dfrac{D}{r}$

$D = 165$ and $r = 55$: $\qquad t = \dfrac{165}{55} = 3$

9. Switch sides: $\qquad\qquad 2l + 2w = P$

Subtract $2w$ from both sides: $\quad 2l = P - 2w$

Divide both sides by 2: $\qquad l = \dfrac{P - 2w}{2}$

$P = 60$ and $w = 12$: $\qquad l = \dfrac{60 - 2 \cdot 12}{2} = 18$

10. $-3y = 15x$
$y = -5x$

11. $-y = -6x - 7$
$y = 6x + 7$

12. $y - 2 = -4x + 3$
$y = -4x + 5$

13. $3y - 7 = 9x + 5$
$3y = 9x + 12$
$y = 3x + 4$

14. Switch sides: $\qquad\qquad lw = A$

Divide both sides by l: $\qquad w = \dfrac{A}{l}$

$A = 90$ and $l = 15$: $\qquad w = \dfrac{90}{15} = 6$

15. Switch sides: $\qquad\qquad 2\pi r = C$

Divide both sides by 2π: $\qquad r = \dfrac{C}{2\pi}$

$C = 31.4$: $\qquad r = \dfrac{31.4}{2 \cdot 3.14} = 5$

16. Switch sides: $\qquad\qquad \dfrac{1}{2}bh = A$

Multiply both sides by 2: $\qquad bh = 2A$

Divide both sides by b: $\qquad h = \dfrac{2A}{b}$

$A = 24$ and $b = 6$: $\qquad h = \dfrac{2 \cdot 24}{6} = 8$

17. Switch sides: $\qquad\qquad \pi r^2 h = V$

Divide both sides by πr^2: $\qquad h = \dfrac{V}{\pi r^2}$

$V = 785$ and $r = 5$: $\qquad h = \dfrac{785}{3.14 \cdot 5^2} = 10$

18. Switch sides: $\qquad\qquad 2\pi rh + 2\pi r^2 = SA$
Subtract $2\pi r^2$ from both sides: $2\pi rh = SA - 2\pi r^2$

Divide both sides by $2\pi r$: $\qquad h = \dfrac{SA - 2\pi r^2}{2\pi r}$

$SA = 942$ and $r = 10$: $\qquad h = \dfrac{942 - 2\pi \cdot 10^2}{2\pi \cdot 10} = 5$

19. Switch sides: $\qquad\qquad \dfrac{9}{5}C + 32 = F$

Subtract 32 from both sides: $\qquad \dfrac{9}{5}C = F - 32$

Multiply both sides by 5/9: $\qquad C = \dfrac{5}{9}(F - 32)$

$F = 50$: $\qquad C = \dfrac{5}{9}(50 - 32) = 10$

20. Switch sides: $\qquad\qquad Prt = I$

Divide both sides by Pr: $\qquad t = \dfrac{I}{Pr}$

$P = 1200$, $I = 360$, $r = 0.06$: $\qquad t = \dfrac{360}{1200 \cdot 0.06} = 5$

21. Multiply by 5.
$4x - 2y = -5$
$-2y = -4x - 5$
$y = 2x + \dfrac{5}{2}$

22. Multiply by 6.
$3x + 4y = 3y$
$4y = -3x + 3y$
$y = -3x$

23. Multiply by 5.
$y - 5 + 5x = 10x + 4$
$y - 5 = 5x + 4$
$y = 5x + 9$

24. Multiply by 9.
$4x + 3y = 3x + 2y$
$3y = -x + 2y$
$y = -x$

LESSON 13

1. 20   **2.** 9   **3.** -13 **4.** 2

5. $x - 4$

6. $-22x + 44$

7. $x = -7$

8. $x = -4$

9. $x = 5$

10. $x = 1/2$

11. $x = -7$

12. $x = 3$

13. $x = -1$

14. $x = -3$

15. $x = 4$

16. $x = -8$

17. $x = -3/4$

18. $x = -2$

19. $x = 1/2$ or $x = -1/2$

20. $x = 2$ or $x = -2$

21. $x = 7$ or $x = 3$

22. $x = 4$ or $x = 3$

23. No solution

24. Infinitely many solutions

25. 5, 6, and 7

26. 280 miles

27. 20 liters

28. $h = \dfrac{3V}{\pi r^2} = \dfrac{3 \cdot 157}{\pi \cdot 5^2} = 6$

29. 0.3

30. $2 \times 3 \times 3 \times 3$

31. GCF = 8

32. LCM = 48

33. Quadrant 4

LESSON 14

1. Solution

2. Not a solution

3. Solution
$2 + 2(1) = 4$ is true.

4. $-2 + 2y = 4$
$y = 3$

5.

x	y
-2	3
0	1
3	-2

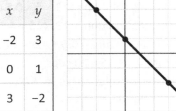

6. $-6 = -3(2)$ is true, so it is a solution.

7. $4 + 4(-3) = -8$ is true, so it is a solution.

8. $y = -3 + 5 = 2$

9. $3 - 2y = 7$
$y = -2$

10. $4 = x - 2$
$x = 6$

11. $5x - 3(-3) = 9$
$x = 0$

12.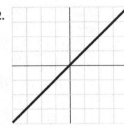

13.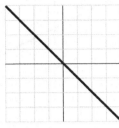

14.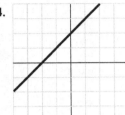

15.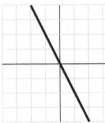

16.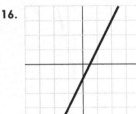

17.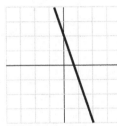

18.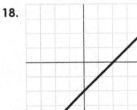

19.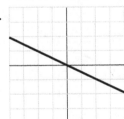

20.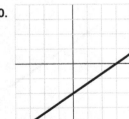

LESSON 15

1. Undefined

2. Positive

3. Negative

4. Zero

5. You can use any two points on the line.
Rise = 2 and run = 1, so slope = 2/1 = 2.

You could say that rise = –2, run = –1, and slope = (–2)/(–1) = 2.

6. (2, 4) and (–3, 1)
$$\frac{1 - 4}{-3 - 2} = \frac{3}{5}$$

7. (–1, –2) and (1, 2)
$$\frac{2 - (-2)}{1 - (-1)} = 2$$

8. (0, 1) and (3, 0)
$$\frac{0 - 1}{3 - 0} = -\frac{1}{3}$$

9. (1, 0) and (3, 3)
$$\frac{3 - 0}{3 - 1} = \frac{3}{2}$$

10. (–1, 3) and (3, –1)
$$\frac{-1 - 3}{3 - (-1)} = -1$$

11. (–2, –1) and (–1, 2)
$$\frac{2 - (-1)}{-1 - (-2)} = 3$$

12. (0, –1) and (2, 0)
$$\frac{0 - (-1)}{2 - 0} = \frac{1}{2}$$

13. (–2, 2) and (3, –2)
$$\frac{-2 - 2}{3 - (-2)} = -\frac{4}{5}$$

14. (0, –2) and (2, 2)
$$\frac{2 - (-2)}{2 - 0} = 2$$

15. (–1, 1) and (2, –1)
$$\frac{-1 - 1}{2 - (-1)} = -\frac{2}{3}$$

16. $\dfrac{8 - 5}{3 - 0} = 1$

17. $\dfrac{3 - 2}{-1 - 4} = -\dfrac{1}{5}$

18. $\dfrac{-5 - 7}{2 - (-1)} = -4$

19. $\dfrac{4 - 6}{2 - 3} = 2$

20. $\dfrac{4 - 4}{-2 - 1} = 0$

21. $\dfrac{7 - (-3)}{6 - 4} = 5$

LESSON 16

1. See the second example in Lesson 16.

2. Slope = 2

3. (0, 1)

4. $m = 5, b = -4$

5. $m = 0, b = 6$

6. $m = 2$, y-int = –1

7. $m = -1$, y-int = 2

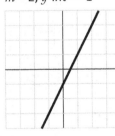

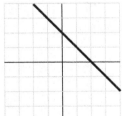

8. $m = 1$, y-int = 2

9. $m = -1$, y-int = 3

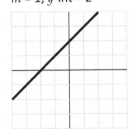

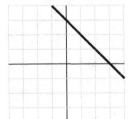

10. $m = 2$, y-int $= -3$

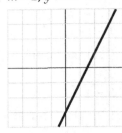

11. $m = -1$, y-int $= -1$

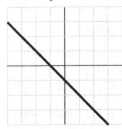

12. $m = -2$, y-int $= 2$

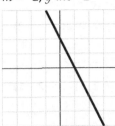

13. $m = 4$, y-int $= 0$

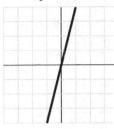

14. $m = 1$, y-int $= -3$

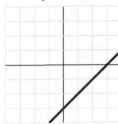

15. $m = -1/2$, y-int $= 1$

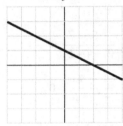

16. $m = 1/4$, y-int $= -1$

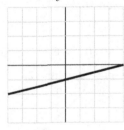

17. $m = 3/4$, y-int $= -1$

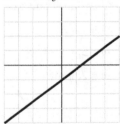

18. $m = -2/3$, y-int $= -2$

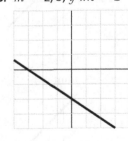

19. $m = 1/2$, y-int $= 3$

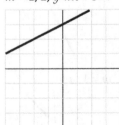

LESSON 17

1. See the second example in Lesson 17.

2. (3, 0)

3. Quadrants 1, 2, and 4

4. $y = 3x - 2$

5. $y = -\dfrac{1}{2}x + 2$

6. $2y = -x + 2$

$y = -\dfrac{1}{2}x + 1$

7. $3y = -4x + 6$

$y = -\dfrac{4}{3}x + 2$

8.

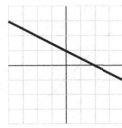

See Problem 6.
Slope: $-1/2$
y-intercept: 1
1st point: (0, 1)
2nd point: $(-4, 3)$, $(-2, 2)$,
   $(2, 0)$, or $(4, -1)$

9. $y = -x + 4$

10. $y = -5x - 4$

11. $4y = -x + 8$

$y = -\dfrac{1}{4}x + 2$

12. $-5y = -2x + 10$

$y = \dfrac{2}{5}x - 2$

13. $m = -1$, y-int $= 2$

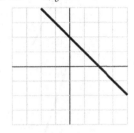

14. $m = 4$, y-int $= -4$

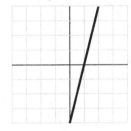

15. $m = 1/2$, y-int $= 0$

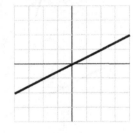

16. $m = 3$, y-int $= 3$

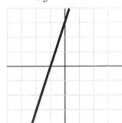

17. $m = -1/4$, y-int $= 2$

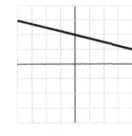

18. $m = -2/3$, y-int $= 1$

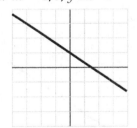

19. $m = 5/3$, y-int $= -2$

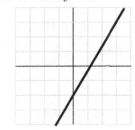

20. $m = -2$, y-int $= -1$

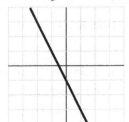

21. $m = -1/3$, y-int $= -2$

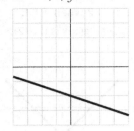

LESSON 18

1. Slope $m = -4/3$, y-intercept $= 4$

2. See the second example in Lesson 18.

3. The line crosses the x-axis at $(3, 0)$.

4. $x - 0 = -4$
   $x = -4$

   $0 - y = -4$
   $y = 4$

   x-int $= -4$, y-int $= 4$

5. $2x + 3(0) = 6$
   $x = 3$

   $2(0) + 3y = 6$
   $y = 2$

   x-int $= 3$, y-int $= 2$

6.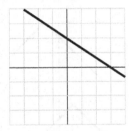

   See Problem 5.
   x-intercept: 3
   y-intercept: 2
   Two points: $(3, 0)$ and $(0, 2)$

7. $x - 4(0) = 8$
   $x = 8$

   $0 - 4y = 8$
   $y = -2$

   x-int $= 8$, y-int $= -2$

8. $5x + 3(0) = -15$
   $x = -3$

   $5(0) + 3y = -15$
   $y = -5$

   x-int $= -3$, y-int $= -5$

9. x-int $= -2$, y-int $= 2$

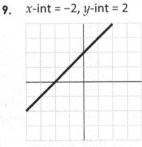

10. x-int $= 2$, y-int $= -1$

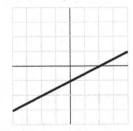

11. x-int $= 1$, y-int $= 3$

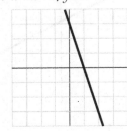

12. x-int $= -3$, y-int $= 2$

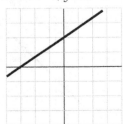

13. x-int $= -3$, y-int $= -3$

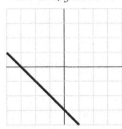

14. x-int $= -1$, y-int $= 4$

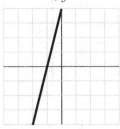

15. x-int $= -1$, y-int $= 1$

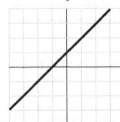

16. x-int $= 3$, y-int $= -4$

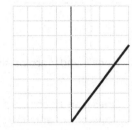

17. x-int $= -3$, y-int $= 1$

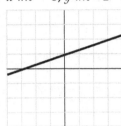

18. x-int $= 1$, y-int $= 2$

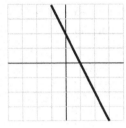

19. x-int $= -4$, y-int $= -1$

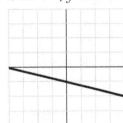

20. x-int $= 2$, y-int $= 3$

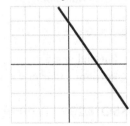

LESSON 19

1. $m = 0$

2. $m = undefined$

3. $y = -x - 2$; $m = -1$

4. $y = -\frac{1}{2}x$; $m = -\frac{1}{2}$

5. $y = \frac{5}{3}x - 2$; $m = \frac{5}{3}$

6. $y = -\frac{3}{4}x - 1$; $m = -\frac{3}{4}$

7.

8.

9. $y = x$
   $y = -x + 5$
   Perpendicular

10. $y = 2x + 1$
    $y = 2x - 3$
    Parallel

11.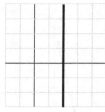

12.

13.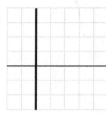

14.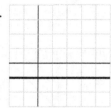

15. Lines b and d are parallel because they both have a slope of −2

16. Lines a and c are perpendicular because line a has a slope of 2/3 and line c has a slope of −3/2.

17. $y = -x + 5$
$y = -x + 3$
Parallel

18. $y = -3x + 1$
$y = \frac{1}{3}x - 3$
Perpendicular

19. $y = \frac{2}{3}x - 3$
$y = -\frac{3}{2}x + 4$
Perpendicular

20. $y = -\frac{2}{5}x + 2$
$y = -\frac{5}{2}x - 5$
Neither

21. $y = 5x - 1$
Parallel $m = 5$
Perpendicular $m = -1/5$

22. $y = \frac{4}{3}x - 1$
Parallel $m = 4/3$
Perpendicular $m = -3/4$

LESSON 20

1. See the graphs in the next section.

2. (0, 1)

3. (2, 0)

4. $x = 3$ makes $|x - 3| = 0$.
$y = -1$ when $x = 3$.
The vertex is (3, −1).

5.

Vertex: (3, −1)

Left-side point:
(2, 0), (1, 1), (0, 2), (−1, 3), ...

Right-side point:
(4, 0), (5, 1), (6, 2), ...

6. $x = 0$ makes $|x| = 0$.
$y = 0$ when $x = 0$.
The vertex is (0, 0).

7. $x = 0$ makes $|x| = 0$.
$y = 3$ when $x = 0$.
The vertex is (0, 3).

8. $x = -2$ makes $|x + 2| = 0$.
$y = 0$ when $x = -2$.
The vertex is (−2, 0).

9. $x = -1$ makes $|x + 1| = 0$.
$y = 0$ when $x = -1$.
The vertex is (−1, 0).

10. $x = 1$ makes $|x - 1| = 0$.
$y = 3$ when $x = 1$.
The vertex is (1, 3).

11. $x = 3$ makes $|x - 3| = 0$.
$y = -2$ when $x = 3$.
The vertex is (3, −2).

12.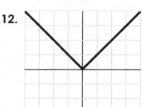

13.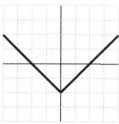

14.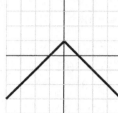

15.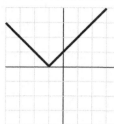

16.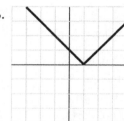

17.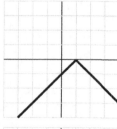

18.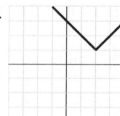

19.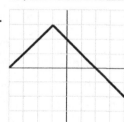

20.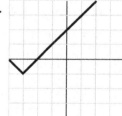

LESSON 21

1. (−1, −3), (0, −2), (3, 1)

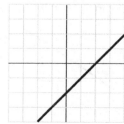

2. (−2, 3), (0, 2), (4, 0)

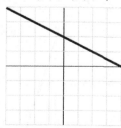

3. 1/5

4. −1

5. $m = 1$, y-int = -1

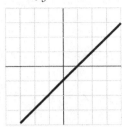

6. $m = 2$, y-int = 3

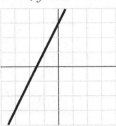

7. $m = -1/2$, y-int = 1

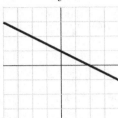

8. $m = -1/3$, y-int = 2

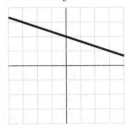

9. x-int = -1, y-int = 2

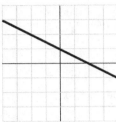

10. x-int = 3, y-int = 4

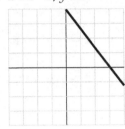

11. Vertex $(2, 0)$

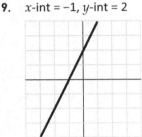

12. Vertex $(-1, -3)$

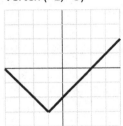

13. Perpendicular

14. Parallel

15. Neither

16. Perpendicular

17. 5

18. 4.52

19. 0.096

20. 1.8

21. $-1/6$

22. 2/3

LESSON 22

1–2. See the first and second examples in Lesson 16.

3. $m = 1/2$

4. $m = -1$

5. $(0, -1)$, $(2, 0)$, ...
$m = 1/2$, y-int = -1
$y = \dfrac{1}{2}x - 1$

6. $(0, 3)$, $(3, 0)$, ...
$m = -1$, y-int = 3
$y = -x + 3$

7. $(0, -3)$, $(1, -1)$, ...
$m = 2$, y-int = -3
$y = 2x - 3$

8. $(0, 1)$, $(2, 0)$, ...
$m = -1/2$, y-int = 1
$y = -\dfrac{1}{2}x + 1$

9. $(0, -1)$, $(4, 2)$, ...
$m = 3/4$, y-int = -1
$y = \dfrac{3}{4}x - 1$

10. $(0, -1)$, $(-1, 0)$, ...
$m = -1$, y-int = -1
$y = -x - 1$

11. $(0, 0)$, $(1, 4)$, ...
$m = 4$, y-int = 0
$y = 4x$

12. $(0, 2)$, $(1, 0)$, ...
$m = -2$, y-int = 2
$y = -2x + 2$

13. $(0, -2)$, $(3, 0)$, ...
$m = 2/3$, y-int = -2
$y = \dfrac{2}{3}x - 2$

14. $(0, -2)$, $(3, 3)$, ...
$m = 5/3$, y-int = -2
$y = \dfrac{5}{3}x - 2$

15. $(0, -1)$, $(1, -3)$, ...
$m = -2$, y-int = -1
$y = -2x - 1$

16. $(0, -3)$, $(3, 0)$, ...
$m = 1$, y-int = -3
$y = x - 3$

17. $(0, 0)$, $(2, -1)$, ...
$m = -1/2$, y-int = 0
$y = -\dfrac{1}{2}x$

18. $(0, 2)$, $(-2, 0)$, ...
$m = 1$, y-int = 2
$y = x + 2$

19. $(0, -2)$, $(-3, 0)$, ...
$m = -2/3$, y-int = -2
$y = -\dfrac{2}{3}x - 2$

20. $(0, -1)$, $(4, 0)$, ...
$m = 1/4$, y-int = -1
$y = \dfrac{1}{4}x - 1$

LESSON 23

1. See the first example in Lesson 22.

2. Parallel $m = 2$, perpendicular $m = -1/2$

3. $m = \dfrac{-3 - 7}{-2 - 3} = 2$
$7 = 2(3) + b$
$b = 1$
$y = 2x + 1$

4. $m = \dfrac{-4 - (-1)}{7 - 4} = -1$
$-1 = -1(4) + b$
$b = 3$
$y = -x + 3$

5. $-2 = 1(6) + b$
$b = -8$
$y = x - 8$

6. $-3 = -5(1) + b$
$b = 2$
$y = -5x + 2$

7. Given $m = -1/4$
Parallel $m = -1/4$
$0 = -\dfrac{1}{4}(8) + b$
$b = 2$
$y = -\dfrac{1}{4}x + 2$

8. Given $m = 3/2$
Perpendicular $m = -2/3$
$3 = -\dfrac{2}{3}(3) + b$
$b = 5$
$y = -\dfrac{2}{3}x + 5$

9. $8 = 5(1) + b$

$b = 3$

$y = 5x + 3$

10. $-5 = \frac{1}{2}(8) + b$

$b = -9$

$y = \frac{1}{2}x - 9$

11. $m = \frac{8 - 5}{2 - 1} = 3$

$5 = 3(1) + b$

$b = 2$

$y = 3x + 2$

12. $m = \frac{-2 - (-2)}{9 - 5} = 0$

$-2 = 0(5) + b$

$b = -2$

$y = -2$

13. $m = \frac{3 - (-9)}{1 - (-2)} = 4$

$3 = 4(1) + b$

$b = -1$

$y = 4x - 1$

14. $m = \frac{17 - (-4)}{8 - (-6)} = \frac{3}{2}$

$17 = \frac{3}{2}(8) + b$

$b = 5$

$y = \frac{3}{2}x + 5$

15. Given $m = 3$
Parallel $m = 3$
$4 = 3(-1) + b$
$b = 7$
$y = 3x + 7$

16. Given $m = 1$
Perpendicular $m = -1$
$8 = -1(2) + b$
$b = 10$
$y = -x + 10$

17. Given $m = 1/5$
Parallel $m = 1/5$
$-1 = \frac{1}{5}(5) + b$
$b = -2$
$y = \frac{1}{5}x - 2$

18. Given $m = -3$
Perpendicular $m = 1/3$
$0 = \frac{1}{3}(9) + b$
$b = -3$
$y = \frac{1}{3}x - 3$

19. $4 = 0(-1) + b$
$b = 4$
$y = 4$

20. $9 = -2(-3) + b$
$b = 3$
$y = -2x + 3$

21. $m = \frac{7 - (-1)}{3 - 1} = 4$

$-1 = 4(1) + b$
$b = -5$
$y = 4x - 5$

22. $m = \frac{-3 - 2}{-1 - 0} = 5$

$2 = 5(0) + b$
$b = 2$
$y = 5x + 2$

23. $m = \frac{5 - 2}{-4 - 2} = -\frac{1}{2}$

$2 = -\frac{1}{2}(2) + b$

$b = 3$

$y = -\frac{1}{2}x + 3$

24. $m = \frac{-4 - (-4)}{3 - 7} = 0$

$-4 = 0(7) + b$

$b = -4$

$y = -4$

LESSON 24

1. $y = -x + 3$

2. $y = 4x - 3$

3. $y = \frac{2}{3}x + 1$

4. $y = 2x + 5$

5. $y - 7 = -2(x + 2)$

$y = -2x + 3$

6. $y - 2 = \frac{3}{4}(x - 4)$

$y = \frac{3}{4}x - 1$

7. $m = \frac{8 - 3}{6 - 1} = 1$

$y - 3 = x - 1$

$y = x + 2$

8. $m = \frac{10 - 4}{4 - 2} = 3$

$y - 4 = 3(x - 2)$

$y = 3x - 2$

9. Use any points to find the slope: $m = -1$.
The marked point is $(1, -2)$.
$y - (-2) = -(x - 1)$

10. $m = 3/2$; $(2, 1)$

$y - 1 = \frac{3}{2}(x - 2)$

11. $m = -1/2$; $(-2, 2)$

$y - 2 = -\frac{1}{2}(x + 2)$

12. $y - 5 = 2(x - 1)$

$y = 2x + 3$

13. $y + 1 = \frac{2}{5}(x - 10)$

$y = \frac{2}{5}x - 5$

14. $m = \frac{3 - 9}{-1 - 2} = 2$

$y - 9 = 2(x - 2)$

$y = 2x + 5$

15. $m = \frac{-5 - (-1)}{-3 - 9} = \frac{1}{3}$

$y + 1 = \frac{1}{3}(x - 9)$

$y = \frac{1}{3}x - 4$

16. Given $m = -1$
Parallel $m = -1$
$y - 2 = -(x - 6)$
$y = -x + 8$

17. Given $m = -1/6$
Perpendicular $m = 6$
$y - 1 = 6(x + 1)$
$y = 6x + 7$

18. $y + 2 = 4(x - 3)$

$y = 4x - 14$

19. $y - 1 = \frac{1}{4}(x + 2)$

$y = \frac{1}{4}x + \frac{3}{2}$

20. $m = \frac{-4 - 5}{2 - (-1)} = -3$

$y - 5 = -3(x + 1)$

$y = -3x + 2$

21. $m = \frac{7 - (-2)}{4 - (-2)} = \frac{3}{2}$

$y + 2 = \frac{3}{2}(x + 2)$

$y = \frac{3}{2}x + 1$

LESSON 25

1. $y - 1 = 4(x - 3)$

2. $y + 5 = -(x - 2)$

3. $y - 4 = \frac{1}{2}(x + 5)$

4. $y - 6 = 2(x - 3)$

5. $2x + y = 4$

6. $2y = x + 6$
$-x + 2y = 6$
$x - 2y = -6$

7. $6y = -x + 6$
$y = -\frac{1}{6}x + 1$

8. $y - 4 = \frac{2}{3}x - 4$
$y = \frac{2}{3}x$

9. $4x + y = 3$

10. $5y = 3x + 10$
$-3x + 5y = 10$
$3x - 5y = -10$

11. $y - 2 = 4(x + 1)$
$y = 4x + 6$
$4x - y = -6$

12. $y + 3 = -3(x - 4)$
$y = -3x + 9$
$3x + y = 9$

13. $m = \frac{3 - (-1)}{5 - (-3)} = \frac{1}{2}$
$y + 1 = \frac{1}{2}(x + 3)$
$y = \frac{1}{2}x + \frac{1}{2}$
$x - 2y = -1$

14. $m = \frac{2 - 8}{-6 - 3} = \frac{2}{3}$
$y - 8 = \frac{2}{3}(x - 3)$
$y = \frac{2}{3}x + 6$
$2x - 3y = -18$

15. Given $m = -1$
Parallel $m = -1$
$y - 0 = -(x - 2)$
$y = -x + 2$
$x + y = 2$

16. Given $m = -1/4$
Perpendicular $m = 4$
$y - 5 = 4(x - 2)$
$y = 4x - 3$
$4x - y = 3$

17. $y + 3 = -5x + 5$
$5x + y = 2$

18. $2y + 16 = x + 6$
$-x + 2y = -10$
$x - 2y = 10$

19. $y + 2 = -\frac{1}{3}(x - 6)$
$y = -\frac{1}{3}x$
$x + 3y = 0$

20. $y - 1 = \frac{3}{4}(x + 8)$
$y = \frac{3}{4}x + 7$
$3x - 4y = -28$

21. $m = \frac{-2 - 6}{1 - 0} = -8$
$y - 6 = -8(x - 0)$
$y = -8x + 6$
$8x + y = 6$

22. $m = \frac{-5 - 7}{1 - 5} = 3$
$y - 7 = 3(x - 5)$
$y = 3x - 8$
$3x - y = 8$

23. Given $m = 4/7$
Parallel $m = 4/7$
$y + 1 = \frac{4}{7}(x + 1)$
$y = \frac{4}{7}x - \frac{3}{7}$
$4x - 7y = 3$

24. Given $m = -5/3$
Perpendicular $m = 3/5$
$y - 2 = \frac{3}{5}(x - 4)$
$y = \frac{3}{5}x - \frac{2}{5}$
$3x - 5y = 2$

LESSON 26

1. $y = -3$

2. $y = 8$

3. $x = 7$

4. $x = 3$

5. Slope $m = 2$
y-intercept $= 1$

6. Slope $m = 5$
y-intercept $= -4$

7. a. $m = 38$ and $b = 40$, so $y = 38x + 40$.
b. When $x = 3$, $y = 154$. It will cost $154.
c. When $y = 116$, $x = 2$. It took 2 hours.

8. a. $m = 9$ and $b = 15$, so $y = 9x + 15$.
b. When $x = 3$, $y = 42$. It will cost $42.
c. When $y = 78$, $x = 7$. You can rent a bike for 7 hours.

9. a. $m = 1.5$ and $b = 8$, so $y = 1.5x + 8$.
b. When $x = 20$, $y = 38$. It will cost $38.
c. When $y = 29$, $x = 14$. It traveled 14 miles.

10. a. $m = -9$ and $b = 360$, so $y = -9x + 360$.
b. When $x = 15$, $y = 225$. There will be 225 gallons.
c. When $y = 0$, $x = 40$. It will take 40 minutes.

11. a. $m = 2.5$ and $b = 7$, so $y = 2.5x + 7$.
b. When $x = 12$, $y = 37$. It will cost $37.
c. When $y = 62$, $x = 22$. You can order 22 magazines.

12. a. $m = -30$ and $b = 750$, so $y = -30x + 750$.
b. When $x = 6$, $y = 570$. It is 570 feet above sea level.
c. When $y = 0$, $x = 25$. It will take 25 hours.

13. a. $m = -1200$ and $b = 32000$, so $y = -1200x + 32000$.
b. When $x = 10$, $y = 20000$. It is 20,000 feet above ...
c. When $y = 26000$, $x = 5$. It will take 5 minutes.

14. a. $m = 6700 - 1200 = 5500$ and $b = 2800$,
so $y = 5500x + 2800$.
b. When $x = 3$, $y = 19300$. It will be $19,300.
c. Solve $5500x + 2800 = 50000$, and you get $x = 8.58...$
It will take 9 months.

LESSON 27

1. $y = 2$
2. $y = -6$
3. $x = 7$
4. $x = 7$
5. $2x + y = 4$
6. $4x - y = -2$

7. a. $3x$ = points form multiple-choice questions
   $5y$ = points from short-answer questions
   Total points = 100, so $3x + 5y = 100$.
   b. When $x = 20$, $y = 8$. There are 8 5-point questions.

8. a. $6.8x$ = cost of beef
   $4.4x$ = cost of pork
   Total cost = 56, so $6.8x + 4.4y = 56$.
   b. When $y = 5$, $x = 5$. She can buy 5 pounds of beef.

9. a. $0.1x$ = amount from dimes
   $0.05y$ = amount from nickels
   Total amount = 1.80, so $0.1x + 0.05y = 1.80$.
   b. When $x = 15$, $y = 6$. She has 6 nickels.

10. a. $5x$ = amount from fives
    $10y$ = amount from tens
    Total amount = 80, so $5x + 10y = 80$.
    b. When $x = 8$, $y = 4$. She has 4 tens.

11. a. $2x$ = points form multiple-choice questions
    $5y$ = points from short-answer questions
    Total points = 100, so $2x + 5y = 100$.
    b. When $y = 6$, $x = 35$. There are 35 2-point questions.

12. a. $5x$ = cost of popcorn
    $4y$ = cost of sodas
    Total cost = 45, so $5x + 4y = 45$.
    b. When $x = 6.2$, $y = 3.5$. Sodas costs $3.50 each.

13. a. $20x$ = amount earned from selling muffins
    $46y$ = amount earned from selling cookies
    Total amount earned = 113, so $20x + 46y = 113$.
    b. When $y = 1.5$, $x = 2.2$. Muffins cost $2.20 each.

14. a. $7x$ = cost of adult tickets
    $5y$ = cost of child tickets
    Total cost = 81, so $7x + 5y = 81$.
    b. When $x = 8$, $y = 5$. Child tickets cost $5 each.

15. a. $4x$ = cost of flour
    $6.5y$ = cost of sugar
    Total cost = 55, so $4x + 6.5y = 55$.
    b. When $x = 4$, $y = 6$. He can buy 6 bags of sugar.

16. a. $4x$ = number of seats from 4-seat tables
    $8y$ = number of seats from 8-seat tables
    Total number of seats = 96, so $4x + 8y = 96$.
    b. When $y = 6$, $x = 12$. 12 tables seat 4 people.

LESSON 28

1. $y = -x + 2$
2. $y = 4x - 4$
3. $y = 2x + 4$
4. $y = 5x - 1$
5. $y = 3x - 3$
6. $y = -2x + 8$
7. $y - 0 = -(x - 3)$
8. $y - 4 = 2(x - 5)$
9. $y + 7 = 4(x + 2)$
10. $y + 8 = -5(x - 3)$
11. $5x - y = 6$
12. $4x - 5y = -35$
13. $x - 5y = -10$
14. $x + 2y = 12$

15. a. $y = 1.6x + 5$
    b. $29
    c. 25 miles
16. a. $y = 32x + 58$
    b. $218
    c. 12 months

17. a. $0.25x + 0.1y = 2.30$
    b. 8 dimes
18. a. $3x + 2y = 20$
    b. $3 per bag

19. $0.2 \cdot 80 = 16$
20. $40/100 = 2/5$

21. $17/50 = 0.34 = 34\%$
22. 100,000 centimeters

23. 100 cm: 3 ft = x cm: 1.2 ft
    About 40 cm

LESSON 29

1-2. See the second example in Lesson 29.

3. The graph is a vertical line passing through (2, 0).

4. It is a solution because it satisfies both the equations.

5.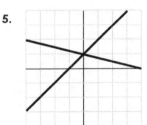
   Intersection: (0, 1)
   Solution: (0, 1)

6. $1 + 3(-1) = -2$
   $4(1) - (-1) = 5$
   Solution
7. $2 + 1 = 3$
   $2(2) - 1 \neq -3$
   Not a solution

8. Solution: (1, -1)
   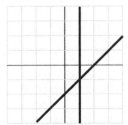
9. Solution: (0, 2)
   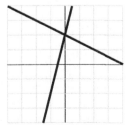

10. Solution: (–2, 0)

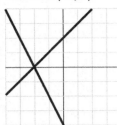

11. Solution: (3, 2)

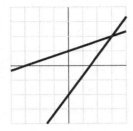

12. Solution: (–1, 1)

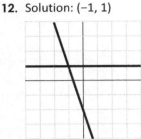

13. Solution: (0, –1)

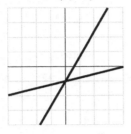

14. Solution: (3, –1)

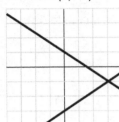

15. Solution: (–1, –1)

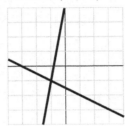

16. Solution: (3, –4)

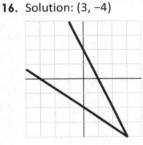

LESSON 30

1-3.

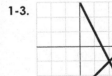

The lines intersect at (2, –1), so the solution to the system is (2, –1).

4. Solve eq1 for x: $x = -y + 3$

Plug eq1 into eq2: $2(-y + 3) + y = 6$

Solve eq2 to find y: $-y + 6 = 6$

                        $y = 0$

Use eq1 to find x: $x = -0 + 3 = 3$

Write the solution: Solution: (3, 0)

5. Solve eq2 for y: $y = 3x - 7$

Plug eq2 into eq1: $2x + 3(3x - 7) = 1$

Solve eq1 to find x: $11x - 21 = 1$

                        $x = 2$

Use eq2 to find y: $y = 3(2) - 7 = -1$

Write the solution: Solution: (2, –1)

6. $x = y + 4$

$(y + 4) + 3y = -8$

$4y + 4 = -8$

$y = -3$

$x = -3 + 4 = 1$

Solution: (1, –3)

7. $y = -4x - 3$

$-2x + (-4x - 3) = 9$

$-6x - 3 = 9$

$x = -2$

$y = -4(-2) - 3 = 5$

Solution: (–2, 5)

8. $y = -2$

$3x + 5(-2) = -7$

$3x - 10 = -7$

$x = 1$

Solution: (1, –2)

9. $3x + (x + 3) = 11$

$4x + 3 = 11$

$x = 2$

$y = 2 + 3 = 5$

Solution: (2, 5)

10. $x = -y + 5$

$(-y + 5) + 3y = 1$

$2y + 5 = 1$

$y = -2$

$x = -(-2) + 5 = 7$

Solution: (7, –2)

11. $x = -3y$

$2(-3y) - y = 7$

$-7y = 7$

$y = -1$

$x = -3(-1) = 3$

Solution: (3, –1)

12. $x = 2y - 2$

$(2y - 2) + 3y = 8$

$5y - 2 = 8$

$y = 2$

$x = 2(2) - 2 = 2$

Solution: (2, 2)

13. $y = -2x - 7$

$-2x + (-2x - 7) = 9$

$-4x - 7 = 9$

$x = -4$

$y = -2(-4) - 7 = 1$

Solution: (–4, 1)

14. $y = -3x + 4$

$5x + 2(-3x + 4) = 8$

$-x + 8 = 8$

$x = 0$

$y = -3(0) + 4 = 4$

Solution: (0, 4)

15. $x = 4y - 7$

$2(4y - 7) - 5y = -5$

$3y - 14 = -5$

$y = 3$

$x = 4(3) - 7 = 5$

Solution: (5, 3)

16. $x = 2y$

$3(2y) - 4y = 2$

$2y = 2$

$y = 1$

$x = 2(1) = 2$

Solution: (2, 1)

17. $x = 4$

$6(4) + 5y = 4$

$y = -4$

Solution: (4, –4)

18. $y = -5x - 4$

$7x + 8(-5x - 4) = 1$

$-33x - 32 = 1$

$x = -1$

$y = -5(-1) - 4 = 1$

Solution: (–1, 1)

19. $y = 2x + 10$

$4x + 5(2x + 10) = 8$

$14x + 50 = 8$

$x = -3$

$y = 2(-3) + 10 = 4$

Solution: (–3, 4)

20. $x = -3y + 4$
$4(-3y + 4) + 5y = -12$
$-7y + 16 = -12$
$y = 4$
$x = -3(4) + 4 = -8$
Solution: $(-8, 4)$

21. $y = -2x + 3$
$2x - 3(-2x + 3) = 31$
$8x - 9 = 31$
$x = 5$
$y = -2(5) + 3 = -7$
Solution: $(5, -7)$

22. $x = -2y$
$5(-2y) - 2y = 24$
$-12y = 24$
$y = -2$
$x = -2(-2) = 4$
Solution: $(4, -2)$

23. $y = 4x + 8$
$4x - 9(4x + 8) = 24$
$-32x - 72 = 24$
$x = -3$
$y = 4(-3) + 8 = -4$
Solution: $(-3, -4)$

24. $x = -4y + 14$
$7(-4y + 14) - 5y = 32$
$-33y + 98 = 32$
$y = 2$
$x = -4(2) + 14 = 6$
Solution: $(6, 2)$

25. $y = 3x + 9$
$-5x + 2(3x + 9) = 19$
$x + 18 = 19$
$x = 1$
$y = 3(1) + 9 = 12$
Solution: $(1, 12)$

26. $y = 9x + 5$
$3x - 4(9x + 5) = -20$
$-33x - 20 = -20$
$x = 0$
$y = 9(0) + 5 = 5$
Solution: $(0, 5)$

27. $x = 2y + 5$
$9(2y + 5) - 4y = -11$
$14y + 45 = -11$
$y = -4$
$x = 2(-4) + 5 = -3$
Solution: $(-3, -4)$

LESSON 31 ·······································

1. Solution: $(1, -2)$

2. Solution: $(-8, 7)$

3. Add eq1 to eq2: $6x = 12$
Solve for x: $x = 2$
Plug x into eq1: $2 + y = 5$
Solve for y: $y = 3$
Write the solution: Solution: $(2, 3)$

4. Subtract eq2 from eq1 × 3: $3x - 3y = -12$
$\underline{- (3x - 2y = -7)}$
$-y = -5$
Solve for y: $y = 5$
Plug y into eq1: $x - 5 = -4$
Solve for x: $x = 1$
Write the solution: Solution: $(1, 5)$

5. Multiply eq1 by 2: $8x - 6y = -4$
Multiply eq2 by 3: $\underline{+ (9x + 6y = 21)}$
Add the equations: $17x \quad\quad = 17$
Solve for x: $x = 1$
Plug x into eq1: $4(1) - 3y = -2$
Solve for y: $y = 2$
Write the solution: Solution: $(1, 2)$

6. eq1 + eq2
$9x = -9$
$x = -1$
$7(-1) + y = 0$
$y = 7$
Solution: $(-1, 7)$

7. eq1 + eq2
$5x = 5$
$x = 1$
$2(1) + y = 7$
$y = 5$
Solution: $(1, 5)$

8. eq1 + eq2
$-y = 2$
$y = -2$
$x - 4(-2) = 11$
$x = 3$
Solution: $(3, -2)$

9. eq1 − eq2
$-3y = 9$
$y = -3$
$x - (-3) = 7$
$x = 4$
Solution: $(4, -3)$

10. eq1 × 3 + eq2
$5x = 5$
$x = 1$
$1 - y = -1$
$y = 2$
Solution: $(1, 2)$

11. eq1 × 2 + eq2
$13x = 0$
$x = 0$
$5(0) + y = -4$
$y = -4$
Solution: $(0, -4)$

12. eq1 × 3 − eq2
$-2y = 0$
$y = 0$
$x + 0 = 3$
$x = 3$
Solution: $(3, 0)$

13. eq1 × 2 − eq2
$-3y = 6$
$y = -2$
$x + 3(-2) = -1$
$x = 5$
Solution: $(5, -2)$

14. eq1 × 3 − eq2 × 4
$-19x = 38$
$x = -2$
$3(-2) + 4y = 6$
$y = 3$
Solution: $(-2, 3)$

15. eq1 × 5 − eq2 × 6
$-y = -5$
$y = 5$
$6x - 5(5) = -7$
$x = 3$
Solution: $(3, 5)$

16. eq1 + eq2
$2y = -2$
$y = -1$
$2x + (-1) = 3$
$x = 2$
Solution: $(2, -1)$

17. eq1 × 3 − eq2
$11y = 22$
$y = 2$
$3x + 2(2) = 4$
$x = 0$
Solution: $(0, 2)$

18. eq1 − eq2
$y = -3$
$3x + (-3) = 9$
$x = 4$
Solution: $(4, -3)$

19. eq1 × 2 − eq2
$x = -1$
$3(-1) + 2y = 7$
$y = 5$
Solution: $(-1, 5)$

20. eq1 × 2 − eq2 × 3
$-11y = 11$
$y = -1$
$3x + 2(-1) = 7$
$x = 3$
Solution: $(3, -1)$

21. eq1 × 3 − eq2 × 2
$31y = -31$
$y = -1$
$2x + 9(-1) = 3$
$x = 6$
Solution: $(6, -1)$

LESSON 32 ···

1. See the second example in Lesson 29.

2. See the first example in Lesson 30.

3. See the first example in Lesson 31.

4. $1 + 3(1) = 4$
$8(1) - 3(1) = 5$
Solution

5. $3(3) + 2(-2) = 5$
$8(3) - 5(-2) \neq 14$
Not a solution

6. Solution: (0, –2)

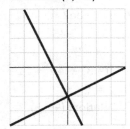

7. Solution: (2, 2)

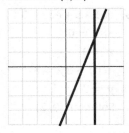

8. $y = -2x + 7$
$3x - 5(-2x + 7) = 4$
$13x - 35 = 4$
$x = 3$
$y = -2(3) + 7 = 1$
Solution: (3, 1)

9. $y = 5x - 3$
$3x + (5x - 3) = 13$
$8x - 3 = 13$
$x = 2$
$y = 5(2) - 3 = 7$
Solution: (2, 7)

10. eq1 + eq2
$7y = 28$
$y = 4$
$x + 3(4) = 16$
$x = 4$
Solution: (4, 4)

11. eq1 × 2 – eq2 × 3
$-7x = -35$
$x = 5$
$4(5) + 3y = -1$
$y = -7$
Solution: (5, –7)

12. eq1 × 2 – eq2
$7y = 28$
$y = 4$
$x + 2(4) = 10$
$x = 2$
Solution: (2, 4)

13. eq1 × 3 – eq2
$2x = 10$
$x = 5$
$2(5) + y = 7$
$y = -3$
Solution: (5, –3)

14. $y = x - 4$
$5x + 2(x - 4) = 6$
$7x - 8 = 6$
$x = 2$
$y = 2 - 4 = -2$
Solution: (2, –2)

15. eq1 × 2 – eq2
$-17y = 0$
$y = 0$
$2x - 7(0) = -4$
$x = -2$
Solution: (–2, 0)

16. eq1 × 2 – eq2
$13y = 26$
$y = 2$
$2x + 5(2) = 10$
$x = 0$
Solution: (0, 2)

17. eq1 + eq2 × 2
$11x = 66$
$x = 6$
$5(6) - 10y = 0$
$y = 3$
Solution: (6, 3)

18. eq1 × 4 – eq2 × 3
$y = 4$
$3x - 5(4) = -5$
$x = 5$
Solution: (5, 4)

19. $x = y + 8$
$3(y + 8) + 8y = -9$
$11y + 24 = -9$
$y = -3$
$x = -3 + 8 = 5$
Solution: (5, –3)

20. $x = -2y - 1$
$4(-2y - 1) + 9y = -9$
$y - 4 = -9$
$y = -5$
$x = -2(-5) - 1 = 9$
Solution: (9, –5)

21. eq1 + eq2
$7x = 28$
$x = 4$
$5(4) - y = 18$
$y = 2$
Solution: (4, 2)

22. eq1 – eq2
$-y = 5$
$y = -5$
$x + 2(-5) = -8$
$x = 2$
Solution: (2, –5)

23. eq1 × 2 – eq2
$9y = -18$
$y = -2$
$2x + 7(-2) = -4$
$x = 5$
Solution: (5, –2)

24. $y = 6x - 11$
$7x + 3(6x - 11) = -8$
$25x - 33 = -8$
$x = 1$
$y = 6(1) - 11 = -5$
Solution: (1, –5)

25. eq1 × 5 – eq2 × 4
$-3y = -12$
$y = 4$
$4x + 9(4) = -4$
$x = -10$
Solution: (–10, 4)

26. eq1 × 7 + eq2 × 3
$41x = 41$
$x = 1$
$5(1) - 3y = -4$
$y = 3$
Solution: (1, 3)

27. eq1 + eq2
$5x = 0$
$x = 0$
$3(0) + 5y = 30$
$y = 6$
Solution: (0, 6)

LESSON 33 ···

1. Solution: (2, 0)

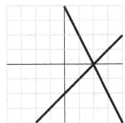

2. Solution: none

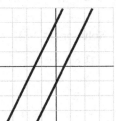

3. Solution: infinitely many

4. $m1 = 1/2, b1 = -1$
$m2 = 1/2, b2 = -5$
No solution

5. $m1 = 3$
$m2 = -1/3$
One solution

6. $m1 = -4/3, b1 = 2$
$m2 = -4/3, b2 = 2$
Infinitely many solutions

7. $m1 = -2/5, b1 = 1$
$m2 = -2/5, b2 = -1$
No solution

8. $y = x + 2$
$3x - (x + 2) = 2$
$2x - 2 = 2$
$x = 2$
$y = 2 + 2 = 4$
Solution: (2, 4)

9. $x = 2y + 9$
$-2(2y + 9) + 4y = 5$
$0y - 18 = 5$
$0y = 23$
No solution

10. eq1 + eq2 × 3
$13x = 26$
$x = 2$
$3(2) - y = 5$
$y = 1$
Solution: (2, 1)

11. eq1 - eq2
$4y = -12$
$y = -3$
$2x - (-3) = 7$
$x = 2$
Solution: (2, -3)

12. $x = 2y - 3$
$(2y - 3) - 2y = 5$
$0y - 3 = 5$
$0y = 8$
No solution

13. eq1 × 2 - eq2
$0y = 0$
Infinitely many solutions

14. eq1 × 4 + eq2
$7x = 7$
$x = 1$
$3(1) - y = -2$
$y = 5$
Solution: (1, 5)

15. eq1 + eq2 × 3
$14y = 42$
$y = 3$
$-x + 4(3) = 16$
$x = -4$
Solution: (-4, 3)

16. $x = y + 9$
$3(y + 9) - 2y = 22$
$y + 27 = 22$
$y = -5$
$x = -5 + 9 = 4$
Solution: (4, -5)

17. eq1 × 5 + eq2 × 2
$23x = 23$
$x = 1$
$3(1) + 2y = 1$
$y = -1$
Solution: (1, -1)

18. eq1 × 2 + eq2
$11y = 22$
$y = 2$
$-x + 4(2) = 9$
$x = -1$
Solution: (-1, 2)

19. eq1 + eq2
$5y = 10$
$y = 2$
$x + 3(2) = 9$
$x = 3$
Solution: (3, 2)

20. eq1 × 2 + eq2
$0 = 11$
No solution

21. $y = -4$
$3x - 2(-4) = 11$
$x = 1$
Solution: (1, -4)

22. eq1 × 2 - eq2
$17y = 0$
$y = 0$
$2x + 7(0) = -6$
$x = -3$
Solution: (-3, 0)

23. $y = 2x + 3$
$-5x + 3(2x + 3) = 11$
$x + 9 = 11$
$x = 2$
$y = 2(2) + 3 = 7$
Solution: (2, 7)

24. eq1 × 2 + eq2
$0 = -7$
No solution

25. eq1 × 3 + eq2
$0 = 13$
No solution

26. eq1 × 5 + eq2 × 3
$38x = 0$
$x = 0$
$4(0) + 3y = 6$
$y = 2$
Solution: (0, 2)

27. eq1 + eq2 × 2
$15x = -45$
$x = -3$
$3(-3) + 4y = 11$
$y = 5$
Solution: (-3, 5)

LESSON 34

1–5. See the examples in Lesson 9.

6. x = number of adults
y = number of children
A total of 10 tickets, so $x + y = 10$.
Total cost = 78, so $9x + 7y = 78$.
Solve the system, and you get $x = 4$ and $y = 6$.
There were 4 adults and 6 children in the group.

7. x = number of 4-point questions
y = number of 8-point questions
A total of 20 questions, so $x + y = 20$.
Total points = 100, so $4x + 8y = 100$.
Solve the system, and you get $x = 15$ and $y = 5$.
There are 15 4-point questions and 5 8-point questions.

8. x = larger integer, y = smaller integer
$3x + y = 3$, $x - 3y = 11$
$x = 2, y = -3$
The integers are 2 and -3.

9. x = number of dimes, y = number of nickels
$x + y = 17$, $0.1x + 0.05y = 1.3$
$x = 9, y = 8$
Max has 9 dimes and 8 nickels.

10. x = number of fives, y = number of tens
$x + y = 27$, $5x + 10y = 205$
$x = 13, y = 14$
Mr. Kim has 13 fives and 14 tens.

11. x = Mark's age, y = Dale's age
$x = y - 5$, $2(x - 5) = y - 5$
$x = 10, y = 15$
Mark is 10 years old. Dale is 15 years old.

12. x = price of an apple, y = price of a pear

$5x + 4y = 9.2$, $3x + 2y = 5$

$x = 0.8$, $y = 1.3$

Apples are \$0.80 each. Pears are \$1.30 each.

13. x = number of 2-point questions

y = number of 5-point questions

$x + y = 35$, $2x + 5y = 100$

$x = 25$, $y = 10$

There are 25 2-point questions and 10 5-point questions.

14. x = number of 4-seat tables

y = number of 6-seat tables

$x + y = 12$, $4x + 6y = 58$

$x = 7$, $y = 5$

Seven tables seat 4 people. Five tables seat 6 people.

15. x = what Leah paid, y = what Vicky paid

$x + y = 550$, $x = y + 70$

$x = 310$, $y = 240$

Leah paid \$310. Vicky paid \$240.

16. x = tens place digit, y = ones place digit

$x + y = 5$, $10x + y - 9 = 10y + x$

$x = 3$, $y = 2$

The number is 32.

17. x = number of nickels, y = number of quarters

$x = y + 5$, $0.05x + 0.25y = 2.65$

$x = 13$, $y = 8$

Lynn has 13 nickels and 8 quarters.

18. x = Joey's age, y = Anna's age

$x = 3y$, $x + 5 = 2(y + 5)$

$x = 15$, $y = 5$

Joey is 15 years old. Anna is 5 years old.

19. x = number of roses, y = number of lilies

$x + y = 24$, $2.2x + 1.8y = 48$

$x = 12$, $y = 12$

Josh used 12 roses and 12 lilies.

LESSON 35 ·······························

1–5. See the examples in Lesson 10.

6. x = time spent in bus 1

y = time spent in bus 2

Total travel time = 3.5 hours, so $x + y = 3.5$.

Distance traveled in bus 1 + distance traveled in bus 2 = 235, so $70x + 65y = 235$.

Solve the system, and you get $x = 1.5$ and $y = 2$.

Logan spent 1.5 hours in the first bus and 2 hours in the second bus.

7. x = speed of the plane in still air

y = speed of the wind

$x + y$ = speed of the plane flying with the wind

$x - y$ = speed of the plane flying against the wind

Distance with the wind = 1440, so $4(x + y) = 1440$.

Distance against the wind = 1440, $6(x - y) = 1440$.

Solve the system, and you get $x = 300$ and $y = 60$.

The speed of the airplane in still air would be 300 mph, and the speed of the wind was 60 mph.

8. x = time spent in the train, y = time spent in the car

$x + y = 5.5$, $67x + 120y = 554$

$x = 2$, $y = 3.5$

He spent 2 hours in the train and 3.5 hours in the car.

9. x = time spent in bus 1, y = time spent in bus 2

$x + y = 4$, $72x + 66y = 273$

$x = 1.5$, $y = 2.5$

Jessie traveled $72 \times 1.5 = 108$ miles in the first bus and $66 \times 2.5 = 165$ miles in the second bus.

10. x = speed of the plane in still air, y = speed of the wind

$7(x + y) = 2240$, $8(x - y) = 2240$

$x = 300$, $y = 20$

The speed of the airplane in still air would be 300 mph, and the speed of the wind was 20 mph.

11. x = speed of the boat in still water

y = speed of the current

$2(x + y) = 56$, $4(x - y) = 56$

$x = 21$, $y = 7$

The speed of the boat in still water would be 21 km/h, and the speed of the current was 7 km/h.

12. x = speed of train 1, y = speed of train 2

$y = x + 25$, $2x + 2y = 530$

$x = 120$, $y = 145$

One travels at 120mph and the other at 145mph.

13. x = speed of bus 1, y = speed of bus 2

$x = y + 20$, $2.5x = 3y$

$x = 120$, $y = 100$

Bus 1 took 2.5 hours at 120 km/h, so the distance between the two cities is $120 \times 2.5 = 300$ km.

LESSON 36

1–5. See the examples in Lesson 11.

6. x = amount of 10% solution
y = amount of 55% solution
Amount of the mixture = 30, so $x + y = 30$.
Alcohol in 10% solution + alcohol in 55% solution
= alcohol in the mixture, so $0.1x + 0.55y = 0.37 \times 30$.
Solve the system, and you get $x = 12$ and $y = 18$.
12 liters of the 10% solution and 18 liters of the 55% solution should be used.

7. x = amount of 42% solution
y = amount of 20% solution
Amount of the mixture = 22 so $x + y = 22$.
Acid in 42% solution + acid in 20% solution
= acid in the mixture, so $0.42x + 0.2y = 0.27 \times 22$.
Solve the system, and you get $x = 7$ and $y = 15$.
Seven ounces of the 42% solution and 15 ounces of the 20% solution should be used.

8. x = amount of chocolate
y = amount of nuts
Amount of the mixture = 8, so $x + y = 8$.
Cost of chocolate + cost of nuts
= cost of the mixture, so $5x + 3y = 4.50 \times 8$.
Solve the system, and you get $x = 6$ and $y = 2$.
Six pounds of chocolate and 2 pounds of nuts should be used.

9. x = amount of coffee A
y = amount of coffee B
Amount of the mixture = 20, so $x + y = 20$.
Cost of coffee A + cost of coffee B
= cost of the mixture, so $12x + 8y = 9.60 \times 20$.
Solve the system, and you get $x = 8$ and $y = 12$.
Eight pounds of coffee A and 12 pounds of coffee B should be mixed.

10. x = amount of 30% solution
y = amount of 50% solution
$x + y = 20$, $0.3x + 0.5y = 0.44 \times 20$
$x = 6$, $y = 14$
Six gallons of the 30% solution and 14 gallons of the 50% solution should be used.

11. x = amount of 50% solution
y = amount of 65% solution
$x + y = 24$, $0.5x + 0.65y = 0.6 \times 24$
$x = 8$, $y = 16$
Eight ounces of the 50% solution and 16 ounces of the 65% solution should be used.

12. x = amount of 10% juice, y = amount of 15% juice
$x + y = 15$, $0.1x + 0.15y = 0.13 \times 15$
$x = 6$, $y = 9$
Six cups of the 10% juice and 9 cups of the 15% juice should be mixed.

13. x = amount of 45% solution
y = amount of 80% solution
$x + y = 14$, $0.45x + 0.8y = 0.65 \times 14$
$x = 6$, $y = 8$
Six milliliters of the 45% solution and 8 milliliters of the 80% solution should be used.

14. x = amount of pretzels, y = amount of cereal
$x + y = 10$, $2.5x + 2y = 2.2 \times 10$
$x = 4$, $y = 6$
Four pounds of pretzels and 6 pounds of cereal should be used.

15. x = amount of white rice, y = amount of wild rice
$x + y = 5$, $1.1x + 2.4y = 1.88 \times 5$
$x = 2$, $y = 3$
Two pounds of white rice and 3 pounds of wild rice are in the bag.

16. x = amount of beef, y = amount of pork
$x + y = 25$, $6.9x + 4.9y = 142.50$
$x = 10$, $y = 15$
The cook used 10 pounds of ground beef and 15 pounds of ground pork.

LESSON 37

1. Solution

2. Not a solution

3. Solution: (–2, 2)

4. Solution: (3, 3)

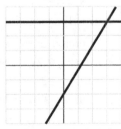

5. (9, 7)   **6.** (7, 1)   **7.** (2, 5)   **8.** (3, 5)

9. (1, 1)   **10.** (4, –2)   **11.** (6, 3)   **12.** (8, 6)

13. (5, 0)   **14.** Infinite   **15.** None   **16.** (1, –3)

17. (4, –6)   **18.** (–2, 4)

19. Muffins: $2.10 each
Cookies: $1.50 each

20. Boat: 30 mph
Current: 10 mph

21. 15% solution: 2 liters
60% solution: 8 liters

22. True

23. $9 + 8 = 17$

24. $-1000 + 3 = -997$

25. $\sqrt{(4 \cdot 7)} = 2\sqrt{7}$

26. $6^2 + 8^2 = x^2$
$x^2 = 100$, so $x = 10$.

LESSON 38

1. $2 < 5$

2. $-2 > -5$

3. $x = 2$

4. $x = -3$

5. $x = 5$

6. $x = -1$

7.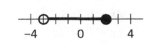

8.

9. $x < 3$

10. $-3x \leq -12$
$x \geq 4$

11.

12.

13. $-2x \leq -4$
$x \geq 2$

14. $5x + 17 < 17$
$5x < 0$
$x < 0$

15. $x > -24$

16. $x > -8$

17. $16x + 25 \leq -39$
$16x \leq -64$
$x \leq -4$

18. $18 - 3x < 45$
$-3x < 27$
$x > -9$

19. $-2x - 12 \geq -8$
$-2x \geq 4$
$x \leq -2$

20. $3x - 6 \leq 19 - 2x$
$5x \leq 25$
$x \leq 5$

21. Multiply both sides by 3.
$18 - x > 21$
$-x > 3$
$x < -3$

22. Multiply both sides by 4.
$20x - 3 < 1$
$20x < 4$
$x < 1/5$

23. Multiply both sides by 5.
$-10 + 4x \geq 3$
$4x \geq 13$
$x \geq 13/4$

24. Multiply both sides by 6.
$2x - 6x + 1 \leq -1$
$-4x + 1 \leq -1$
$-4x \leq -2$
$x \geq 1/2$

25. $2(9 + x) \leq 54$
$x \leq 18$
At most 18 cm

26. $0.25x > 2000$
$x > 8000$
More than $8,000

27. $(87 + 88 + x)/3 \geq 90$
$x \geq 95$
At least 95

1. $x \leq -6$

2. $x < 3$

3.

4.

5.

6. $-9 < 3x \leq 6$
$-3 < x \leq 2$

7. $5x > 10$ or $-2x < -10$
$x > 2$ or $x > 5$
$x > 2$

8.

9.

10.

11. $-28 \leq 4x < -16$
$-7 \leq x < -4$

12. $5x < 25$ or $3x > 21$
$x < 5$ or $x > 7$

13. $14 < x \leq 36$

14. $x < -15$ or $x > -6$

15. $-10 \leq -5x < 3$
$-\dfrac{3}{5} < x \leq 2$

16. $2x \leq -10$ or $4x \leq -12$
$x \leq -5$ or $x \leq -3$
$x \leq -3$

17. Multiply all sides by 12.
$-12 < 4x + 12 < 9$
$-24 < 4x < -3$
$-6 < x < -\dfrac{3}{4}$

18. $x - 4 < -4$ or
$1 - 4x \geq 5$
$x < 0$ or $x \leq -1$
$x < 0$

19 $-8 < 8x \leq 24$
$-1 < x \leq 3$

20. $x > 7$ and $3x < 15$
$x > 7$ and $x < 5$
No solution

21. $-11 \leq 3x - 14 < 10$
$3 \leq 3x < 24$
$1 \leq x < 8$

22. $7x < 0$ or $-6x < 6$
$x < 0$ or $x > -1$
True for all x

23. Multiply all sides by 4.
$-8 < x + 20 \leq 24$
$-28 < x \leq 4$

24. $x - 7 \leq -6$ and
$1 - 5x > 6$
$x \leq 1$ and $x < -1$
$x < -1$

LESSON 40

1. $x = 4$ or $x = 10$

2. $x = -1$ or $x = 2$

3.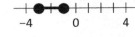

4.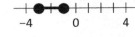

5.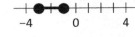

6. $3|x + 2| \le 3$
$|x + 2| \le 1$
$-1 \le x + 2 \le 1$
$-3 \le x \le -1$

7. $3|2x - 5| > 9$
$|2x - 5| > 3$
$2x - 5 < -3$ or
$2x - 5 > 3$
$2x < 2$ or $2x > 8$
$x < 1$ or $x > 4$

8.

9.

10.

11. $-2 < 4x - 3 < 2$
$1 < 4x < 5$
$\dfrac{1}{4} < x < \dfrac{5}{4}$

12. $|5 - 2x| \ge 2$
$5 - 2x \le -2$ or
$5 - 2x \ge 2$
$x \le \dfrac{3}{2}$ or $x \ge \dfrac{7}{2}$

13. $-20 < 5x < 20$
$-4 < x < 4$

14. $x + 4 \le -7$ or
$x + 4 \ge 7$
$x \le -11$ or $x \ge 3$

15. $|8 - x| > 4$
$8 - x < -4$ or
$8 - x > 4$
$x < 4$ or $x > 12$

16. $-12 < 9 - 3x < 12$
$-21 < -3x < 3$
$-1 < x < 7$

17. $|4x| \ge 2$
$4x \le -2$ or $4x \ge 2$
$x \le -\dfrac{1}{2}$ or $x \ge \dfrac{1}{2}$

18. $|7x - 6| \le -4$
No solution
An absolute value can never be negative.

19. Multiply both sides by 5.
$|x - 6| < 10$
$-10 < x - 6 < 10$
$-4 < x < 16$

20. Multiply both sides by 3.
$|x| + 12 > 6$
$|x| > -6$
True for all x

21. $|x + 4| > -4$
True for all x

22. $-2x + 8 < -20$ or
$-2x + 8 > 20$
$x < -6$ or $x > 14$

23. $|1 - 5x| \ge 1$
$1 - 5x \le -1$ or
$1 - 5x \ge 1$
$x \le 0$ or $x \ge \dfrac{2}{5}$

24. Multiply both sides by 5.
$2|2 - x| - 45 \ge -35$
$|2 - x| \ge 5$
$2 - x \le -5$ or
$2 - x \ge 5$
$x \le -3$ or $x \ge 7$

LESSON 41

1. See the second example in Lesson 16.

2. See the second example in Lesson 17.

3. $2(1) + 3(2) = 6$ is false, so it is not a solution.

4. $2 + 2(-3) \le 4$ is true, so it is a solution.

5. $y > x - 1$

6. $y \le -\dfrac{1}{2}x + 2$

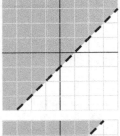

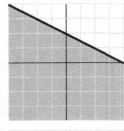

7.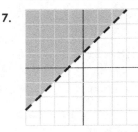

8.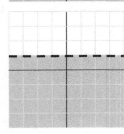

9.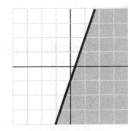

10.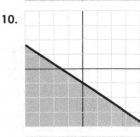

11.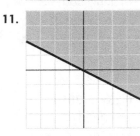

12.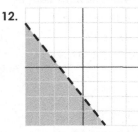

13.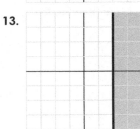

14.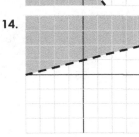

15.

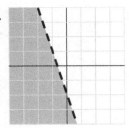

LESSON 42

1–2. See the first graph and second example in Lesson 41.

3. $2(1) - 3(2) > 3$ is false, so it is not a solution.

4.

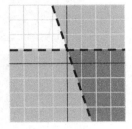

5. Not a solution

It does not satisfy the first equation.

6. Not a solution

It does not satisfy the second equation.

7.

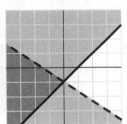

8.

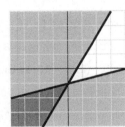

9.

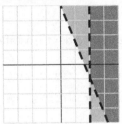

10.

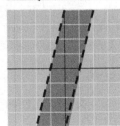

11.

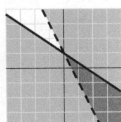

12.

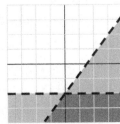

13.

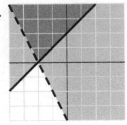

14.

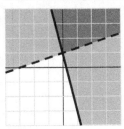

15.

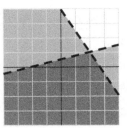

LESSON 43

1. $x \leq 1/5$

2. $x > -3$

3. $x \leq 15$

4. $x < -8$

5. $x \leq 15$

6. $x > -3/2$

7. $x \geq -2$

8. $-1 < x \leq 3$

9. $x > -1$

10. $x < 2$ or $x > 3$

11. $-12 < x \leq 12$

12. $x \leq 20$

13. $-7 < x < 3$

14. $-2 \leq x \leq 2$

15. $x < -1$ or $x > 2$

16. $x \leq 4$ or $x \geq 8$

17.

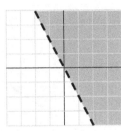

18.

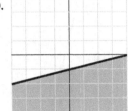

19.

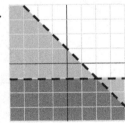

20.

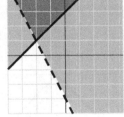

21.

22.

23. $\dfrac{1}{5^2} = \dfrac{1}{25}$

24. $x^{6-4-3} = x^{-1} = \dfrac{1}{x}$

25. $(x^{5-2})^3 = x^{3 \times 3} = x^9$

26. 1.25×10^{-6}

27. 2×10^{11}

LESSON 44

1. $1,000$

2. -11

3. $x = 2$

4. $x = 18$

5. $x = 9/10$

6. $x = -11$

7. $x = 8$ or $x = -10$

8. $x = 0$ or $x = 4$

9. $(3, -2)$

10. $(1, 1)$

11. $x \leq 3$

12. $x > 1$

13. $-2 < x \leq 3$

14. $x \geq -3$

15. $-7 \leq x \leq 1$

16. $x < 2/3$ or $x > 2$

17. 9, 10, 11

18. $25

19. 18 minutes

20. 3 hours

21. 5 liters

22. 2 pounds

23. Mike is 14 years old.
Jason is 5 years old.

24. Plane: 325 mph
Wind: 25 mph

25. 30% solution: 3 gallons
50% solution: 9 gallons

26. Coffee A: 4 pounds
Coffee B: 6 pounds

LESSON 45

1. $m = 3$

2. $m = 0$

3.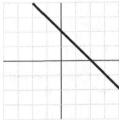

4.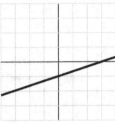

5.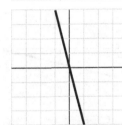

6.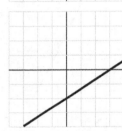

7.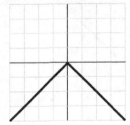

8.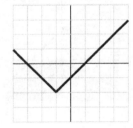

9. $y = 3x - 8$
$3x - y = 8$

10. $y = -\dfrac{1}{2}x - 3$
$x + 2y = -6$

11. $y = -x + 5$
$x + y = 5$

12. $y = 5x + 2$
$5x - y = -2$

13. $y = -2x + 7$
$2x + y = 7$

14. $y = \dfrac{3}{2}x - 2$
$3x - 2y = 4$

15.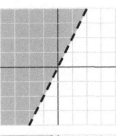

16.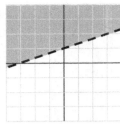

17.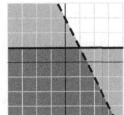

18.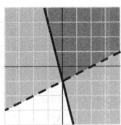

19.

20.

LESSON 46

1. B   2. D   3. D   4. C   5. D   6. A

7. C   8. B   9. C   10. B   11. B   12. B

13. A   14. B   15. D   16. A   17. C

Worked-out solutions to selected problems:

2. $x = 3$, so $x + 3 = 6$.

5. $7 = 3c - 5$, so $c = 4$.

6. $x = -2$ or $x = 5$

7. $x = 3$ and $y = -2$

9. 2 quarts = 4 pints = 8 cups, so Josh needs 6 more cups.

10. $45 \times (2/5) = 18$, so there are 18 males and 27 females.

13. 1 km = 1,000 m and 350 m = 0.35 km

14. x = Kate's age now
$x - 2$ = Kate's age two years ago
$18 - 2 = 2(x - 2)$; $x = 10$
Kate is 10 years old. Mark is 8 years older than Kate.

LESSON 47

1. C   2. A   3. B   4. C   5. C   6. A

7. B   8. A   9. C   10. B   11. C   12. C

13. C   14. D   15. A   16. C   17. C

Worked-out solutions to selected problems:

2. $0.4x = 16$ and $(2/3)y = 12$
$x = 40$ and $y = 18$, so $x - 2y = 40 - 36 = 4$

3. Multiply both sides by 12, then solve $6x + 3 = 4$.

4. $|x - 7| = -1 < 0$, so there is no solution.

8. Slope $= (k - 4)/(3 + 1) = -3$, so k = -8.

10. $20 \times 3 + 0.1x = 105$; $x = 450$

11. 40×60 minutes = 2400 words/hour
2400/200 = 12 pages/hour

12. t = time it will take bus 2 to overtake bus 1

$60(t + 1) = 70t$; $t = 6$

Bus 2 leaves the station at 2 PM and it will take 6 hours to overtake bus 1, so the answer is 8 PM.

15. 1 liter = 1,000 milliliters and 0.2 liters = 200 milliliters

200/60 = 3.3333...., so she can fill up 3 bottles.

17. x = number of 4-seat tables

y = number of 6-seat tables

$x + y = 15$ and $4x + 6y = 70$; $x = 10$ and $y = 5$

There are 10 4-seat tables and 5 6-seat tables.

LESSON 48

1. Function

2. Not a function
Input 3 has two outputs.

3. Function

4. Function

5. Not a function
The vertical line test fails.

6. Function

7. Function

8. Function

9. Not a function (input 4)

10. Function

11. Function

12. Not a function (input 1)

13. Function

14. Not a function (input 7)

15. Function

16. Function

17. Function

18. Function

19. Not a function
The vertical line test fails.

20. Function

21. Not a function

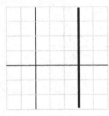

22. Function

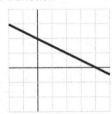

23. Function

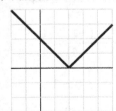

24. Function

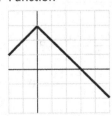

LESSON 49

1. Function

2. Not a function

3. D: {−1, 0, 1, 3, 4}
R: {−1, 0, 1, 3}
Function

4. D: $0 \leq x < 4$
R: $−1 < y \leq 3$
Function

5. a. D is the dependent variable.
t is the independent variable.

b. The range is {4, 8, 12}.

6. D: {−1, 0, 1, 2, 3, 4}
R: {0, 1, 2}
Function

7. D: $−1 \leq x < 4$
R: $−1 \leq y \leq 3$
Function

8. D: $−1 \leq x \leq 4$
R: $−2 \leq y \leq 3$
Not a function

9. D: $x \geq −1$
R: $y \geq −1$
Function

10. Dependent variable: C
Independent variable: e
Range: {6, 12, 18}

11. Dependent variable: C
Independent variable: h
Range: {24, 33, 42}

12. Dependent variable: w
Independent variable: m
Range: {190, 180, 170}

13. Dependent variable: C
Independent variable: m
Range: {9.5, 11, 12.5}

14. $3 < y < 8$

15. $1 \leq y < 9$

16. $y = -\dfrac{1}{5}x - 1$
$-2 < y \leq -1$

17. $y = \dfrac{2}{3}x - 2$
$-4 \leq y \leq 2$

18. $0 \leq y \leq 5$

19. $0 \leq y < 6$

LESSON 50

1. $y = -x + 7$

2. $y = -\dfrac{1}{4}x - 2$

3. $-y = -x + 2$
$y = x - 2$

4. $y = -2x^2 + 7$

5. $f(-5) = -5 + 1 = -4$

6. $g(4) = 4^2 - 4 = 12$

7. $y = 2$ at $x = 0$.
$g(0) = 2$

8. $y = -1$ at $x = 3$.
$g(3) = -1$

9. $y = -x - 9$

10. $-3y = -x + 6$
$y = \dfrac{1}{3}x - 2$

11. $-4y = -x^2$
$y = \dfrac{1}{4}x^2$

12. $2xy = 4$
$y = \dfrac{2}{x}$

13. $f(-2) = 0$
$f(0) = 2$
$f(4) = 6$

14. $g(-2) = 9$
$g(0) = 1$
$g(4) = -15$

15. $h(-2) = 5$
$h(0) = 3$
$h(4) = 1$

16. $k(-2) = 11$
$k(0) = 7$
$k(4) = 23$

17. $x + 2 = 7$
$x = 5$

18. $1 - 4x = 13$
$x = -3$

19. $|x - 3| = 3$
$x - 3 = 3$ or
$x - 3 = -3$
$x = 6$ or $x = 0$

20. $x^2 + 7 = 56$
$x^2 = 49$
$x = 7$ or $x = -7$

21. $p(-3) = 2$
$n = 2$

22. $p(3) = -1$
$n = -1$

23. $p(-4) = 1$
$n = -4$

24. $q(0) = 0, q(2) = 0$
$n = 0, n = 2$

25. $p(0) = 3, q(1) = 1$
$n = 3 + 1 = 4$

26. $p(1) = 4, q(-2) = -2$
$n = 4(-2) = -8$

27. $3 + 7 = 10$

28. $3 + (-15) \div 5 = 0$

29. $h(-7) = 10$

30. $4 + k(4)$
$= 4 + 23 = 27$

LESSON 51

1. $m = 1/2$

2. $m = -1$

3. $y = -x + 2$

4. $y = 2x - 1$

5. $y = -\dfrac{1}{2}x + 2$

6. $y = \dfrac{2}{3}x - 1$

7. $y = 2x + 3$

8. $y = -7x + 5$

9. Linear; $y = -2x + 4$

10. Nonlinear

11. Linear; $y = 2$

12. Nonlinear

13. $-3y = -6x$
$y = 2x$
Linear

14. $-y = -x^2 + 2x$
$y = x^2 - 2x$
Nonlinear

15. $xy = -x + 3$
$y = \dfrac{-x + 3}{x}$
Nonlinear

16. $-5y = -x - 10$
$y = \dfrac{1}{5}x + 2$
Linear

17. Nonlinear

18. Linear; $y = -x + 5$

19. Nonlinear

20. Nonlinear

21. Linear; $y = 4x - 8$

22. Linear; $y = -x + 3$

23. Nonlinear

24. $xy = 5$
$y = 5/x$
Nonlinear

25. $-y = -x - 6$
$y = x + 6$
Linear

26. $-3y = -9x + 6$
$y = 3x - 2$
Linear

27. $-y = -x^2 - x$
$y = x^2 + x$
Nonlinear

28. Linear; $y = 3x - 4$

29. Nonlinear

30. Linear; $y = 5$

31. Linear; $y = -x + 3$

LESSON 52

1. Quadratic

2. Linear

3. Exponential

4. None of these

5. Quadratic

6. Linear

7. None of these

8. Exponential

9. Quadratic
Second difference = 8

10. Exponential
Common ratio = 4

11. Exponential

12. Quadratic

13. Linear

14. Quadratic

15. $y = x^2 - 2$

16. $y = -x + 4$

17. $y = -2x^2$

18. $y = 2^x + 1$

19. Exponential
Common ratio = 2

20. None of these

21. Linear
First difference = 4

22. Quadratic
Second difference = 8

23. None of these

24. Linear
First difference = ~3

LESSON 53

1. $m = -6$

2. $m = 3/4$

3. $g(4) = 0$

4. $g(-2) = 3$

5. $h(-1) = -1$

6. $h(4) = 2$

7. $\dfrac{9 - 4}{1 - 0} = 5$

8. $\dfrac{9 - 1}{1 - (-1)} = 4$

9. $\dfrac{16 - 1}{2 - (-1)} = 5$

10. $\dfrac{16 - 0}{2 - (-2)} = 4$

11. $\dfrac{3 - 1}{5 - 1} = \dfrac{1}{2}$

12. $\dfrac{1 - (-1)}{2 - 0} = 1$

13. $\dfrac{h(3) - h(1)}{3 - 1} = \dfrac{112 - 240}{3 - 1} = -64 \, feet \, per \, second$

14. $\dfrac{9 - 9}{3 - (-3)} = 0$

15. $\dfrac{1 - 25}{1 - (-5)} = -4$

16. $\dfrac{0 - (-3)}{3 - 2} = 3$

17. $\dfrac{1 - (-1)}{4 - (-4)} = \dfrac{1}{4}$

18. $\dfrac{-1 - (-1)}{2 - (-2)} = 0$

19. $\dfrac{2 - 3}{1 - 0} = -1$

20. $\dfrac{1 - 49}{4 - (-4)} = -6$

21. $\dfrac{54 - (-2)}{3 - (-1)} = 14$

22. $\dfrac{-7 - (-1)}{2 - (-1)} = -2$

23. $\dfrac{12 - 4}{4 - 0} = 2$

24. $\dfrac{h(4) - h(0)}{4 - 0} = \dfrac{8 - 8}{4 - 0} = 0 \, feet \, per \, second$

LESSON 54

1. $(-5, 1), (3, 2), (-2, 5), (0, 7)$

2. $(4, -2), (0, 0), (4, 2), (8, 4)$

3. $g(1) = 2$
   $g^{-1}(2) = 1$

4. $g(4) = -1$
   $g^{-1}(-1) = 4$

5. $y = -x + 3$
   $x = -y + 3$
   $y = -x + 3$
   $f^{-1}(x) = -x + 3$

6. $y = 2x - 6$
   $x = 2y - 6$
   $y = \frac{1}{2}x + 3$
   $g^{-1}(x) = \frac{1}{2}x + 3$

7. $y = -\frac{1}{3}x + 1$

   $x = -\frac{1}{3}y + 1$

   $y = -3x + 3$
   $h^{-1}(x) = -3x + 3$

8. $(1, -5), (0, 0), (-1, 5), (-2, 10)$

9. $(0.5, -1), (2, 1), (8, 3), (32, 5)$

10. $f(-1) = 0$
    $f^{-1}(0) = -1$

11. $f(-2) = 1$
    $f^{-1}(1) = -2$

12. $f(0) = -1$
    $f(2) = -3$
    $f^{-1}(-3) = 2$
    $-1 + 2 = 1$

13. $g(4) = 4$
    $g^{-1}(4) = 4$

14. $g(3) = 2$
    $g^{-1}(2) = 3$

15. $g(1) = -2$
    $g(2) = 0$
    $g^{-1}(0) = 2$
    $-2 - 2 = -4$

16. $x = y - 2$
    $y = x + 2$
    $f^{-1}(x) = x + 2$

17. $x = \frac{1}{4}y$

    $y = 4x$
    $g^{-1}(x) = 4x$

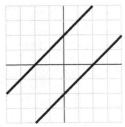

18. $y = x + 7$
    $x = y + 7$
    $y = x - 7$
    $p^{-1}(x) = x - 7$

19. $y = 3x - 2$
    $x = 3y - 2$
    $y = \frac{1}{3}x + \frac{2}{3}$
    $q^{-1}(x) = \frac{1}{3}x + \frac{2}{3}$

20. $y = \frac{5 - 2x}{6}$

    $x = \frac{5 - 2y}{6}$

    $y = -3x + \frac{5}{2}$

    $r^{-1}(x) = -3x + \frac{5}{2}$

21. $y = \frac{1}{4}x + \frac{1}{2}$

    $x = \frac{1}{4}y + \frac{1}{2}$

    $y = 4x - 2$
    $s^{-1}(x) = 4x - 2$

22. $p^{-1}(9) = 2$
    $q^{-1}(1) = 1$
    $2 + 1 = 3$

23. $p(3) = 10$
    $r(1) = 1/2$
    $r^{-1}(1/2) = 1$
    $10 + 1 = 11$

24. $r^{-1}(-1/2) = 4$
    $q^{-1}(4) = 2$
    $4 \times 2 = 8$

25. $s^{-1}(3) = 10$
    $p^{-1}(10) = 3$
    $r^{-1}(1/2) = 1$
    $3 - 1 = 2$

LESSON 55

1. Function

2. Function

3. Function

4. Not a function

5. D: $\{-1, 0, 1, 2, 3, 4\}$
   R: $\{-1, 0, 1, 2, 3\}$

6. D: $-1 < x < 4$
   R: $-2 \le y < 3$

7. D: $-1 \le x < 4$
   R: $-2 \le y \le 3$

8. D: $-1 \le x \le 4$
   R: $-2 < y < 3$

9. $f(-1) = -1$
   $f(0) = 3$
   $f(5) = 23$

10. $g(-1) = -8$
    $g(0) = -9$
    $g(5) = 16$

11. Linear; $y = (-2/3)x$

12. Quadratic

13. Exponential

14. Linear; $y = -x + 2$

15. None of these

16. Quadratic

17. 12

18. 7

19. 1

20. $-1/10$

21. $f^{-1}(x) = x - 5$

22. $g^{-1}(x) = \frac{1}{2}x + \frac{1}{2}$

23. $h^{-1}(x) = \frac{3}{2}x - 3$

24. $k^{-1}(x) = 5x - \frac{1}{2}$

25. Rectangle, Square

26. Not a polygon
    (no straight side)

27. No $(5^2 + 6^2 \ne 9^2)$

28. $80 + 69 + x = 180$
    $x = 31$

29. Alternate exterior angles
    $x = 72$

LESSON 56

1. $m = 2$, y-int = 0

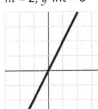

2. $m = -1$, y-int = 1

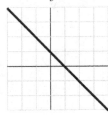

3. The graph of $y = 2x$ represents a direct variation.

4. $y = -x$
   Direct variation ($k = -1$)

5. $y = 5/x$
   Not direct variation

6. $12 = 4k$, so $k = 3$ and $y = 3x$.
   When $x = 6$, $y = 18$.

7. $2 = 8k$, so $k = 1/4$ and $y = (1/4)x$.
   When $y = -1$, $x = -4$.

8. x = time, y = distance
   $1700 = 5k$, so $k = 340$ and $y = 340x$.
   When $x = 12$, $y = 4080$.
   It will travel 4,080 meters.

9. x = shadow's length, y = object's height
   $12 = 18k$, so $k = 2/3$ and $y = (2/3)x$.
   When $y = 16$, $x = 24$.
   The shadow is 24 feet long.

10. $y = -2x$
    Direct variation ($k = -2$)

11. $y = 1/x$
    Not direct variation

12. $y = (1/2)x$
    Direct variation ($k = 1/2$)

13. $y = -2x + 3$
    Not direct variation

14. $8 = 2k$, so $k = 4$ and $y = 4x$.
    When $x = 3$, $y = 12$.

15. $6 = 9k$, so $k = 2/3$ and $y = (2/3)x$.
    When $y = 4$, $x = 6$.

16. x = area, y = cost
    $50 = 400k$, so $k = 1/8$ and $y = (1/8)x$.
    When $x = 500$, $y = 62.5$.
    It will cost $62.50.

17. x = amount of soda, y = number of calories
    $150 = 12k$, so $k = 25/2$ and $y = (25/2)x$.
    When $x = 20$, $y = 250$.
    There will be 250 calories.

18. x = weight on Mars, y = weight on Earth
    $50 = 19k$, so $k = 50/19$ and $y = (50/19)x$.
    When $y = 80$, $x = 30.4$.
    It will weigh about 30.4 pounds.

LESSON 57

1. $y = -12$

2. 6 gallons

3. $y = -3/x$
   Inverse variation ($k = -3$)

4. $y = 3x$
   Direct variation ($k = 3$)

5. $k = 2 \times 6 = 12$, so $xy = 12$.
   When $x = 4$, $y = 3$.

6. $k = -2 \times 5 = -10$, so $xy = -10$.
   When $y = -10$, $x = 1$.

7. x = age, y = resale value
   $k = 2 \times 18000 = 36000$, so $xy = 36000$.
   When $x = 5$, $y = 7200$.
   It will be $7,200.

8. x = number of people, y = time taken
   $k = 4 \times 3 = 12$, so $xy = 12$.
   When $x = 6$, $y = 2$.
   It will take 2 hours.

9. $y = -2/x$
   Inverse variation ($k = -2$)

10. $y = -2$
    Neither

11. $y = 1/(5x)$
    Inverse variation ($k = 1/5$)

12. $y = (1/3)x$
    Direct variation ($k = 1/3$)

13. $-3 = 3k$, so $k = -1$.
    $y = -x$

14. $0.6 = 2k$, so $k = 0.3$.
    $y = 0.3x$

15. $k = 1 \times 4 = 4$
    $xy = 4$ or $y = 4/x$

16. $k = -2 \times 4 = -8$
    $xy = -8$ or $y = -8/x$

17. $15 = 3k$, so $k = 5$ and $y = 5x$.
    When $y = 30$, $x = 6$.

18. $k = -5 \times 4 = -20$, so $xy = -20$.
    When $x = 2$, $y = -10$.

19. x = time, y = distance
    $72 = (3/4)k$, so $k = 96$ and $y = 96x$.
    When $x = 4$, $y = 384$.
    It will travel 384 miles.

20. x = rate of pumping, y = time to empty the tank
    $k = 12 \times 36 = 432$, so $xy = 432$.
    When $x = 16$, $y = 27$.
    It will take 27 minutes.

21. x = resistance, y = current
    $k = 4 \times 9 = 36$, so $xy = 36$.
    When $x = 12$, $y = 3$.
    It will be 3 amperes.

LESSON 58

1. Arithmetic ($d = 7$)

2. Not arithmetic

3. $a_1 = 9, d = -2$
$a_n = 9 - 2(n - 1)$
$= -2n + 11$

4. $a_1 = 6, d = 9$
$a_n = 6 + 9(n - 1)$
$= 9n - 3$

5. $a_1 = -5, d = 5$
$a_n = -5 + 5(n - 1)$
$= 5n - 10$
$a_{10} = 5(10) - 10 = 40$

6. $a_1 = 4, d = 6$
$a_n = 4 + 6(n - 1)$
$= 6n - 2$
$a_{10} = 6(10) - 2 = 58$

7. Arithmetic ($d = 3$)

8. Not arithmetic

9. Arithmetic ($d = 7$)

10. Arithmetic ($d = -6$)

11. 2, –3, –8, –13, –18

12. 5, 14, 23, 32, 41

13. –1, 3, 7, 11, 15

14. –9, –12, –15, –18, –21

15. $a_1 = -3, d = 5$
$a_n = 5n - 8$
$a_{10} = 42$

16. $a_1 = 8, d = -4$
$a_n = -4n + 12$
$a_{10} = -28$

17. $a_1 = 2, d = 7$
$a_n = 7n - 5$
$a_{10} = 65$

18. $a_1 = -5, d = 4$
$a_n = 4n - 9$
$a_{10} = 31$

19. $a_1 = 3, d = -7$
$a_n = -7n + 10$
$a_{10} = -60$

20. $a_1 = -2, d = 6$
$a_n = 6n - 8$
$a_{10} = 52$

21. $a_1 = 7, d = 3$
$a_n = 3n + 4$
$a_{10} = 34$

22. $a_1 = 23, d = -5$
$a_n = -5n + 28$
$a_{10} = -22$

23. $a_1 = 35, d = -8$
$a_n = -8n + 43$
$a_{10} = -37$

24. $a_1 = -23, d = 3$
$a_n = 3n - 26$
$a_{10} = 4$

25. Find the rule:
$a_1 = 3, d = 4$
$a_n = 4n - 1$
$\Rightarrow$ Find x:
$a_x = 4x - 1 = 35$
$x = 9$

26. $a_1 = 5, d = 3$
$a_n = 3n + 2$
$\Rightarrow$ $a_x = 3x + 2 = 41$
$x = 13$

27. $a_1 = 20, d = -5$
$a_n = -5n + 25$
$\Rightarrow$ $a_x = -5x + 25 = -50$
$x = 15$

28. $a_1 = -60, d = 12$
$a_n = 12n - 72$
$\Rightarrow$ $a_x = 12x - 72 = 192$
$x = 22$

LESSON 59

1. Not geometric

2. Geometric ($r = 2$)

3. $a_1 = 2, r = 2$
$a_n = 2 \cdot 2^{n-1} = 2^n$

4. $a_1 = 4, r = 3$
$a_n = 4(3)^{n-1}$

5. $a_1 = 4, r = -3$
$a_n = 4(-3)^{n-1}$
$a_7 = 4(-3)^6 = 2916$

6. $a_1 = 9, r = 1/3$
$a_n = 9(1/3)^{n-1}$
$a_7 = 9(1/3)^6 = 1/81$

7. Geometric ($r = 4$)

8. Geometric ($r = 1/3$)

9. Not geometric

10. Geometric ($r = -2$)

11. 3, 6, 12, 24, 48

12. 2, 10, 50, 250, 1250

13. 6, –18, 54, –162, 486

14. –5, 10, –20, 40, –80

15. $a_1 = 1, r = 5$
$a_n = (5)^{n-1}$
$a_7 = 15,625$

16. $a_1 = 5, r = -2$
$a_n = 5(-2)^{n-1}$
$a_7 = 320$

17. $a_1 = -4, r = 2$
$a_n = -4(2)^{n-1}$
$a_7 = -256$

18. $a_1 = 5, r = 4$
$a_n = 5(4)^{n-1}$
$a_7 = 20,480$

19. $a_1 = 2, r = 1/4$
$a_n = 2(1/4)^{n-1}$
$a_7 = 1/2,048$

20. $a_1 = 5, r = 1/10$
$a_n = 5(1/10)^{n-1}$
$a_7 = 1/200,000$

21. $a_1 = 3, r = 4$
$a_n = 3(4)^{n-1}$
$a_7 = 12,288$

22. $a_1 = 5, r = -3$
$a_n = 5(-3)^{n-1}$
$a_7 = 3,645$

23. $a_1 = -4, r = -3$
$a_n = -4(-3)^{n-1}$
$a_7 = -2,916$

24. $a_1 = 4, r = 5$
$a_n = 4(5)^{n-1}$
$a_7 = 62,500$

25. Find the rule:
$a_1 = 3, r = 2$
$a_n = 3(2)^{n-1}$
$\Rightarrow$ Find x:
$a_x = 3(2)^{x-1} = 768$
$(2)^{x-1} = 256 = 2^8$
$x = 9$

26. $a_1 = 1, r = -2$
$a_n = (-2)^{n-1}$
$\Rightarrow$ $a_x = (-2)^{x-1} = 1024$
$(-2)^{x-1} = 1024 = (-2)^{10}$
$x = 11$

27. $a_1 = -2, r = 3$
$a_n = -2(3)^{n-1}$
$\Rightarrow$ $a_x = -2(3)^{x-1} = -4374$
$(3)^{x-1} = 2187 = 3^7$
$x = 8$

28. $a_1 = 512, r = 1/2$
$a_n = 512(1/2)^{n-1}$
$\Rightarrow$ $a_x = 512(1/2)^{x-1} = 1$
$(1/2)^{x-1} = 1/512$
$(1/2)^{x-1} = (1/2)^9$
$x = 10$

LESSON 60

1. $a_1 = 15, d = -3$
   $a_n = -3n + 18$

2. $a_1 = 3, r = 4$
   $a_n = 3(4)^{n-1}$

3. $a_1 = 6, d = 9$
   $a_n = 9n - 3$

4. $a_1 = 5, r = -2$
   $a_n = 5(-2)^{n-1}$

5. $a_1 = 7, d = 2$
   $a_1 = 7, a_n = a_{n-1} + 2$

6. $a_1 = 26, \mathrm{d} = -6$
   $a_1 = 26, a_n = a_{n-1} - 6$

7. $a_1 = 1, r = 2$
   $a_1 = 1, a_n = 2a_{n-1}$

8. $a_1 = 2, r = 5$
   $a_1 = 2, a_n = 5a_{n-1}$

9. 5, 13, 21, 29, 37, ...
   $a_1 = 5, d = 8$
   $a_n = 8n - 3$

10. 4, −8, 16, −32, 64, ...
    $a_1 = 4, r = -2$
    $a_n = 4(-2)^{n-1}$

11. 32, 25, 18, 11, 4, ...
    $a_1 = 32, d = -7$
    $a_n = -7n + 39$

12. 5, 15, 45, 135, 405, ...
    $a_1 = 5, r = 3$
    $a_n = 5(3)^{n-1}$

13. 9, 13, 17, 21, 25, ...
    $a_1 = 9, d = 4$
    $a_1 = 9, a_n = a_{n-1} + 4$

14. 3, 6, 12, 24, 48, ...
    $a_1 = 3, r = 2$
    $a_1 = 3, a_n = 2a_{n-1}$

15. 16, 11, 6, 1, -4, ...
    $a_1 = 16, d = -5$
    $a_1 = 16, a_n = a_{n-1} - 5$

16. 2, −6, 18, −54, 162, ...
    $a_1 = 2, r = -3$
    $a_1 = 2, a_n = -3a_{n-1}$

17. Geometric
    $a_1 = 2, r = -4$
    $a_n = 2(-4)^{n-1}$
    $a_1 = 2, a_n = -4a_{n-1}$

18. Arithmetic
    $a_1 = 22, d = -9$
    $a_n = -9n + 31$
    $a_1 = 22, a_n = a_{n-1} - 9$

19. Arithmetic
    $a_1 = 35, d = -10$
    $a_n = -10n + 45$
    $a_1 = 35, a_n = a_{n-1} - 10$

20. Geometric
    $a_1 = 4, r = 5$
    $a_n = 4(5)^{n-1}$
    $a_1 = 4, a_n = 5a_{n-1}$

21. Geometric
    $a_1 = 5, r = -3$
    $a_n = 5(-3)^{n-1}$
    $a_1 = 5, a_n = -3a_{n-1}$

22. Arithmetic
    $a_1 = 13, d = 8$
    $a_n = 8n + 5$
    $a_1 = 13, a_n = a_{n-1} + 8$

23. Arithmetic
    $a_1 = 42, d = 5$
    $a_n = 5n + 37$
    $a_1 = 42, a_n = a_{n-1} + 5$

24. Geometric
    $a_1 = 1, r = 1/2$
    $a_n = (1/2)^{n-1}$
    $a_1 = 1, a_n = (1/2)a_{n-1}$

25. Set up the system:
    $a_1 + 7d = 19$
    $a_1 + 11d = 27$
    Solve the system:
    $a_1 = 5, d = 2$
    → Write the formulas:
    $a_n = 2n + 3$
    $a_1 = 5, a_n = a_{n-1} + 2$

26. $a_1 + 2d = 1$
    $a_1 + 8d = 25$
    $a_1 = -7, d = 4$
    → $a_n = 4n - 11$
    $a_1 = -7, a_n = a_{n-1} + 4$

27. $a_1 + 8d = -13$
    $a_1 + 14d = -31$
    $a_1 = 11, d = -3$
    → $a_n = -3n + 14$
    $a_1 = 11, a_n = a_{n-1} - 3$

28. $a_1 + 4d = 44$
    $a_1 + 9d = 89$
    $a_1 = 8, d = 9$
    → $a_n = 9n - 1$
    $a_1 = 8, a_n = a_{n-1} + 9$

29. $a_1 + 6d = 38$
    $a_1 + 13d = 73$
    $a_1 = 8, d = 5$
    → $a_n = 5n + 3$
    $a_1 = 8, a_n = a_{n-1} + 5$

30. $a_1 + 12d = -40$
    $a_1 + 17d = -70$
    $a_1 = 32, d = -6$
    → $a_n = -6n + 38$
    $a_1 = 32, a_n = a_{n-1} - 6$

LESSON 61

1. Geometric
   $a_n = 5(2)^{n-1}$
   $a_1 = 5, a_n = 2a_{n-1}$

2. Arithmetic
   $a_n = 5n + 5$
   $a_1 = 10, a_n = a_{n-1} + 5$

3. 5200, 5400, 5600, 5800, 6000, ...
   The balance at the end of the first year will be $5,200.
   $a_1 = 5200, d = 5000 \times 0.04 = 200$
   $a_n = 200n + 5000$
   $a_{10} = 200(10) + 5000 = 7000$
   The balance will be $7,000.

4. 5, 6.2, 7.4, 8.6, 9.8, ...
   The height at the beginning of the first year was 5 feet.
   $a_1 = 5, d = 1.2$
   $a_n = 1.2n + 3.8$
   $a_8 = 1.2(8) + 3.8 = 13.4$
   The tree will be 13.4 feet tall.

5. 96, 72, 54, 40.5, 30.375, ...
   The height after the first bounce is 128 × 0.75 = 96 feet.
   $a_1 = 96, r = 0.75$
   $a_n = 96(0.75)^{n-1}$
   $a_7 = 96(0.75)^6 = 17.08 \ldots$
   The ball will rebound to about 17 feet.

6. 18000, 16200, 14580, 13122, 11809.8, ...
   The value after the first year is 20000 × 0.9 = 18000.
   $a_1 = 18000, r = 0.9$
   $a_n = 18000(0.9)^{n-1}$
   $a_6 = 18000(0.9)^5 = 10{,}628.82$
   The value of the car will be about $10,629.

7. $a_1 = -12, d = 7$
   $a_n = 7n - 19$

8. $a_1 = 2, r = 3$
   $a_n = 2(3)^{n-1}$

9. Arithmetic: 72, 76, 80, 84, 88, ...

$a_1 = 72, d = 4$

$a_n = 4n + 68$

$a_7 = 4(7) + 68 = 96$

Her score will be 96%.

10. Geometric: 10, 20, 40, 80, 160, ...

$a_1 = 10, r = 2$

$a_n = 10(2)^{n-1}$

$a_8 = 10(2)^7 = 1280$

There will be 1,280 bacteria.

11. Arithmetic: 62000, 62800, 63600, 64400, 65200, ...

$a_1 = 62000, d = 800$

$a_n = 800n + 61200$

$a_8 = 800(8) + 61200 = 67600$

His salary was $67,600.

12. Geometric: 14400, 11520, 9216, 7372.8, 5898.24, ...

The value after the first year is 18000 × 0.8 = 14400.

$a_1 = 14400, r = 0.8$

$a_n = 14400(0.8)^{n-1}$

$a_7 = 14400(0.8)^6 = 3774.8736$

The value of the car will be about $3,775.

13. Geometric: 33000, 36300, 39930, 43923, ...

The population after the first year will be 30000 + 30000 × 0.1 = 33000.

$a_1 = 33000, r = 1.1$

$a_n = 33000(1.1)^{n-1}$

$a_5 = 33000(1.1)^4 = 48315.3$

The population will be about 48,315.

14. Arithmetic: 5, 7, 9, 11, 13, ...

$a_1 = 5, d = 2$

$a_n = 2n + 3$

$a_{10} = 2(10) + 3 = 23$

She will run 23 km daily.

15. Geometric: 500, 1000, 2000, ...

$a_1 = 500, r = 2$

$a_n = 500(2)^{n-1}$

$a_5 = 500(2)^4 = 8000$

It will have 8,000 hits.

16. Geometric: 52000, 54600, 57330, ...

$a_1 = 52000, r = 1.05$

$a_n = 52000(1.05)^{n-1}$

$a_7 = 52000(1.05)^6 = 69684.97331$

His salary will be about $69,685.

17. Arithmetic: 4, 7, 10, 13, 16, ...

$a_1 = 4, d = 3$

$a_n = 3n + 1$

$a_x = 3x + 1 = 43; x = 14$

He run the full distance in the 14th week.

18. Arithmetic: 180, 360, 540, 720, 900, ...

$a_1 = 180, d = 180$

$a_n = 180n$

Note that the 1st term gives the sum of the interior angles of a triangle (3 sides). The 8th term will give the sum of the interior angles of a decagon (10 sides).

$a_8 = 180(8) = 1440$

LESSON 62

1. $y = 4x$
$y = 12$ at $x = 3$

2. $y = (-4/9)x$
$x = 18$ at $y = -8$

3. 475 kilometers

4. 125 pounds

5. $xy = 12$
$y = 3$ at $x = 4$

6. $xy = 3/2$
$x = 1/2$ at $y = 3$

7. 165 units

8. 280 Hz

9. $a_n = 2n + 6$
$a_{10} = 26$

10. $a_n = 4n - 5$
$a_{10} = 35$

11. $a_n = -3n + 6$
$a_{10} = -24$

12. $a_n = -8n + 3$
$a_{10} = -77$

13. $a_n = 2(3)^{n-1}$
$a_7 = 1458$

14. $a_n = 8(-2)^{n-1}$
$a_7 = 512$

15. $a_n = 2(-5)^{n-1}$
$a_7 = 31250$

16. $a_n = 128(1/2)^{n-1}$
$a_7 = 2$

17. Arithmetic
$a_n = 9n - 1$
$a_1 = 8, a_n = a_{n-1} + 9$

18. Geometric
$a_n = 4(5)^{n-1}$
$a_1 = 4, a_n = 5a_{n-1}$

19. $a_n = 16n + 16$
336 orders

20. $a_n = 9(0.75)^{n-1}$
About 0.68 meter

21. $2:8 = x:20$
$x = 5$

22. $15:12 = 25:x$
$x = 20$ feet

23. $0.5:25 = 1.8:x$
$x = 90$ miles

24. Right 4 units: (1, 1)
Down 2 units: (1, –1)
Across the x-axis: (1, 1)

LESSON 63

1. 2   2. 8   3. 0.1   4. 0.7
5. 1   6. 5   7. −3   8. 0.2
9. 1   10. 2   11. 5   12. −10
13. 1   14. 3   15. 7   16. 12
17. 0.1   18. 0.6   19. 1.1   20. 1.4
21. 0   22. 2   23. 3   24. 10
25. −1   26. −4   27. −5   28. −0.3
29. 0   30. −1   31. −2   32. 2
33. 3   34. −2   35. 10   36. 20

37. $8 - 4 \times (-4) = 24$

38. $5 \times 3 - 9 = 6$

39. $\sqrt{25} + 4 = 5 + 4 = 9$

40. $12 \div 6 - \sqrt{100} = 12 \div 6 - 10 = -8$

41. $(27 - 7)^2 \div 10 = 400 \div 10 = 40$

42. $(9 - 6)^3 \div 27 \times 25 \times 1 = 27 \div 27 \times 25 \times 1 = 25$

43. 2-digit perfect squares: 16, 25, 36, 49, 64, 81
    8 + 1 = 9 and √(81) = 9, so the number is 81.

44. Both digits of 25 are prime and √(25) = 5 is prime, so the number is 25.

45. Divisible by 3 and 5 = multiples of 15
    Not divisible by 10 = not multiples of 10
    So the possible numbers are 15, 45, or 75.
    4 + 5 = 9, so the number is 45.

LESSON 64

1. 5   2. 9   3. −3   4. 2

5. $\sqrt{16 \cdot 2} = 4\sqrt{2}$ 6. $4\sqrt{4 \cdot 7} = 8\sqrt{7}$

7. $\dfrac{\sqrt{27}}{\sqrt{25}} = \dfrac{\sqrt{9 \cdot 3}}{5} = \dfrac{3\sqrt{3}}{5}$ 8. $\dfrac{\sqrt{45}}{\sqrt{64}} = \dfrac{\sqrt{9 \cdot 5}}{8} = \dfrac{3\sqrt{5}}{8}$

9. $\sqrt[3]{8 \cdot 3} = 2\sqrt[3]{3}$ 10. $5\sqrt[3]{-8 \cdot 5} = -10\sqrt[3]{5}$

11. $\dfrac{\sqrt[3]{27 \cdot 3}}{\sqrt[3]{64}} = \dfrac{3\sqrt[3]{3}}{4}$ 12. $\dfrac{\sqrt[3]{8 \cdot 4}}{\sqrt[3]{125}} = \dfrac{2\sqrt[3]{4}}{5}$

13. $\sqrt{2 \cdot 2 \cdot 2 \cdot 2 \cdot 5} = 2 \cdot 2 \cdot \sqrt{5} = 4\sqrt{5}$

14. $\sqrt{2 \cdot 2 \cdot 2 \cdot 2 \cdot 7} = 2 \cdot 2 \cdot \sqrt{7} = 4\sqrt{7}$

15. $\sqrt[3]{3 \cdot 3 \cdot 3 \cdot 5} = 3\sqrt[3]{5}$

16. $\sqrt[3]{5 \cdot 5 \cdot 5 \cdot 2} = 5\sqrt[3]{2}$

17. $\sqrt{4 \cdot 2} = 2\sqrt{2}$ 18. $\sqrt{9 \cdot 2} = 3\sqrt{2}$

19. $\sqrt{4 \cdot 6} = 2\sqrt{6}$ 20. $\sqrt{25 \cdot 2} = 5\sqrt{2}$

21. $7\sqrt{4 \cdot 5} = 14\sqrt{5}$ 22. $2\sqrt{4 \cdot 7} = 4\sqrt{7}$

23. $\sqrt[3]{8 \cdot 5} = 2\sqrt[3]{5}$ 24. $5\sqrt[3]{-8 \cdot 2} = -10\sqrt[3]{2}$

25. $\dfrac{\sqrt{18}}{\sqrt{25}} = \dfrac{\sqrt{9 \cdot 2}}{5} = \dfrac{3\sqrt{2}}{5}$ 26. $\dfrac{3\sqrt{50}}{\sqrt{81}} = \dfrac{3\sqrt{25 \cdot 2}}{9} = \dfrac{5\sqrt{2}}{3}$

27. $\dfrac{\sqrt[3]{8 \cdot 6}}{\sqrt[3]{125}} = \dfrac{2\sqrt[3]{6}}{5}$ 28. $\dfrac{10\sqrt[3]{27 \cdot 3}}{\sqrt[3]{1000}} = 3\sqrt[3]{3}$

29. $\sqrt{4 \cdot 3} = 2\sqrt{3}$ 30. $\sqrt{9 \cdot 3} = 3\sqrt{3}$

31. $\sqrt{9 \cdot 5} = 3\sqrt{5}$ 32. $\sqrt{9 \cdot 7} = 3\sqrt{7}$

33. $9\sqrt{16 \cdot 3} = 36\sqrt{3}$ 34. $2\sqrt{36 \cdot 2} = 12\sqrt{2}$

35. $\sqrt[3]{-27 \cdot 2} = -3\sqrt[3]{2}$ 36. $2\sqrt[3]{27 \cdot 3} = 6\sqrt[3]{3}$

37. $\dfrac{\sqrt{45}}{\sqrt{16}} = \dfrac{\sqrt{9 \cdot 5}}{4} = \dfrac{3\sqrt{5}}{4}$ 38. $\dfrac{4\sqrt{27}}{\sqrt{64}} = \dfrac{4\sqrt{9 \cdot 3}}{8} = \dfrac{3\sqrt{3}}{2}$

39. $\dfrac{\sqrt[3]{27 \cdot 5}}{\sqrt[3]{64}} = \dfrac{3\sqrt[3]{5}}{4}$ 40. $\dfrac{6\sqrt[3]{8 \cdot 4}}{\sqrt[3]{27}} = \dfrac{12\sqrt[3]{4}}{3} = 4\sqrt[3]{4}$

LESSON 65

1. $3\sqrt{2}$ 2. $4\sqrt{5}$ 3. $-2\sqrt[3]{2}$ 4. $9\sqrt[3]{2}$

5. $\sqrt{x^2 \cdot x} = \sqrt{x^2} \cdot \sqrt{x} = x\sqrt{x}$

6. $\sqrt{2^2 \cdot 6 \cdot x^2 \cdot y^2 \cdot y^2 \cdot y^2} = 2xy^3\sqrt{6}$

7. $\dfrac{\sqrt{4^2 \cdot x^2 \cdot x^2 \cdot x}}{\sqrt{5^2 \cdot y^2 \cdot y^2 \cdot y^2 \cdot y^2}} = \dfrac{4x^2\sqrt{x}}{5y^4}$

8. Remember that the 3 is not an exponent.
   $\sqrt[3]{x^3 \cdot x} = \sqrt[3]{x^3} \cdot \sqrt[3]{x} = x\sqrt[3]{x}$

9. $\sqrt[3]{3^3 \cdot x^3 \cdot y^3 \cdot y^3} = 3xy^2$

10. $\dfrac{\sqrt[3]{2^3 \cdot 2 \cdot x^3 \cdot y^2}}{\sqrt[3]{5^3 \cdot z^3}} = \dfrac{2x\sqrt[3]{2y^2}}{5z}$

11. $\sqrt{x^2 \cdot x^2} = x^2$

12. $\sqrt{4^2 \cdot x^2 \cdot x^2 \cdot x^2} = 4x^3$

13. $\sqrt{m \cdot n^2 \cdot n^2 \cdot n^2 \cdot n} = n^3\sqrt{mn}$

14. $\sqrt{5^2 \cdot m^2 \cdot n^2} = 5mn$

15. $\sqrt{p^2 \cdot p \cdot q^2 \cdot q \cdot r} = pq\sqrt{pqr}$

16. $\sqrt{5^2 \cdot 3 \cdot p^2 \cdot q \cdot r} = 5p\sqrt{3qr}$

17. $\dfrac{\sqrt{x^2 \cdot x}}{\sqrt{y^2 \cdot y^2}} = \dfrac{x\sqrt{x}}{y^2}$

18. $\dfrac{\sqrt{6^2 \cdot 2 \cdot x}}{\sqrt{y^2 \cdot y^2 \cdot y^2 \cdot y^2}} = \dfrac{6\sqrt{2x}}{y^4}$

19. $\sqrt[3]{x^3 \cdot x^3} = x^2$

20. $\sqrt[3]{5^3 \cdot x^3 \cdot x^2} = 5x\sqrt[3]{x^2}$

21. $\dfrac{\sqrt[3]{x^3 \cdot x}}{\sqrt[3]{y^3 \cdot y^3 \cdot z^3}} = \dfrac{x\sqrt[3]{x}}{y^2 z}$

22. $\dfrac{\sqrt[3]{(-2)^3 \cdot 4 \cdot x^2 \cdot y^3}}{\sqrt[3]{3^3 \cdot z^3}} = \dfrac{-2y\sqrt[3]{4x^2}}{3z}$

23. $\sqrt{y^2 \cdot y^2 \cdot y} = y^2\sqrt{y}$

24. $\sqrt{2^2 \cdot 3 \cdot y^2} = 2y\sqrt{3}$

25. $\sqrt{a^2 \cdot a^2 \cdot b^2 \cdot b^2} = a^2 b^2$

26. $\sqrt{2^2 \cdot 2 \cdot a^2 \cdot b^2 \cdot b} = 2ab\sqrt{2b}$

27. $\sqrt{s^2 \cdot s \cdot t^2 \cdot t^2 \cdot t^2 \cdot u^2 \cdot u^2} = st^3 u^2\sqrt{s}$

28. $\sqrt{7^2 \cdot 2 \cdot s^2 \cdot s^2 \cdot s^2 \cdot s^2 \cdot t^2 \cdot u^2 \cdot u^2 \cdot u} = 7s^4 tu^2\sqrt{2u}$

29. $\dfrac{\sqrt{x^2 \cdot x^2 \cdot x^2}}{\sqrt{y^2 \cdot z^2}} = \dfrac{x^3}{yz}$

30. $\dfrac{\sqrt{5^2 \cdot 3 \cdot x^2 \cdot x^2 \cdot x^2 \cdot x \cdot z^2 \cdot z}}{\sqrt{6^2 \cdot y^2}} = \dfrac{5x^3 z\sqrt{3xz}}{6y}$

31. $\sqrt[3]{a^3 \cdot a \cdot b} = a\sqrt[3]{ab}$

32. $\sqrt[3]{3^3 \cdot a^3 \cdot b^2} = 3a\sqrt[3]{b^2}$

33. $\dfrac{\sqrt[3]{x^3 \cdot x^3 \cdot x}}{\sqrt[3]{y^3}} = \dfrac{x^2\sqrt[3]{x}}{y}$

34. $\dfrac{\sqrt[3]{(-2)^3 \cdot x^3 \cdot x \cdot y^2}}{\sqrt[3]{z^3 \cdot z^3}} = \dfrac{-2x\sqrt[3]{xy^2}}{z^2}$

LESSON 66

1. $5x - 7$

2. $2x + 4y + 5$

3. $3\sqrt{3}$

4. $6\sqrt{2}$

5. $8\sqrt{7}$

6. $9\sqrt{5}$

7. $(5+1)\sqrt{3} = 6\sqrt{3}$

8. $(2-6)\sqrt{7} = -4\sqrt{7}$

9. $2\sqrt{3} + \sqrt{3} = 3\sqrt{3}$

10. $2\sqrt{6} - \sqrt{6} = \sqrt{6}$

11. $4 \cdot 2\sqrt{2} - 3 \cdot 4\sqrt{2}$
$= 8\sqrt{2} - 12\sqrt{2} = -4\sqrt{2}$

12. $2\sqrt{5} - 2\sqrt{7} + 3 \cdot 3\sqrt{7}$
$= 2\sqrt{5} + 7\sqrt{7}$

13. $2\sqrt{5} - \sqrt{5} = \sqrt{5}$

14. $\sqrt{7} + 2\sqrt{7} = 3\sqrt{7}$

15. $3\sqrt{7} - 2\sqrt{7} = \sqrt{7}$

16. $5\sqrt{3} + 3\sqrt{3} = 8\sqrt{3}$

17. $4\sqrt{3} + 10\sqrt{3} = 14\sqrt{3}$

18. $9\sqrt{10} - 8\sqrt{10} = \sqrt{10}$

19. $6\sqrt{2} - 21\sqrt{2} = -15\sqrt{2}$

20. $8\sqrt{6} - 10\sqrt{6} = -2\sqrt{6}$

21. $5\sqrt{5} + 10\sqrt{5} - 5\sqrt{5}$
$= 10\sqrt{5}$

22. $15\sqrt{2} - 6\sqrt{6} - 14\sqrt{2}$
$= \sqrt{2} - 6\sqrt{6}$

23. $3\sqrt{2} - \sqrt{2} = 2\sqrt{2}$

24. $2\sqrt{2} + 6\sqrt{2} = 8\sqrt{2}$

25. $2\sqrt{3} - 4\sqrt{3} = -2\sqrt{3}$

26. $3\sqrt{5} - 4\sqrt{5} = -\sqrt{5}$

27. $2\sqrt{6} + 3\sqrt{6} = 5\sqrt{6}$

28. $5\sqrt{2} + 7\sqrt{2} = 12\sqrt{2}$

29. $4\sqrt{2} - 3\sqrt{2} = \sqrt{2}$

30. $3\sqrt{11} + 2\sqrt{11} = 5\sqrt{11}$

31. $9\sqrt{5} + 10\sqrt{5} = 19\sqrt{5}$

32. $16\sqrt{5} + 12\sqrt{5} = 28\sqrt{5}$

33. $6\sqrt{2} + 2\sqrt{2} - 12\sqrt{3}$
$= 8\sqrt{2} - 12\sqrt{3}$

34. $9\sqrt{3} + 4\sqrt{5} - 6\sqrt{5}$
$= 9\sqrt{3} - 2\sqrt{5}$

35. $16 \cdot \dfrac{\sqrt{5}}{8} + 2\sqrt{5}$
$= 2\sqrt{5} + 2\sqrt{5} = 4\sqrt{5}$

36. $14 \cdot \dfrac{4}{7} - 13$
$= 8 - 13 = -5$

37. $6 \cdot \dfrac{2\sqrt{3}}{3} - 8 \cdot \dfrac{3\sqrt{3}}{4}$
$= 4\sqrt{3} - 6\sqrt{3} = -2\sqrt{3}$

38. $3 \cdot \dfrac{2\sqrt{2}}{9} + 4 \cdot \dfrac{2\sqrt{2}}{6}$
$= \dfrac{2\sqrt{2}}{3} + \dfrac{4\sqrt{2}}{3} = 2\sqrt{2}$

LESSON 67

1. $2x\sqrt{2x}$

2. $\sqrt{2}$

3. $\sqrt{5 \cdot 10} = \sqrt{50} = 5\sqrt{2}$

4. $3 \cdot 5 \cdot \sqrt{2 \cdot 3} = 15\sqrt{6}$

5. $\sqrt{3} \cdot 5\sqrt{5} - \sqrt{3} \cdot \sqrt{6}$
$= 5\sqrt{15} - \sqrt{18}$
$= 5\sqrt{15} - 3\sqrt{2}$

6. $3\sqrt{6 \cdot 8 \cdot x \cdot x}$
$= 3\sqrt{4^2 \cdot 3 \cdot x^2}$
$= 12x\sqrt{3}$

7. $\sqrt{\dfrac{18}{2}} = \sqrt{9} = 3$ OR $\dfrac{3\sqrt{2}}{\sqrt{2}} = 3$

8. $4\sqrt{\dfrac{5}{20}} = 4\sqrt{\dfrac{1}{4}} = 4 \cdot \dfrac{1}{2} = 2$ OR $\dfrac{4\sqrt{5}}{\sqrt{20}} = \dfrac{4\sqrt{5}}{2\sqrt{5}} = 2$

9. $\sqrt{\dfrac{48x^5 y}{6xy}} = \sqrt{8x^4} = 2x^2\sqrt{2}$

10. $\dfrac{1}{\sqrt{5}} \cdot \dfrac{\sqrt{5}}{\sqrt{5}} = \dfrac{\sqrt{5}}{5}$

11. $\dfrac{4}{\sqrt{2}} \cdot \dfrac{\sqrt{2}}{\sqrt{2}} = \dfrac{4\sqrt{2}}{2} = 2\sqrt{2}$

12. $\dfrac{\sqrt{7}}{\sqrt{3}} \cdot \dfrac{\sqrt{3}}{\sqrt{3}} = \dfrac{\sqrt{21}}{3}$

13. $\dfrac{3\sqrt{5}}{\sqrt{6}} \cdot \dfrac{\sqrt{6}}{\sqrt{6}} = \dfrac{\sqrt{30}}{2}$

14. $\sqrt{15}$

15. $3\sqrt{2 \cdot 2 \cdot 7} = 6\sqrt{7}$

16. $\sqrt{5} \cdot \sqrt{3} - \sqrt{5} \cdot \sqrt{10}$
$= \sqrt{15} - 5\sqrt{2}$

17. $\sqrt{12x^5} = 2x^2\sqrt{3x}$

18. $4\sqrt{\dfrac{15}{60}} = 4\sqrt{\dfrac{1}{4}} = \dfrac{4}{2} = 2$

19. $\sqrt{\dfrac{27x^3}{3x}} = \sqrt{9x^2} = 3x$

20. $\dfrac{2}{\sqrt{2}} \cdot \dfrac{\sqrt{2}}{\sqrt{2}} = \dfrac{2\sqrt{2}}{2} = \sqrt{2}$

21. $\dfrac{4}{\sqrt{6}} \cdot \dfrac{\sqrt{6}}{\sqrt{6}} = \dfrac{4\sqrt{6}}{6} = \dfrac{2\sqrt{6}}{3}$

22. $\dfrac{5}{2\sqrt{5}} \cdot \dfrac{\sqrt{5}}{\sqrt{5}} = \dfrac{5\sqrt{5}}{10} = \dfrac{\sqrt{5}}{2}$

23. $\dfrac{3\sqrt{2}}{\sqrt{3}} \cdot \dfrac{\sqrt{3}}{\sqrt{3}} = \dfrac{3\sqrt{6}}{3} = \sqrt{6}$

24. $\sqrt{2 \cdot 3 \cdot 3} = 3\sqrt{2}$

25. $2\sqrt{5 \cdot 5 \cdot 3} = 10\sqrt{3}$

26. $4\sqrt{2} + \sqrt{2} \cdot 2\sqrt{6}$
$= 4\sqrt{2} + 4\sqrt{3}$

27. $\sqrt{x^{10}} = x^5$

28. $\sqrt{\dfrac{90}{5}} = \sqrt{18} = 3\sqrt{2}$

29. $\sqrt{\dfrac{75x^4y^6}{3x^2y^3}} = \sqrt{25x^2y^3}$
$= 5xy\sqrt{y}$

LESSON 68

1. $x = 3$

2. $x = 6$

3. $\sqrt{x-5} = 2$
$\left(\sqrt{x-5}\right)^2 = 2^2$
$x - 5 = 4$
$x = 9$

4. $\sqrt{2x+4} = 4$
$\left(\sqrt{2x+4}\right)^2 = 4^2$
$2x + 4 = 16$
$x = 6$

5. $\left(\sqrt{x+2}\right)^2 = \left(\sqrt{6-x}\right)^2$
$x + 2 = 6 - x$
$x = 2$

6. $\left(\sqrt{4x-9}\right)^2 = \left(\sqrt{3x}\right)^2$
$4x - 9 = 3x$
$x = 9$

7. $\sqrt[3]{x} = 3$
$\left(\sqrt[3]{x}\right)^3 = 3^3$
$x = 27$

8. $\left(\sqrt[3]{x+6}\right)^3 = \left(\sqrt[3]{2x}\right)^3$
$x + 6 = 2x$
$x = 6$

9. $\sqrt{x} = -3$
$\left(\sqrt{x}\right)^2 = (-3)^2$
$x = 9$
$\sqrt{9} + 7 \neq 4$
No solution

10. $\sqrt{x-5} = -1$
$\left(\sqrt{x-5}\right)^2 = (-1)^2$
$x - 5 = 1$
$x = 6$
$\sqrt{6-5} + 3 \neq 2$
No solution

11. $x + 9 = 36$
$x = 27$

12. $3x + 7 = 25$
$x = 6$

13. $\sqrt{x} = 5$
$x = 25$

14. $5\sqrt{x} = 5$
$\sqrt{x} = 1$
$x = 1$

15. $\sqrt{x-4} = -6$
$x - 4 = 36$
$x = 40$
$\sqrt{40-4} + 8 \neq 2$
No solution

16. $3\sqrt{7x+2} = 12$
$\sqrt{7x+2} = 4$
$7x + 2 = 16$
$x = 2$

17. $x = 2x - 5$
$x = 5$

18. $5x - 1 = 3x + 7$
$x = 4$

19. $\sqrt[3]{x-5} = -2$
$x - 5 = -8$
$x = -3$

20. $x + 4 = 5x - 8$
$x = 3$

21. $\sqrt{x} = 2$
$x = 4$

22. $4x = x + 6$
$x = 2$

23. $\sqrt{4x+1} = 5$
$4x + 1 = 25$
$x = 6$

24. $3\sqrt{x} = -9$
$\sqrt{x} = -3$
$x = 9$
$2 - 3\sqrt{9} \neq 11$
No solution

25. $\sqrt[3]{x+2} = 1$
$x + 2 = 1$
$x = -1$

26. $9x = 2x - 7$
$x = -1$

LESSON 69

1. $x = 4$

2. $x = 11$

3. $3^2 + 3^2 = c^2$
$c^2 = 18$
$c = \sqrt{18} = 3\sqrt{2}$

4. $a^2 + 5^2 = 13^2$
$a^2 = 144$
$a = \sqrt{144} = 12$

5. Hypotenuse = 13
Legs = 5 and x
$5^2 + x^2 = 13^2$
$x^2 = 144$
$x = \sqrt{144} = 12$ feet

6. Hypotenuse = x
Legs = 3 and 6
$3^2 + 6^2 = x^2$
$x^2 = 45$
$x = \sqrt{45} = 3\sqrt{5}$ km

7. $24 = \sqrt{64d}$
$24^2 = 64d$
$d = 9$ feet

8. $\sqrt{(2-1)^2 + (7-5)^2}$
$= \sqrt{1^2 + 2^2}$
$= \sqrt{5}$

9. $6^2 + 8^2 = x^2$
$x^2 = 100$
$x = \sqrt{100} = 10$

10. $6^2 + x^2 = 9^2$
$x^2 = 45$
$x = \sqrt{45} = 3\sqrt{5}$

11. $5^2 + x^2 = 10^2$
$x^2 = 75$
$x = \sqrt{75} = 5\sqrt{3}$

12. x = side length, y = diagonal
Area = 49, so solving $x^2 = 49$ gives $x = 7$.
Side length = 7, so solving $7^2 + 7^2 = y^2$ gives $y = 7\sqrt{2}$.
The diagonal is 7√2 cm long.

13. Hypotenuse = 15, Legs = 12 and x
Solving $12^2 + x^2 = 15^2$ gives $x = 9$.
The perimeter is 15 + 12 + 9 = 36cm.

14. Hypotenuse = 16, Legs = 12 and x
Solving $12^2 + x^2 = 16^2$ gives $x = 4\sqrt{7}$.
The height is 4√7 inches.

15. Hypotenuse = 10, Legs = 8 and x
Solving $8^2 + x^2 = 10^2$ gives $x = 6$.
The bottom is 6 feet from the wall.

16. Plug P = 2 into the formula: $2 = 2\pi\sqrt{\dfrac{L}{32}}$

Switch sides, and
divide both sides by 2π: $\sqrt{\dfrac{L}{32}} = \dfrac{1}{\pi}$

Square both sides: $\dfrac{L}{32} = \dfrac{1}{\pi^2}$

Multiply both sides by 32: $L = \dfrac{32}{\pi^2}$

LESSON 70

1. 4   **2.** -2 **3.** 3   **4.** 2

5. $2\sqrt{2}$ **6.** $2\sqrt[3]{3}$ **7.** $\dfrac{2\sqrt{3}}{5}$ **8.** $\dfrac{2\sqrt[3]{2}}{3}$

9. $x^2\sqrt{x}$ **10.** $xy\sqrt[3]{x}$ **11.** $\dfrac{x}{y^3}$ **12.** $\dfrac{x\sqrt[3]{x^2}}{y^3}$

13. $5\sqrt{5}$ **14.** $4\sqrt{2}$ **15.** 4   **16.** $5x^2\sqrt{2}$

17. $4\sqrt{2}$ **18.** $\sqrt{6}$

19. $x = 7$ **20.** $x = 4$

21. $x = 10$ **22.** No solution

23. $x = 30$ **24.** $x = 1$

25. $x = 3\sqrt{2}$ **26.** $x = 13$

27. Area = 8.5 × 5 = 42.5 in^2

28. Area = (6 + 10) × 5 × 1/2 = 40 m^2

29. Area = rectangle + triangle
= (6 × 5) +(6 × 4 × 1/2) = 42 in^2

30. Area = rectangle − triangle
= (18 × 11) − (8 × 6 × 1/2) = 174 ft^2

LESSON 71

1. 1   **2.** 32   **3.** -81 **4.** -64

5. 1   **6.** 1   **7.** -2 **8.** -4

9. $\dfrac{1}{9^2} = \dfrac{1}{81}$ **10.** $\dfrac{1}{(-4)^3} = -\dfrac{1}{64}$

11. $3^2 = 9$ **12.** $(-2)^5 = -32$

13. $\dfrac{2^4}{4^2} = 1$ **14.** $\dfrac{3^3}{9^2} = \dfrac{1}{3}$

15. 1   **16.** -36

17. $\dfrac{1}{2^5} = \dfrac{1}{32}$ **18.** $\dfrac{1}{(-3)^3} = -\dfrac{1}{27}$

19. $2^3 = 8$ **20.** $3^4 = 81$

21. $(-2)^1 = -2$ **22.** $10^2 = 100$

23. $\dfrac{5^9}{5^7} = 25$ **24.** $\dfrac{4^3}{4^5} = \dfrac{1}{16}$

25. $\dfrac{1}{2^2 \cdot 5^2} = \dfrac{1}{100}$ **26.** $\dfrac{(-9)^5}{27^4} = -\dfrac{1}{9}$

27. 1   **28.** 121

29. $\dfrac{1}{1^1} = 1$ **30.** $-\dfrac{1}{5^3} = -\dfrac{1}{125}$

31. $3^3 = 27$ **32.** $5^2 = 25$

33. $(-7)^2 = 49$ **34.** $(-10)^3 = -1000$

35. $\dfrac{3^5}{3^5} = 1$ **36.** $\dfrac{7^7}{7^5} = 49$

37. $\dfrac{3^6}{6^4} = \dfrac{9}{16}$ **38.** $\dfrac{(-18)^3}{(-3)^5} = 24$

39. $2^7 = 2^x$ **40.** $4^2 = 4^x$
$x = 7$ $x = 2$

41. $3^6 = 3^x \cdot 3^3$ **42.** $7^2 = 7^2 \cdot 7^x$
$x = 3$ $x = 0$

43. $\dfrac{1}{6^3} = \dfrac{6^x}{6^2}$ **44.** $\dfrac{1}{2^7} = \dfrac{2^x}{2^5}$
$x = -1$ $x = -2$

LESSON 72

1. 1   **2.** 1/64   **3.** −81   **4.** 1/1000

5. $3 \cdot 5 \cdot x^{4+2} = 15x^6$ **6.** $3x^{6-4}y^{1+2} = 3x^2y^3$

7. $\frac{4}{2} \cdot x^{4-2} = 2x^2$ **8.** $\frac{5}{-5} \cdot x^{4-2}y^{5-2} = -x^2y^3$

9. $5x^{-4+2} = 5x^{-2} = \frac{5}{x^2}$ **10.** $x^{2-1-3-2} = x^{-4} = \frac{1}{x^4}$

11. $a^{3+2} = a^5$ **12.** $a^{4-7} = a^{-3}$

13. $a^{8-4} = a^4$ **14.** $a^{6-8} = a^{-2}$

15. $4x^{8-5} = 4x^3$ **16.** $14x^{3-5} = 14x^{-2} = \frac{14}{x^2}$

17. $x^{8-2}y^{-2+5} = x^6y^3$ **18.** $-27x^{2-4}y^5 = \frac{-27y^5}{x^2}$

19. $-5x^{5+2-4} = -5x^3$ **20.** $3x^{-4+5-3} = 3x^{-2} = \frac{3}{x^2}$

21. $4x^{5-2-4} = 4x^{-1} = \frac{4}{x}$ **22.** $10x^{3+2-(-1)} = 10x^6$

23. $\frac{1}{3}x^{3-3}y^{-1-(-5)} = \frac{1}{3}x^0y^4 = \frac{y^4}{3}$

24. $-3x^{4-3}y^{5-7} = -3xy^{-2} = -\frac{3x}{y^2}$

25. $5^{9-7} = 5^2 = 25$

26. $15^{3+7-9} = 15^1 = 15$

27. $(-16)^{7-6} = -16$

28. $8^{7-5} \cdot 4^{3-6} = 8^2 \cdot 4^{-3} = \frac{8^2}{4^3} = 1$

LESSON 73

1. $6x^7$ **2.** $7/x^2$ **3.** x **4.** $-2x^4$

5. $x^{-1 \times 5} = x^{-5} = \frac{1}{x^5}$ **6.** $x^{-3 \times -2} = x^6$

7. $(-3)^2x^2 = 9x^2$ **8.** $5^{-1}x^{-1}y^{-1} = \frac{1}{5xy}$

9. $\frac{3^3}{x^3} = \frac{27}{x^3}$ **10.** $\frac{5^{-2}}{x^{-2}} = \frac{x^2}{5^2} = \frac{x^2}{25}$

11. $2^4x^{2 \times 4}y^{-1 \times 4} = \frac{16x^8}{y^4}$ **12.** $\frac{x^{-2}}{y^{2 \times -2}} = \frac{x^{-2}}{y^{-4}} = \frac{y^4}{x^2}$

13. $2^3a^{2 \times 3} = 8a^6$ **14.** $(-1)^{-5}a^{4 \times -5} = -a^{-20}$

15. $\frac{a^2}{2^2} = \frac{1}{4}a^2$ **16.** $\frac{3^{-2}}{a^{-2}} = \frac{a^2}{3^2} = \frac{1}{9}a^2$

17. $8^2x^{5 \times 2} = 64x^{10}$ **18.** $3^3x^{-4 \times 3} = \frac{27}{x^{12}}$

19. $2^{-5}x^{3 \times -5} = \frac{1}{32x^{15}}$ **20.** $4^{-3}x^{-5 \times -3} = \frac{x^{15}}{64}$

21. $(-3)^4x^4y^4 = 81x^4y^4$ **22.** $7^2x^{3 \times 2}y^{-5 \times 2} = \frac{49x^6}{x^{10}}$

23. $\frac{x^{2 \times 2}}{10^2} = \frac{x^4}{100}$ **24.** $\frac{(-1)^3}{x^{-5 \times 3}} = \frac{-1}{x^{-15}} = -x^{15}$

25. $\frac{1}{x^{3 \times 3}y^{-4 \times 3}} = \frac{1}{x^9y^{-12}} = \frac{y^{12}}{x^9}$

26. $\frac{y^{3 \times -2}}{9^{-2}x^{4 \times -2}} = \frac{y^{-6}}{9^{-2}x^{-8}} = \frac{9^2x^8}{y^6} = \frac{81x^8}{y^6}$

27. $\frac{9^{4 \times 3}}{9^{10}} = \frac{9^{12}}{9^{10}} = 9^2 = 81$ **28.** $\frac{4^2 \cdot 8^2}{4^3} = \frac{8^2}{4} = 16$

29. $\frac{7^{2 \times 7}}{7^{15}} = \frac{7^{14}}{7^{15}} = \frac{1}{7}$ **30.** $\frac{6^7 \cdot 12^3}{6^5 \cdot 12^5} = \frac{6^2}{12^2} = \frac{1}{4}$

LESSON 74

1–7. Answers will vary. See Lessons 71 through 73.

8. $3^{-3}x^{-3} \cdot x^0 = \frac{1}{27x^3}$

9. $(3x^{-3})^4 = 3^4x^{-12} = \frac{81}{x^{12}}$

10. $x^8y^4 \cdot x^{-5}y^3 = x^3y^7$

11. $\frac{x^{12}y^{12}}{x^{-4}y^4} = x^{16}y^8$

12. $(3xy^{-3})^{-3} = 3^{-3}x^{-3}y^9 = \frac{y^9}{27x^3}$

13. $\left(\frac{x^2y^4}{4x^5y^2}\right)^2 = \left(\frac{y^2}{4x^3}\right)^2 = \frac{y^4}{16x^6}$

14. a^3 **a.** a^3 b. a^7 c. a^{-3} **d.** a^3

15. $\frac{s^6}{t^6}$ a. $\frac{t^6}{s^6}$ **b.** $\frac{s^6}{t^6}$ **c.** $\frac{s^6}{t^6}$ d. $\frac{t^6}{s^6}$

16. $\frac{x}{y}$ **a.** $\frac{x}{y}$ b. $\frac{y}{x}$ **c.** $\frac{x}{y}$ d. $\frac{1}{xy}$

17. $7x^{-1-3-2} = 7x^{-6} = \dfrac{7}{x^6}$ **18.** $35x^{-4+3} = 35x^{-1} = \dfrac{35}{x}$

19. $9x \cdot 9^{-3}x^9 = \dfrac{x^{10}}{81}$ **20.** $x^5 \cdot (-2)^3 x^6 = -8x^{11}$

21. $xy^{-2} \cdot 2^2 x^6 y^2 = 4x^7$ **22.** $7^3 x^3 y^{12} \cdot 7^{-2} x^4 y^{-6}$
$= 7x^7 y^6$

23. $3x^{5-2+4-4} = 3x^3$ **24.** $\dfrac{25^2 x^6 y^4}{5^3 x^6 y^3} = 5y$

25. $3x^{-2+4-2} = 3x^0 = 3$ **26.** $8x^{-5+2} = 8x^{-3} = \dfrac{8}{x^3}$

27. $x^7 \cdot 2^{-5} x^{-5} = \dfrac{x^2}{32}$ **28.** $x^{-5} \cdot (-4)^2 x^{10} = 16x^5$

29. $x^5 y^{-3} \cdot x^{-8} y^4 = \dfrac{y}{x^3}$ **30.** $x^3 y^{-12} \cdot x^{-4} y^{12} = \dfrac{1}{x}$

LESSON 75

1. 1   **2.** 1/100   **3.** 10,000   **4.** 1/1,000

5. 10^8 **6.** 10^{-5} **7.** 10^{-4} **8.** 10^{-1}

9. Yes   **10.** No; 14 > 10

11. 23,000   **12.** 0.0000328

13. 1.59×10^9 **14.** 3.2×10^{-7}

15. $(3 \times 5) \times 10^{2+3}$ **16.** $(3/4) \times 10^{6-2}$
$= 15 \times 10^5$ $= 0.75 \times 10^4$
$= 1.5 \times 10^6$ $= 7.5 \times 10^3$

17. 1,500   **18.** 0.0000916

19. 1.95×10^9 **20.** 5×10^{-7}

21. $(6 \times 9) \times 10^{2+7}$ **22.** $(1.1 \times 3) \times 10^{-5+3}$
$= 54 \times 10^9$ $= 3.3 \times 10^{-2}$
$= 5.4 \times 10^{10}$

23. $(5 \times 4) \times 10^{6-3}$ **24.** $(2.3 \times 5) \times 10^{-4-4}$
$= 20 \times 10^3$ 11.5×10^{-8}
$= 2 \times 10^4$ $= 1.15 \times 10^{-7}$

25. $\dfrac{8}{5} \times 10^{-4-(-7)}$ **26.** $\dfrac{4}{5} \times 10^{-2-3}$
$= 1.6 \times 10^3$ $= 0.8 \times 10^{-5}$
$= 8 \times 10^{-6}$

27. $(1.4 \times 5) \times 10^{-8+3}$ **28.** $(3 \times 8) \times 10^{3+7}$
$= 7 \times 10^{-5}$ $= 24 \times 10^{10}$
$= 2.4 \times 10^{11}$

29. $\dfrac{2.5}{5} \times 10^{4-(-3)}$ **30.** $\dfrac{1.5}{3} \times 10^{4-9}$
$= 0.5 \times 10^7$ $= 0.5 \times 10^{-5}$
$= 5 \times 10^6$ $= 5 \times 10^{-6}$

LESSON 76

1. 7   **2.** 3   **3.** 2   **4.** 9

5. $3^{1/2}$ **6.** $6^{3/5}$ **7.** $\sqrt{7}$ **8.** $\sqrt[3]{4^2}$

9. $(5^2)^{1/2} = 5^1 = 5$ OR $\sqrt{25} = 5$

10. $(4^3)^{2/3} = 4^2 = 16$ OR $\left(\sqrt[3]{64}\right)^2 = 4^2 = 16$

11. $(6^2)^{-1/2} = 6^{-1} = \dfrac{1}{6}$ OR $\dfrac{1}{36^{1/2}} = \dfrac{1}{\sqrt{36}} = \dfrac{1}{6}$

12. $\dfrac{1^{3/2}}{(10^2)^{3/2}} = \dfrac{1}{10^3} = \dfrac{1}{1000}$ OR $\dfrac{1}{\left(\sqrt{100}\right)^3} = \dfrac{1}{10^3} = \dfrac{1}{1000}$

13. $2^{1/2}$ **14.** $8^{5/6}$ **15.** $3^{2/9}$ **16.** $6^{2/7}$

17. $\sqrt{3}$ **18.** $\sqrt{7^3}$ **19.** $\sqrt[3]{5^4}$ **20.** $\sqrt[5]{8}$

21. $(3^2)^{1/2} = 3^1 = 3$ OR $\sqrt{9} = 3$

22. $(2^3)^{1/3} = 2^1 = 2$ OR $\sqrt[3]{8} = 2$

23. $(2^2)^{5/2} = 2^5 = 32$ OR $\left(\sqrt{4}\right)^5 = 2^5 = 32$

24. $(3^3)^{2/3} = 3^2 = 9$ OR $\left(\sqrt[3]{27}\right)^2 = 3^2 = 9$

25. $(5^2)^{-1/2} = 5^{-1} = \dfrac{1}{5}$ OR $\dfrac{1}{25^{1/2}} = \dfrac{1}{\sqrt{25}} = \dfrac{1}{5}$

26. $(4^3)^{-1/3} = 4^{-1} = \dfrac{1}{4}$ OR $\dfrac{1}{64^{1/3}} = \dfrac{1}{\sqrt[3]{64}} = \dfrac{1}{4}$

27. $(4^2)^{-3/2} = 4^{-3} = \dfrac{1}{64}$ OR $\dfrac{1}{16^{3/2}} = \dfrac{1}{\left(\sqrt{16}\right)^3} = \dfrac{1}{64}$

28. $(5^3)^{-2/3} = 5^{-2} = \dfrac{1}{25}$ OR $\dfrac{1}{125^{2/3}} = \dfrac{1}{\left(\sqrt[3]{125}\right)^2} = \dfrac{1}{25}$

29. $\dfrac{1}{(2^3)^{5/3}} = \dfrac{1}{2^5} = \dfrac{1}{32}$ OR $\dfrac{1}{\left(\sqrt[3]{8}\right)^5} = \dfrac{1}{2^5} = \dfrac{1}{32}$

30. $\dfrac{1}{(2^6)^{1/6}} = \dfrac{1}{2^1} = \dfrac{1}{2}$ OR $\dfrac{1}{\sqrt[6]{64}} = \dfrac{1}{2}$

31. $\dfrac{1}{(3^3)^{4/3}} = \dfrac{1}{3^4} = \dfrac{1}{81}$ OR $\dfrac{1}{\left(\sqrt[3]{27}\right)^4} = \dfrac{1}{3^4} = \dfrac{1}{81}$

32. $\dfrac{1}{(10^3)^{1/3}} = \dfrac{1}{10}$ OR $\dfrac{1}{\sqrt[3]{1000}} = \dfrac{1}{10}$

33. $(2^2)^{1/2} = 2^1 = 2$ OR $\sqrt{4} = 2$

34. $(3^4)^{1/4} = 3^1 = 3$ OR $\sqrt[4]{81} = 3$

35. $(2^5)^{3/5} = 2^3 = 8$ OR $\left(\sqrt[5]{32}\right)^3 = 2^3 = 8$

36. $(4^3)^{2/3} = 4^2 = 16$ OR $\left(\sqrt[3]{64}\right)^2 = 4^2 = 16$

37. $(2^3)^{-1/3} = 2^{-1} = \dfrac{1}{2}$ OR $\dfrac{1}{8^{1/3}} = \dfrac{1}{\sqrt[3]{8}} = \dfrac{1}{2}$

38. $(6^2)^{-1/2} = 6^{-1} = \dfrac{1}{6}$ OR $\dfrac{1}{36^{1/2}} = \dfrac{1}{\sqrt{36}} = \dfrac{1}{6}$

39. $(3^3)^{-4/3} = 3^{-4} = \dfrac{1}{81}$ OR $\dfrac{1}{27^{4/3}} = \dfrac{1}{\left(\sqrt[3]{27}\right)^4} = \dfrac{1}{81}$

40. $(10^4)^{-5/4} = 10^{-5} = \dfrac{1}{10^5} = \dfrac{1}{100000}$

OR $\dfrac{1}{10000^{5/4}} = \dfrac{1}{\left(\sqrt[4]{10000}\right)^5} = \dfrac{1}{10^5} = \dfrac{1}{100000}$

41. $\sqrt[4]{2^3} = 2^{3/4} = 2^n$
$n = 3/4$

42. $\sqrt[3]{5^2} = 5^{2/3} = 5^{2n}$
$2n = 2/3$
$n = 1/3$

43. $\sqrt{2^5} = 2^{5/2} = 2^{n+2}$
$n + 2 = 5/2$
$n = 1/2$

44. $3^{4/5} = (3^2)^{n/5} = 3^{2n/5}$
$2n/5 = 4/5$
$n = 2$

45. $(6^2)^{2/3} = 6^{4/3} = 6^{n/3}$
$n/3 = 4/3$
$n = 4$

46. $4^{3/4} = (4^3)^n = 4^{3n}$
$3n = 3/4$
$n = 1/4$

LESSON 77 ·······················

1. $6x^2$ **2.** $8/x$ **3.** $x^3/3$ **4.** x^{12}

5. $5^{1/3 + 1/4} = 5^{7/12}$ **6.** $4^{1/5 \times 5/2} = 4^{1/2} = 2$

7. $x^{3/5 - 1/2} = x^{1/10}$ **8.** $\left(3^3 x^{1/2}\right)^{1/3} = 3x^{1/6}$

9. $\sqrt{2} \cdot \sqrt[3]{2^2} = 2^{1/2} \cdot 2^{2/3} = 2^{7/6} = \sqrt[6]{2^7} = 2\sqrt[6]{2}$

10. $\dfrac{\sqrt[4]{10^3}}{\sqrt{10}} = \dfrac{10^{3/4}}{10^{1/2}} = 10^{1/4} = \sqrt[4]{10}$

11. $\sqrt[3]{\sqrt[5]{2^3}} = \left(2^{3/5}\right)^{1/3} = 2^{1/5} = \sqrt[5]{2}$

12. $x^{1/4} \cdot x^{1/3} = x^{7/12} = \sqrt[12]{x^7}$

13. $\dfrac{x^{5/8}}{x^{1/2}} = x^{1/8} = \sqrt[8]{x}$ **14.** $\left(x^{2/3}\right)^{1/4} = x^{1/6} = \sqrt[6]{x}$

15. $3^{3/4 + 1/4} = 3^1 = 3$ **16.** $x^{1/3 + 2/5} = x^{11/15}$

17. $8^{1/2 \times 1/3} = 8^{1/6}$
$= 2^{3 \times 1/6} = 2^{1/2}$

18. $\left(2^2 x^{4/5}\right)^{5/2}$
$= 2^5 x^2 = 32x^2$

19. $125^{5/6 - 1/2} = 125^{1/3}$
$= (5^3)^{1/3} = 5$

20. $\left(2^6 x^{1/2}\right)^{1/2}$
$= 2^3 x^{1/4} = 8x^{1/4}$

21. $\sqrt{3} \cdot \sqrt[4]{3^2}$
$= 3^{1/2} \cdot 3^{2/4} = 3^1 = 3$

22. $x^{1/6} \cdot x^{2/6} = x^{1/2}$
$= \sqrt{x}$

23. $\sqrt[3]{2^2} \cdot \sqrt[6]{2^5}$
$= 2^{2/3} \cdot 2^{5/6} = 2^{3/2}$
$= \sqrt{2^3} = 2\sqrt{2}$

24. $x^{3/4} \cdot x^{1/2} = x^{5/4}$
$= \sqrt[4]{x^5} = x\sqrt[4]{x}$

25. $\sqrt[3]{\sqrt{2^6}} = \left(2^{6/2}\right)^{1/3} = 2$

26. $\left(x^{5/7}\right)^{1/5} = x^{1/7} = \sqrt[7]{x}$

27. Left: $3^{n+1/3}$
Right: $(3^3)^{1/3} = 3^1$
$n + 1/3 = 1$
$n = 2/3$

28. Left: $2^{2 \times 1/3 \times 1/2} = 2^{1/3}$
Right: $n^{1/3}$
$n = 2$

29. Left: $x^{1/4+n}$
Right: $x^{3/4}$
$1/4 + n = 3/4$
$n = 1/2$

30. Left: $x^{2n/5}$
Right: $x^{1/10}$
$2n/5 = 1/10$
$n = 1/4$

31. Left: $\left(x^{1/3}\right)^{1/2} = x^{1/6}$
Right: $x^{2/3-n}$
$2/3 - n = 1/6$
$n = 1/2$

32. Left: $(x^3)^{1/6} = x^{1/2}$
Right: $x^{n/6}$
$n/6 = 1/2$
$n = 3$

LESSON 78 ·······················

1. Exponential **2.** Linear

3. Quadratic **4.** Quadratic

5. Exponential **6.** Linear

7. Growth ($b = 3 > 1$) **8.** Decay ($b = 0.5 < 1$)

9. Growth ($b = 1.5 > 1$) **10.** Neither

11. $a = 50,000$ and $b = 1.05$, so $y = 50,000(1.05)^x$.
When $x = 7$, $y = 50,000(1.05)^7 = 70355.02\ldots$
His salary will be about $70,355.

12. $a = 50{,}000$ and $b = 0.95$, so $y = 50{,}000(0.95)^x$.
When $x = 7$, $y = 50{,}000(0.95)^7 = 34916.86\ldots$
The population will be about 34,917.

13. Neither   **14.** Decay ($b = 0.9 < 1$)

15. Growth ($b = 3 > 1$)   **16.** Decay ($b = 0.1 < 1$)

17. Decay ($b = 0.9 < 1$)
$a = 15{,}000$ and $b = 0.9$, so $y = 15{,}000(0.9)^x$.
When $x = 10$, $y = 15{,}000(0.9)^{10} = 5230.17\ldots$
The value will be about $5,230.

18. Growth ($b = 1.04 > 1$)
$a = 3{,}000$ and $b = 1.04$, so $y = 3{,}000(1.04)^x$.
When $x = 8$, $y = 3{,}000(1.04)^8 = 4105.70\ldots$
The balance will be about $4,106.

19. Growth ($b = 2 > 1$)
$a = 10$ and $b = 2$, so $y = 10(2)^x$.
When $x = 10$, $y = 10(2)^{10} = 10240$.
There will be 10,240 bacteria.

(Note that $x = 10$, not 5, because bacteria double every 30 minutes. Bacteria double 10 times in 5 hours.)

20. Decay ($b = 0.86 < 1$)
$a = 1{,}013$ and $b = 0.86$, so $y = 1{,}013(0.86)^x$.
When $x = 5$, $y = 1{,}013(0.86)^5 = 476.54\ldots$
The pressure will be about 477 millibars.

LESSON 79

1. 1   **2.** 1/8   **3.** 16   **4.** 1/3

5. $8x^2$ **6.** $-6/x^3$ **7.** $4/x^4$ **8.** $xy/3$

9. $16x^8$ **10.** x^{12}/y^9 **11.** $-x^{15}/8$ **12.** $x^6y^6/27$

13. $2x^{18}$ **14.** $32x^7y^9$ **15.** $27/x^4$ **16.** $-2x^4y$

17. 3.2×10^{-5} **18.** 2.5×10^2

19. 7   **20.** 9   **21.** 1/2   **22.** 1/1000

23. 5   **24.** $3^{1/3}$ **25.** 3   **26.** $4x^{1/3}$

27. $y = 8000(1.05)^x$ **28.** $y = 40000(0.97)^x$
About $9,724   About 34,349

29. $C = 2\pi r = 2 \times 3.14 \times 6 = 37.68$ cm

30. $r = 10/2 = 5$
$A = \pi r^2 = 3.14 \times 5^2 = 78.5$ in^2

31. $V = \pi r^2 h = 3.14 \times 10^2 \times 5 = 1{,}570$ in^3

32. $V = \pi r^2 h/3 = 3.14 \times 4^2 \times 3 \times 1/3 = 50.24$ m^3

LESSON 80

1. Polynomial

2. Not a polynomial ($4x^{-2}$ is not a monomial.)

3. Polynomial

4. $4x^2 - 2x + 7$ (Degree: 2, Leading: 4)

5. $-x^3 - 6x^2 - x + 4$ (Degree:3, Leading: −1)

6. $3x^5 - 2x^4 + x + 5$ (Degree: 5, Leading: 3)

7. $x^2 + (3x + 7x) + (-1 + 5) = x^2 + 10x + 4$

8. $(3x^2 - 4x^2) + (6x - x) + (1 - (-2))$
$= -x^2 + 5x + 3$

9.
$$\begin{array}{r} 3x^2 + 2x + 5 \\ +\ \ 2x^2 - 6x - 3 \\ \hline 5x^2 - 4x + 2 \end{array}$$

10.
$$\begin{array}{r} 2x^2 +\ x + 2 \\ -\ \ \ \ \ \ \ \ (4x + 3) \\ \hline 2x^2 - 3x - 1 \end{array}$$

11. Polynomial

12. Not a polynomial ($\sqrt{x}$ is not a monomial.)

13. Not a polynomial ($5x^{-4}$ is not a monomial.)

14. $5x^2 - 2x + 4$ (Degree:2, Leading: 5)

15. $x^3 + 4x + 5$ (Degree: 3, Leading: 1)

16. $-x^4 + 4x^3 - 5x^2 + x$ (Degree: 4, Leading: −1)

17. $(3x + x) + (1 - 5) = 4x - 4$

18. $(4x - 3x) + (3 - (-2)) = x + 5$

19. $x^2 + (-2x + 2x) + (4 - 5) = x^2 - 1$

20. $-(-5x^2) + (3x - x) + (7 - 4) = 5x^2 + 2x + 3$

21. $(5x^2 - x^2) + (x - 4x) + (6 + 2) = 4x^2 - 3x + 8$

22. $(x^3 - 2x^3) - x^2 + (5x - (-3x)) + (2 - 1)$
$= -x^3 - x^2 + 8x + 1$

23. $(2x - 3x) + (7 + 1) = -x + 8$

24. $(-x - 6x) + (8 - 5) = -7x + 3$

25. $-x^2 + (-x + 6x) + (9 - 3) = -x^2 + 5x + 6$

26. $5x^2 + (-x - 4x) + (3 - (-2)) = 5x^2 - 5x + 5$

27. $(x^2 + x^2) + (2x + x) + (1 + 5) = 2x^2 + 3x + 6$

28. $(x^2 - 4x^2) + (x - x) + (9 - 8) = -3x^2 + 1$

29. $(-2x^2 - x^2) + (-4x - (-2x)) + (5 - (-1))$
$= -3x^2 - 2x + 6$

30. $x^3 + (x^2 + x^2) + (2x - 4x) + 7$
$= x^3 + 2x^2 - 2x + 7$

LESSON 81

1. $2 \cdot 8 \cdot x^{1+2} = 16x^3$

2. $-4 \cdot 5 \cdot x^{5+3} = -20x^8$

3. $3x(2x) + 3x(1) = 6x^2 + 3x$

4. $(-3x^2)(x^3) + (-3x^2)(-2x) + (-3x^2)(1)$
   $= -3x^5 + 6x^3 - 3x^2$

5. $x(x+2) + 1(x+2)$
   $= x^2 + 2x + x + 2$
   $= x^2 + 3x + 2$

6. $2x(x-3) + 5(x-3)$
   $= 2x^2 - 6x + 5x - 15$
   $= 2x^2 - x - 15$

7. $x^2 + 3x + 2x + 6$
   $= x^2 + 5x + 6$

8. $x^2 - 2x + 2x - 4$
   $= x^2 - 4$

9. $3x^2 - 2x - 12x + 8$
   $= 3x^2 - 14x + 8$

10.

	x	-2
x	x^2	$-2x$
3	$3x$	-6

Add up each product:
$x^2 - 2x + 3x - 6$
$= x^2 + x - 6$

11.

	$2x$	-3
x	$2x^2$	$-3x$
-1	$-2x$	3

Add up each product:
$2x^2 - 3x - 2x + 3$
$= 2x^2 - 5x + 3$

12. $2x^5$

13. $-12x^7$

14. $5x(3x) + 5x(-2)$
    $= 15x^2 - 10x$

15. $x(x^2) + x(x) + x(5)$
    $= x^3 + x^2 + 5x$

16. $x^2 + 3x + 8x + 24$
    $= x^2 + 11x + 24$

17. $x^2 - 4x + 7x - 28$
    $= x^2 + 3x - 28$

18. $2x^2 + 2x + 5x + 5$
    $= 2x^2 + 7x + 5$

19. $4x^2 - x - 8x + 2$
    $= 4x^2 - 9x + 2$

20. $9x^2 - 6x + 6x - 4$
    $= 9x^2 - 4$

21. $6x^2 + 9x - 2x - 3$
    $= 6x^2 + 7x - 3$

22. $5x^4$

23. $-15x^5$

24. $(-2x)(x^2) + (-2x)(4x) + (-2x)(-3)$
    $= -2x^3 - 8x^2 + 6x$

25. $4x^3(x^3) + 4x^3(-4x^2) + 4x^3(2x) + 4x^3(-8)$
    $= 4x^6 - 16x^5 + 8x^4 - 32x^3$

26. $x^2 - 5x + 5x - 25$
    $= x^2 - 25$

27. $x^2 - 3x - 2x + 6$
    $= x^2 - 5x + 6$

28. $3x^2 - x - 18x + 6$
    $= 3x^2 - 19x + 6$

29. $3x^2 - 9x + x - 3$
    $= 3x^2 - 8x - 3$

30. $10x^2 + 6x + 5x + 3$
    $= 10x^2 + 11x + 3$

31. $16x^2 - 12x + 12x - 9$
    $= 16x^2 - 9$

LESSON 82

1. $8x^5$

2. $-x^3 + 5x^2 - x$

3. $x^2 - 8x + 12$

4. $2x^2 + 5x - 3$

5. $x^3 + x^2 + 4x + 2x^2 + 2x + 8$
   $= x^3 + 3x^2 + 6x + 8$

6. $x^3 - 3x^2 - 5x^2 + 15x + 4x - 12$
   $= x^3 - 8x^2 + 19x - 12$

7. $x^4 - 2x^3 + x^2 - x^3 + 2x^2 - x + x^2 - 2x + 1$
   $= x^4 - 3x^3 + 4x^2 - 3x + 1$

8.

	x	4
x	x^2	$4x$
-3	$-3x$	-12

Add up all the areas:
$x^2 + 4x - 3x - 12$
$= x^2 + x - 12$

9.

	x	2
x^2	x^3	$2x^2$
$3x$	$3x^2$	$6x$
-2	$-2x$	-4

Add up all the areas:
$x^3 + 2x^2 + 3x^2 + 6x$
$-2x - 4$
$= x^3 + 5x^2 + 4x - 4$

10.

	x^2	$-3x$	1
$2x^2$	$2x^4$	$-6x^3$	$2x^2$
x	x^3	$-3x^2$	x
1	x^2	$-3x$	1

Add up all the areas:
$2x^4 - 6x^3 + 2x^2 + x^3 - 3x^2 + x + x^2 - 3x + 1$
$= 2x^4 - 5x^3 - 2x + 1$

11. $x^2 + x + 3x + 3$
    $= x^2 + 4x + 3$

12. $x^2 + 5x - 6x - 30$
    $= x^2 - x - 30$

13. $2x^2 - 4x - x + 2$
    $= 2x^2 - 5x + 2$

14. $20x^2 + 12x - 15x - 9$
    $= 20x^2 - 3x - 9$

15. $x^3 - x^2 + x + x^2 - x + 1 = x^3 + 1$

16. $4x^3 + 12x^2 - 8x + 3x^2 + 9x - 6$
    $= 4x^3 + 15x^2 + x - 6$

17. $x^3 + 5x^2 - 3x^2 - 15x + x + 5$
    $= x^3 + 2x^2 - 14x + 5$

18. $6x^3 - 14x^2 - 3x^2 + 7x - 15x + 35$
    $= 6x^3 - 17x^2 - 8x + 35$

19. $x^4 + 4x^3 + 5x^2 + x^3 + 4x^2 + 5x + x^2 + 4x + 5$
    $= x^4 + 5x^3 + 10x^2 + 9x + 5$

20. $2x^4 - x^3 + 3x^2 - 10x^3 + 5x^2 - 15x + 2x^2 - x + 3$
    $= 2x^4 - 11x^3 + 10x^2 - 16x + 3$

21. $(x-1)(x+5)$
    $= x^2 + 5x - x - 5 = x^2 + 4x - 5$

22. $(x + 1)(x^2 + 2x + 1)$
$= x^3 + 2x^2 + x + x^2 + 2x + 1$
$= x^3 + 3x^2 + 3x + 1$

23. $(x + 3)(2x^2 - x + 3)$
$= 2x^3 - x^2 + 3x + 6x^2 - 3x + 9$
$= 2x^3 + 5x^2 + 9$

24. $5x^2(x^3 + 2x^2 - 3x + 1)$
$= 5x^5 + 10x^4 - 15x^3 + 5x^2$

25. $x^2 - 7x + 2x - 14$
$= x^2 - 5x - 14$

26. $x^2 - 2x - 2 + 4$
$= x^2 - 4x + 4$

27. $4x^2 + 16x - x - 4$
$= 4x^2 + 15x - 4$

28. $6x^2 + 15x + 14x + 35$
$= 6x^2 + 29x + 35$

29. $x^3 + 3x^2 - 5x - 4x^2 - 12x + 20$
$= x^3 - x^2 - 17x + 20$

30. $10x^3 + 15x^2 - 10x - 6x^2 - 9x + 6$
$= 10x^3 + 9x^2 - 19x + 6$

31. $x^3 + 2x^2 - 2x^2 - 4x + 4x + 8$
$= x^3 + 8$

32. $8x^3 - 4x^2 - 4x^2 + 2x + 2x - 1$
$= 8x^3 - 8x^2 + 4x - 1$

33. $x^4 - x^3 + 4x^2 + x^3 - x^2 + 4x + 3x^2 - 3x + 12$
$= x^4 + 6x^2 + x + 12$

34. $9x^4 - 9x^3 - 6x^2 - 3x^3 + 3x^2 + 2x - 6x^2 + 6x + 4$
$= 9x^4 - 12x^3 - 9x^2 + 8x + 4$

LESSON 83

1. $a^2 + 2ab + b^2$

2. $a^2 - 2ab + b^2$

3. $a^2 - b^2$

4. $x^2 + 2 \cdot x \cdot 2 + 2^2$
$= x^2 + 4x + 4$

5. $x^2 + 2 \cdot x \cdot 3 + 3^2$
$= x^2 + 6x + 9$

6. $(4x)^2 + 2 \cdot 4x \cdot 1 + 1^2$
$= 16x^2 + 8x + 1$

7. $(3x)^2 + 2 \cdot 3x \cdot 2 + 2^2$
$= 9x^2 + 12x + 4$

8. $x^2 - 2 \cdot x \cdot 1 + 1^2$
$= x^2 - 2x + 1$

9. $x^2 - 2 \cdot x \cdot 5 + 5^2$
$= x^2 - 10x + 25$

10. $(6x)^2 - 2 \cdot 6x \cdot 1 + 1^2$
$= 36x^2 - 12x + 1$

11. $(4x)^2 - 2 \cdot 4x \cdot 3 + 3^2$
$= 16x^2 - 24x + 9$

12. $x^2 - 4^2$
$= x^2 - 16$

13. $x^2 - 8^2$
$= x^2 - 64$

14. $(2x)^2 - 1^2$
$= 4x^2 - 1$

15. $(7x)^2 - 2^2$
$= 49x^2 - 4$

16. $(50 + 2)^2$
$= 50^2 + 2 \cdot 50 \cdot 2 + 2^2$
$= 2500 + 200 + 4$
$= 2704$

17. $(70 - 3)^2$
$= 70^2 - 2 \cdot 70 \cdot 3 + 3^2$
$= 4900 - 420 + 9$
$= 4489$

18. $(30 + 2)(30 - 2)$
$= 30^2 - 2^2$
$= 900 - 4$
$= 896$

19. $x^2 + 2 \cdot x \cdot 4 + 4^2$
$= x^2 + 8x + 16$

20. $(3x)^2 + 2 \cdot 3x \cdot 1 + 1^2$
$= 9x^2 + 6x + 1$

21. $x^2 - 2 \cdot x \cdot 3 + 3^2$
$= x^2 - 6x + 9$

22. $(5x)^2 - 2 \cdot 5x \cdot 4 + 4^2$
$= 25x^2 - 40x + 16$

23. $x^2 - 1^2$
$= x^2 - 1$

24. $(8x)^2 - 5^2$
$= 64x^2 - 25$

25. $(20 + 1)^2$
$= 20^2 + 2 \cdot 20 \cdot 1 + 1^2$
$= 400 + 40 + 1$
$= 441$

26. $(80 - 2)^2$
$= 80^2 - 2 \cdot 80 \cdot 2 + 2^2$
$= 6400 - 320 + 4$
$= 6084$

27. $(80 + 1)(80 - 1)$
$= 80^2 - 1^2$
$= 6400 - 1$
$= 6399$

28. $(200 - 10)(200 + 10)$
$= 200^2 - 10^2$
$= 40000 - 100$
$= 39900$

29. $x^2 + 2 \cdot x \cdot 6 + 6^2$
$= x^2 + 12x + 36$

30. $(2x)^2 + 2 \cdot 2x \cdot 5 + 5^2$
$= 4x^2 + 20x + 25$

31. $x^2 - 2 \cdot x \cdot 7 + 7^2$
$= x^2 - 14x + 49$

32. $(3x)^2 - 2 \cdot 3x \cdot 2 + 2^2$
$= 9x^2 - 12x + 4$

33. $x^2 - 2 \cdot x \cdot 8 + 8^2$
$= x^2 - 16x + 64$

34. $(6x)^2 + 2 \cdot 6x \cdot 1 + 1^2$
$= 36x^2 + 12x + 1$

35. $x^2 - 9^2$
$= x^2 - 81$

36. $(4x)^2 - 1^2$
$= 16x^2 - 1$

LESSON 84

1. $a^2 + 2ab + b^2$

2. $a^2 - 2ab + b^2$

3. $a^2 - b^2$

4. $x^2 + 2x + 1$

5. $x^2 - 4x + 4$

6. $x^2 - 9$

7. $4x^2 + 4x + 1$

8. $9x^2 - 12x + 4$

9. $25x^2 - 16$

10. $x^2 - 2 \cdot x \cdot 4 + 4^2$
$= x^2 - 8x + 16$

11. $x^2 + 3x - x - 3$
$= x^2 + 2x - 3$

12. $x^2 - 2x + 6x - 12$
$= x^2 + 4x - 12$

13. $x^2 + 2 \cdot x \cdot 9 + 9^2$
$= x^2 + 18x + 81$

14. $x^2 + 3x + 4x + 12$
$= x^2 + 7x + 12$

15. $x^2 - 7x + 2x - 14$
$= x^2 - 5x - 14$

16. $x^2 + 2 \cdot x \cdot 3 + 3^2$
$= x^2 + 6x + 9$

17. $x^2 + x + 9x + 9$
$= x^2 + 10x + 9$

18. $x^2 - 2^2$
$= x^2 - 4$

19. $x^2 - 2 \cdot x \cdot 8 + 8^2$
$= x^2 - 16x + 64$

20. $x^2 - x - 4x + 4$
$= x^2 - 5x + 4$

21. $x^2 - 9^2$
$= x^2 - 81$

22. $(3x)^2 + 2 \cdot 3x \cdot 1 + 1^2$
$= 9x^2 + 6x + 1$

23. $(9x)^2 - 2 \cdot 9x \cdot 1 + 1^2$
$= 81x^2 - 18x + 1$

24. $2x^2 - 6x - x + 3$
$= 2x^2 - 7x + 3$

25. $(2x)^2 - 5^2$
$= 4x^2 - 25$

26. $3x^2 - 18x + x - 6$
$= 3x^2 - 17x - 6$

27. $4x^2 + x + 20x + 5$
$= 4x^2 + 21x + 5$

28. $12x^2 + 8x - 21x - 14$
$= 12x^2 - 13x - 14$

29. $(5x)^2 - 2 \cdot 5x \cdot 4 + 4^2$
$= 25x^2 - 40x + 16$

30. $x^2 + 2 \cdot x \cdot 2 + 2^2$
$= x^2 + 4x + 4$

31. $x^2 - 2x + x - 2$
$= x^2 - x - 2$

32. $x^2 - 4^2$
$= x^2 - 16$

33. $x^2 - 5x + 2x - 10$
$= x^2 - 3x - 10$

34. $x^2 - 2 \cdot x \cdot 7 + 7^2$
$= x^2 - 14x + 49$

35. $x^2 + 5x + 3x + 15$
$= x^2 + 8x + 15$

36. $x^2 + 3x - 9x - 27$
$= x^2 - 6x - 27$

37. $x^2 + 2 \cdot x \cdot 6 + 6^2$
$= x^2 + 12x + 36$

38. $5x^2 + 2x + 5x + 2$
$= 5x^2 + 7x + 2$

39. $(2x)^2 - 9^2$
$= 4x^2 - 81$

40. $(4x)^2 + 2 \cdot 4x \cdot 7 + 7^2$
$= 16x^2 + 56x + 49$

41. $8x^2 - 4x + 6x - 3$
$= 8x^2 + 2x - 3$

42. $9x^2 - 12x - 6x + 8$
$= 9x^2 - 18x + 8$

43. $30x^2 + 36x - 5x - 6$
$= 30x^2 + 31x - 6$

44. $(7x)^2 + 2 \cdot 7x \cdot 2 + 2^2$
$= 49x^2 + 28x + 4$

45. $(4x)^2 - 7^2$
$= 16x^2 - 49$

46. $(x + 1)(x + 2)$

47. $(x + 1)(x + 3)$

48. $(x - 1)(x + 2)$

49. $(x - 2)(x + 3)$

50. $(x - 2)(x - 3)$

51. $(x - 2)(x - 5)$

52. $(x - 1)^2$

53. $(2x + 1)^2$

54. $(x + 8)(x - 8)$

55. $(4x + 5)(4x - 5)$

LESSON 85 ·······································

1. $x^{5-3} = x^2$

2. $\dfrac{16}{4} \cdot x^{3-2} = 4x$

3. $\dfrac{x^3}{x} - \dfrac{5x^2}{x} + \dfrac{x}{x}$
$= x^2 - 5x + 1$

4. $\dfrac{2x^6}{2x^3} - \dfrac{6x^5}{2x^3} + \dfrac{4x^4}{2x^3} - \dfrac{2x^3}{2x^3}$
$= x^3 - 3x^2 + 2x - 1$

5.
$$\begin{array}{r} x + 1 \\ x + 2 \enclose{longdiv}{x^2 + 3x + 2} \\ \underline{x^2 + 2x} \\ x + 2 \\ \underline{x + 2} \\ 0 \end{array}$$
Answer: $x + 1$

6.
$$\begin{array}{r} x - 3 \\ 2x + 1 \enclose{longdiv}{2x^2 - 5x - 3} \\ \underline{2x^2 + x} \\ -6x - 3 \\ \underline{-6x - 3} \\ 0 \end{array}$$
Answer: $x - 3$

7. $\dfrac{6}{3} \cdot x^{5-1} = 2x^4$

8. $\dfrac{4x^6}{4x^3} - \dfrac{16x^5}{4x^3} + \dfrac{8x^4}{4x^3}$
$= x^3 - 4x^2 + 2x$

9.
$$\begin{array}{r} x + 2 \\ x + 3 \enclose{longdiv}{x^2 + 5x + 6} \\ \underline{x^2 + 3x} \\ 2x + 6 \\ \underline{2x + 6} \\ 0 \end{array}$$
Answer: $x + 2$

10.
$$\begin{array}{r} x - 1 \\ x - 1 \enclose{longdiv}{x^2 - 2x + 1} \\ \underline{x^2 - x} \\ -x + 1 \\ \underline{-x + 1} \\ 0 \end{array}$$
Answer: $x - 1$

11.
$$\begin{array}{r} x - 4 \\ x - 4 \enclose{longdiv}{x^2 - 8x + 16} \\ \underline{x^2 - 4x} \\ -4x + 16 \\ \underline{-4x + 16} \\ 0 \end{array}$$
Answer: $x - 4$

12.
$$\begin{array}{r} x - 2 \\ x - 6 \enclose{longdiv}{x^2 - 8x + 12} \\ \underline{x^2 - 6x} \\ -2x + 12 \\ \underline{-2x + 12} \\ 0 \end{array}$$
Answer: $x - 2$

13.
$$\begin{array}{r} 3x + 1 \\ x - 3 \enclose{longdiv}{3x^2 - 8x - 3} \\ \underline{3x^2 - 9x} \\ x - 3 \\ \underline{x - 3} \\ 0 \end{array}$$
Answer: $3x + 1$

14.
$$\begin{array}{r} 2x + 1 \\ x + 2 \enclose{longdiv}{2x^2 + 5x + 2} \\ \underline{2x^2 + 4x} \\ x + 2 \\ \underline{x + 2} \\ 0 \end{array}$$
Answer: $2x + 1$

15.
$$\begin{array}{r} x - 2 \\ 4x + 1 \enclose{longdiv}{4x^2 - 7x - 2} \\ \underline{4x^2 + x} \\ -8x - 2 \\ \underline{-8x - 2} \\ 0 \end{array}$$
Answer: $x - 2$

16.
$$\begin{array}{r} 2x - 3 \\ 5x + 3 \enclose{longdiv}{10x^2 - 9x - 9} \\ \underline{10x^2 + 6x} \\ -15x - 9 \\ \underline{-15x - 9} \\ 0 \end{array}$$
Answer: $2x - 3$

17. $\dfrac{12}{-2} \cdot x^{6-2} = -6x^4$

18. $\dfrac{15x^2}{5x} - \dfrac{10x}{5x} = 3x - 2$

19. $\dfrac{9x^4}{x^2} + \dfrac{4x^2}{x^2} = 9x^2 + 4$

20. $\dfrac{2x^3}{-2x} - \dfrac{8x^2}{-2x} + \dfrac{6x}{-2x}$
$= -x^2 + 4x - 3$

21.

$$
\begin{array}{r}
x + 5 \\
x + 2\overline{\smash{\big)}\ x^2 + 7x + 10} \\
\underline{x^2 + 2x} \\
5x + 10 \\
\underline{5x + 10} \\
0
\end{array}
$$

Answer: $x + 5$

22.

$$
\begin{array}{r}
x + 7 \\
x - 4\overline{\smash{\big)}\ x^2 + 3x - 28} \\
\underline{x^2 - 4x} \\
7x - 28 \\
\underline{7x - 28} \\
0
\end{array}
$$

Answer: $x + 7$

23.

$$
\begin{array}{r}
5x + 4 \\
x + 1\overline{\smash{\big)}\ 5x^2 + 9x + 4} \\
\underline{5x^2 + 5x} \\
4x + 4 \\
\underline{4x + 4} \\
0
\end{array}
$$

Answer: $5x + 4$

24.

$$
\begin{array}{r}
4x - 1 \\
x + 5\overline{\smash{\big)}\ 4x^2 + 19x - 5} \\
\underline{4x^2 + 20x} \\
-x - 5 \\
\underline{-x - 5} \\
0
\end{array}
$$

Answer: $4x - 1$

25.

$$
\begin{array}{r}
4x + 3 \\
2x - 1\overline{\smash{\big)}\ 8x^2 + 2x - 3} \\
\underline{8x^2 - 4x} \\
6x - 3 \\
\underline{6x - 3} \\
0
\end{array}
$$

Answer: $4x + 3$

26.

$$
\begin{array}{r}
2x + 4 \\
3x + 2\overline{\smash{\big)}\ 6x^2 + 16x + 8} \\
\underline{6x^2 + 4x} \\
12x + 8 \\
\underline{12x + 8} \\
0
\end{array}
$$

Answer: $2x + 4$

27.

$$
\begin{array}{r}
2x + 1 \\
x^2 - x\overline{\smash{\big)}\ 2x^3 - x^2 - x} \\
\underline{2x^3 - 2x^2} \\
x^2 - x \\
\underline{x^2 - x} \\
0
\end{array}
$$

Answer: $2x + 1$

28.

$$
\begin{array}{r}
x^2 + 3 \\
x^2 + 3\overline{\smash{\big)}\ x^4 + 6x^2 + 9} \\
\underline{x^4 + 3x^2} \\
3x^2 + 9 \\
\underline{3x^2 + 9} \\
0
\end{array}
$$

Answer: $x^2 + 3$

29.

$$
\begin{array}{r}
x^2 + 2x + 1 \\
x + 2\overline{\smash{\big)}\ x^3 + 4x^2 + 5x + 2} \\
\underline{x^3 + 2x^2} \\
2x^2 + 5x \\
\underline{2x^2 + 4x} \\
x + 2 \\
\underline{x + 2} \\
0
\end{array}
$$

Answer: $x^2 + 2x + 1$

30.

$$
\begin{array}{r}
4x - 3 \\
x^2 - x + 2\overline{\smash{\big)}\ 4x^3 - 7x^2 + 11x - 6} \\
\underline{4x^3 - 4x^2 + 8x} \\
-3x^2 + 3x - 6 \\
\underline{-3x^2 + 3x - 6} \\
0
\end{array}
$$

Answer: $4x - 3$

LESSON 86 ⋯⋯⋯⋯⋯⋯⋯⋯⋯

1. $-2x^5$

2. $x - 2$

3.

$$
\begin{array}{r}
x - 3 \\
x + 2\overline{\smash{\big)}\ x^2 - x - 5} \\
\underline{x^2 + 2x} \\
-3x - 5 \\
\underline{-3x - 6} \\
1
\end{array}
$$

Answer:

$x - 3 + \dfrac{1}{x + 2}$

4.

$$
\begin{array}{r}
x - 2 \\
x - 1\overline{\smash{\big)}\ x^2 - 3x + 5} \\
\underline{x^2 - x} \\
-2x + 5 \\
\underline{-2x + 2} \\
3
\end{array}
$$

Answer:

$x - 2 + \dfrac{3}{x - 1}$

5.

$$
\begin{array}{r}
3x - 2 \\
x + 2\overline{\smash{\big)}\ 3x^2 + 4x + 2} \\
\underline{3x^2 + 6x} \\
-2x + 2 \\
\underline{-2x - 4} \\
6
\end{array}
$$

Answer:

$3x - 2 + \dfrac{6}{x + 2}$

6.

$$
\begin{array}{r}
2x + 3 \\
3x - 1\overline{\smash{\big)}\ 6x^2 + 7x + 7} \\
\underline{6x^2 - 2x} \\
9x + 7 \\
\underline{9x - 3} \\
10
\end{array}
$$

Answer:

$2x + 3 + \dfrac{10}{3x - 1}$

7.

$$
\begin{array}{r}
x + 4 \\
x - 4\overline{\smash{\big)}\ x^2 + 0x - 15} \\
\underline{x^2 - 4x} \\
4x - 15 \\
\underline{4x - 16} \\
1
\end{array}
$$

Answer:

$x + 4 + \dfrac{1}{x - 4}$

8.

$$
\begin{array}{r}
2x + 3 \\
2x + 1\overline{\smash{\big)}\ 4x^2 + 8x + 0} \\
\underline{4x^2 + 2x} \\
6x + 0 \\
\underline{6x + 3} \\
-3
\end{array}
$$

Answer:

$2x + 3 - \dfrac{3}{2x + 1}$

9. Correct: $(x + 3)(x + 3) - 2 = x^2 + 6x + 7$

10. Incorrect: $(x + 4)(x + 1) - 5 \neq x^2 + 5x + 9$

11. Correct: $(x - 3)(3x + 1) + 6 = 3x^2 - 8x + 3$

12. Incorrect: $(5x - 2)(4x - 1) + 2 \neq 20x^2 - 13x + 9$

13. $\dfrac{8}{4} \cdot x^{5-1} = 2x^4$

14. $\dfrac{x^4}{x} - \dfrac{2x^2}{x} = x^3 - 2x$

15.

$$
\begin{array}{r}
x + 2 \\
x - 7\overline{\smash{\big)}\ x^2 - 5x - 14} \\
\underline{x^2 - 7x} \\
2x - 14 \\
\underline{2x - 14} \\
0
\end{array}
$$

Answer: $x + 2$

16.

$$
\begin{array}{r}
x + 3 \\
x + 3\overline{\smash{\big)}\ x^2 + 6x + 9} \\
\underline{x^2 + 3x} \\
3x + 9 \\
\underline{3x + 9} \\
0
\end{array}
$$

Answer: $x + 3$

17.

$$
\begin{array}{r}
x + 3 \\
x - 4 \overline{\smash{\big)}\ x^2 - x - 5} \\
\underline{x^2 - 4x} \\
3x - 5 \\
\underline{3x - 12} \\
7
\end{array}
$$

Answer:

$$x + 3 + \frac{7}{x - 4}$$

18.

$$
\begin{array}{r}
x + 4 \\
x + 2 \overline{\smash{\big)}\ x^2 + 6x + 7} \\
\underline{x^2 + 2x} \\
4x + 7 \\
\underline{4x + 8} \\
-1
\end{array}
$$

Answer:

$$x + 4 - \frac{1}{x + 2}$$

29.

$$
\begin{array}{r}
x - 2 \\
x + 3 \overline{\smash{\big)}\ x^2 + x - 10} \\
\underline{x^2 + 3x} \\
-2x - 10 \\
\underline{-2x - 6} \\
-4
\end{array}
$$

Answer:

$$x - 2 - \frac{4}{x + 3}$$

30.

$$
\begin{array}{r}
x - 1 \\
x + 5 \overline{\smash{\big)}\ x^2 + 4x + 0} \\
\underline{x^2 + 5x} \\
-x + 0 \\
\underline{-x - 5} \\
5
\end{array}
$$

Answer:

$$x - 1 + \frac{5}{x + 5}$$

19.

$$
\begin{array}{r}
x \\
2x - 5 \overline{\smash{\big)}\ 2x^2 - 5x + 3} \\
\underline{2x^2 - 5x} \\
3
\end{array}
$$

Answer:

$$x + \frac{3}{2x - 5}$$

20.

$$
\begin{array}{r}
7x + 1 \\
7x - 1 \overline{\smash{\big)}\ 49x^2 + 0x + 1} \\
\underline{49x^2 - 7x} \\
7x + 1 \\
\underline{7x - 1} \\
2
\end{array}
$$

Answer:

$$7x + 1 + \frac{2}{7x - 1}$$

31.

$$
\begin{array}{r}
2x + 1 \\
2x + 1 \overline{\smash{\big)}\ 4x^2 + 4x + 9} \\
\underline{4x^2 + 2x} \\
2x + 9 \\
\underline{2x + 1} \\
8
\end{array}
$$

Answer:

$$2x + 1 + \frac{8}{2x + 1}$$

32.

$$
\begin{array}{r}
3x + 1 \\
3x + 4 \overline{\smash{\big)}\ 9x^2 + 15x - 1} \\
\underline{9x^2 + 12x} \\
3x - 1 \\
\underline{3x + 4} \\
-5
\end{array}
$$

Answer:

$$3x + 1 - \frac{5}{3x + 4}$$

21. $\dfrac{15}{-5} \cdot x^{4-3} = -3x$

22. $\dfrac{3x^6}{3x^3} - \dfrac{9x^5}{3x^3} + \dfrac{6x^3}{3x^3}$

$$= x^3 - 3x^2 + 2$$

23.

$$
\begin{array}{r}
x + 3 \\
x + 6 \overline{\smash{\big)}\ x^2 + 9x + 18} \\
\underline{x^2 + 6x} \\
3x + 18 \\
\underline{3x + 18} \\
0
\end{array}
$$

Answer: $x + 3$

24.

$$
\begin{array}{r}
x + 8 \\
x - 4 \overline{\smash{\big)}\ x^2 + 4x - 32} \\
\underline{x^2 - 4x} \\
8x - 32 \\
\underline{8x - 32} \\
0
\end{array}
$$

Answer: $x + 8$

25.

$$
\begin{array}{r}
x - 5 \\
x + 5 \overline{\smash{\big)}\ x^2 + 0x - 25} \\
\underline{x^2 + 5x} \\
-5x - 25 \\
\underline{-5x - 25} \\
0
\end{array}
$$

Answer: $x - 5$

26.

$$
\begin{array}{r}
x + 7 \\
x + 2 \overline{\smash{\big)}\ x^2 + 9x + 14} \\
\underline{x^2 + 2x} \\
7x + 14 \\
\underline{7x + 14} \\
0
\end{array}
$$

Answer: $x + 7$

27.

$$
\begin{array}{r}
3x + 1 \\
3x + 1 \overline{\smash{\big)}\ 9x^2 + 6x + 1} \\
\underline{9x^2 + 3x} \\
3x + 1 \\
\underline{3x + 1} \\
0
\end{array}
$$

Answer: $3x + 1$

28.

$$
\begin{array}{r}
2x - 3 \\
2x + 3 \overline{\smash{\big)}\ 4x^2 + 0x - 9} \\
\underline{4x^2 + 6x} \\
-6x - 9 \\
\underline{-6x - 9} \\
0
\end{array}
$$

Answer: $2x - 3$

LESSON 87

1. $4x + 2$

2. $6x^2 + 2$

3. $-2x + 8$

4. $7x^2 - 7x + 6$

5. $5x^4$

6. $6x^4 - 2x^3$

7. $x^2 - x - 6$

8. $x^2 + 3x - 28$

9. $2x^2 - 9x - 5$

10. $6x^2 + 17x + 12$

11. $x^3 + 8x^2 + 13x - 10$

12. $x^3 - 8$

13. $8x^3 + 1$

14. $x^4 - x^3 - 3x^2 + x + 2$

15. $x^2 + 6x + 9$

16. $x^2 - 25$

17. $x^2 + 7x + 10$

18. $4x^2 - 4x + 1$

19. $16x^2 - 9$

20. $6x^2 - 11x - 35$

21. $x - 1$

22. $x - 4$

23. $x - 2$

24. $4x - 3$

25. $x + 5 - \dfrac{4}{x + 3}$

26. $x - 2 + \dfrac{3}{2x - 1}$

27. $x + 5 + \dfrac{5}{x - 5}$

28. $3x - 2 - \dfrac{1}{3x + 2}$

29. $V = 8 \times 8 \times 8 = 512 \text{ in}^3$

30. $SA = 6 \text{ squares} = 6 \times (8 \times 8) = 384 \text{ in}^2$

31. $V = 6 \times 5 \times 10 = 300 \text{ in}^3$

32. $SA = 2 \times (6 \times 5) + 2 \times (5 \times 10) + 2 \times (6 \times 10) = 280 \text{ in}^2$

33. $V = (12 \times 12 \times 8)/3 = 384 \text{ ft}^3$

34. $SA = \text{square base} + 4 \text{ triangles}$
$= 12 \times 12 + 4 \times (12 \times 10 \times 1/2) = 384 \text{ ft}^3$

LESSON 88

1. $x = 7$
2. $x < -2$
3. $x = -3$
4. $x > 7$
5. $x = 6$ or $x = 10$
6. $x \leq 0$ or $x \geq 2/5$
7. Kyle is 20 years old. Alex is 15 years old.
8. 45 minutes
9. 9 grams
10. 5.5 hours
11. $(2, -3)$
12. $(-1, 3)$
13. $(2, 3)$
14. $(3, -1)$
15. Time taken from the park to the library = 0.5 hour
    Distance = 40 mph × 0.5 hour = 20 miles
16. Plane: 260 mph
    Wind: 20 mph
17. Candy A: 6 pounds
    Candy B: 12 pounds

18.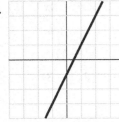

19.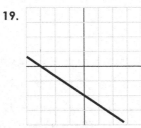

20.

21.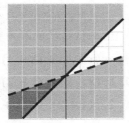

22. $y = \frac{1}{2}x + 1$
    $x - 2y = -2$
23. $y = \frac{1}{3}x + 2$
    $x - 3y = -6$

LESSON 89

1. D: {−1, 0, 1, 3, 4}
   R: {−1, 1, 2, 3}
   Not a function
2. D: $0 \leq x < 4$
   R: $-1 < y \leq 3$
   Function
3. D: $-1 < x < 4$
   R: $-2 \leq y < 3$
   Function
4. D: $x \geq -1$
   R: all values of y
   Not a function
5. $f(-1) = 10$
   $f(0) = 9$
   $f(5) = 4$
6. $g(-1) = 4$
   $g(0) = 1$
   $g(5) = 16$
7. Exponential
   Common ratio = 2
8. Linear; $y = 3x - 5$
   First difference = 3
9. None of these
10. Quadratic
    Second difference = 8

11. 5
12. 80
13. 1
14. −1/8
15. $f^{-1}(x) = x - 3$
16. $g^{-1}(x) = \frac{1}{2}x + 3$
17. $h^{-1}(x) = -2x + \frac{3}{2}$
18. $k^{-1}(x) = 6x - 2$
19. $y = \frac{3}{2}x; y = 9$
20. $xy = 24; y = -6$
21. $1.92
22. 0.8 hour or 48 minutes
23. Geometric
    $a_n = 5(2)^{n-1}$
    $a_1 = 5, a_n = 2a_{n-1}$
24. Arithmetic
    $a_n = 2n + 10$
    $a_1 = 12, a_n = a_{n-1} + 2$
25. Arithmetic
    $a_n = 9n - 16$
    $a_1 = -7, a_n = a_{n-1} + 9$
26. Geometric
    $a_n = (-5)^{n-1}$
    $a_1 = 1, a_n = -5a_{n-1}$
27. $2,240
28. About 1.64 m

LESSON 90

1. 5
2. 3
3. $2\sqrt{6}$
4. $3\sqrt[3]{2}$
5. $x\sqrt{x}$
6. $xy\sqrt[3]{y}$
7. $11\sqrt{2}$
8. $5x^2\sqrt{2}$
9. $6\sqrt{5}$
10. $\sqrt{2x}$
11. $x = 11$
12. No solution
13. $x = 4$
14. $x = -12$
15. $x = 5$
16. $x = 13$
17. 6 feet
18. 1
19. 2
20. $10/x$
21. $16x^{10}$
22. $7/x^{10}$
23. $3x^8$
24. 4
25. −2
26. 1/3
27. 1/25
28. $x^{7/12}$
29. $16x$
30. $2x^{1/4}$
31. $5x^{1/6}$
32. $x^2 - 3x - 18$
33. $2x^3 + 5x^2 - 14x + 3$
34. $x - 7$
35. $x - 2 - \dfrac{4}{x + 2}$

LESSON 91

1. A
2. B
3. B
4. C
5. A
6. C
7. D
8. C
9. B
10. B
11. C
12. D
13. A
14. C
15. B
16. B
17. D

Worked-out solutions to selected problems:

1. $x = -1/3$, so $3x + 1 = 0$.
4. $-3x + 6x = 3x$
5. $2\sqrt{3} - \sqrt{3} = \sqrt{3}$
6. $(2^4)^{-2} = 2^{-8} = (1/2)^8$

7. $a = (1/2) + 2 = 5/2$
$b = (1/4) + 4 = 17/4$
$a + 2b = 11$

9. $3^2 + 3^2 = x^2$
$x^2 = 18$
$x = \sqrt{18} = 3\sqrt{2}$

10. $96/4 = 24$ miles/gallon
$24 \times 3 = 72$ miles

11. 2 yd = 6 ft = 72 in
$72/8 = 9$ strips

17. x = number of 6-point questions
y = number of 8-point questions
$x + y = 16$ and $6x + 8y = 100$
$x = 14$ and $y = 2$, so $x{:}y = 7{:}1$.

LESSON 92

1. B   **2.** B   **3.** D   **4.** C   **5.** A   **6.** C
7. B   **8.** A   **9.** D   **10.** B   **11.** C   **12.** D
13. B   **14.** C   **15.** D   **16.** C   **17.** B

Worked-out solutions to selected problems:

1. $3 + 4x = 5$ or $3 + 4x = -5$
$x = 1/2$ or $x = -2$

4. Square both sides.
$5x - 1 = 3x + 7$
$x = 4$

5.
$$\begin{array}{r} x\ +1 \\ x-4\,\overline{\smash{\big)}\,x^2 - 3x + k} \\ \underline{x^2 - 4x} \\ x + k \\ \underline{x - 4} \\ k + 4 \end{array}$$
Divisible = $k + 4 = 0$
$k = -4$

7. $\dfrac{(2 \cdot 3)^4 \cdot 3^2}{2^4}$
$= \dfrac{2^4 \cdot 3^4 \cdot 3^2}{2^4} = 3^6$

8. $a = 2 \times (1/6) = 1/3$
$b = 3 \times (1/6) = 1/2$
$ab = (1/3)(1/2) = 1/6$

9. $m/n = 3$
$m^2/n^2 = 9$
$m^2 : n^2 = 9{:}1$

10. $20 \times (3/5) = 12$ boys
$20 \times (2/5) = 8$ girls

11. $25 \times 0.4 = 10$
(a whole number)

13. Slope of line $l = -2$
Slope of line $m = 1/2$
$(-2)(1/2) = -1$, so the lines are perpendicular.

15. $16 \le 8x/2 \le 48$
$4 \le x \le 12$

16. x = age, y = value
$k = 2 \times 18000 = 36000$
Equation: $xy = 36000$
When $x = 6$, $y = 6000$.

17. x = speed of the boat
y = speed of the current
$x - y = 16$, $x + y = 20$
$x = 18$, $y = 2$

LESSON 93

1. $6x^6$
2. $2x^5 - 6x^4 - 8x^3$
3. $x^2 + 2x - 15$
4. $x^3 + 7x^2 + 4x - 12$
5. 5
6. $2x$

7. $2x^2 y^2$
8. $5(x + 1)$
9. $2x(2x - 3)$
10. $2x^2 y^2(4x + 3y)$
11. Correct
12. Incorrect
13. $3(x + 2)$
14. $7(2x^2 - 1)$
15. $6x^2(3x^3 + 2)$
16. $3(x^2 - 5x - 3)$
17. $2x(6x^2 + 3x - 4)$
18. $7x^2(4x^2 + 2x + 3)$
19. $y(2x^2 + y - 5)$
20. $4xy(x^2 y^2 + 2xy - 4)$
21. $3(3x - 4)$
22. $x(x + 5)$
23. $4x(4x^2 - 5)$
24. $2(x^2 - 4x + 2)$
25. $x^2(2x^2 + x - 2)$
26. $5x^2(5x^3 + 4x + 2)$
27. $7x(2xy - y + 4)$
28. $x^2 y(7x^2 y + 6x - y)$

LESSON 94

1. $3x^2(x - 3)$
2. $2x(2x^3 + 3x^2 - 6)$
3. $(x + 2)(x + 3)$
4. $(2x^2 - 7)(4x^3 - 3)$
5. $x^2(x + 2) + 4(x + 2) = (x + 2)(x^2 + 4)$
6. $2x^2(x + 5) - 3(x + 5) = (x + 5)(2x^2 - 3)$
7. $2(3x^3 - 4x^2 + 9x - 12)$
$= 2[x^2(3x - 4) + 3(3x - 4)] = 2(3x - 4)(x^2 + 3)$
8. $3x(x^5 + 2x^3 + 4x^2 + 8)$
$= 3x[x^3(x^2 + 2) + 4(x^2 + 2)] = 3x(x^2 + 2)(x^3 + 4)$
9. $x^2(x + 4) + (x + 4) = (x + 4)(x^2 + 1)$
10. $x^2(x - 2) + (x - 2) = (x - 2)(x^2 + 1)$
11. $2x^2(x + 2) - 7(x + 2) = (x + 2)(2x^2 - 7)$
12. $3x^2(x - 5) - 2(x - 5) = (x - 5)(3x^2 - 2)$
13. $x^2(2x - 3) + 4(2x - 3) = (2x - 3)(x^2 + 4)$
14. $x^2(5x - 7) + (5x - 7) = (5x - 7)(x^2 + 1)$
15. $5x^3(6x - 5) - 2(6x - 5) = (6x - 5)(5x^3 - 2)$
16. $2x^3(7x^2 + 2) + 3(7x^2 + 2) = (7x^2 + 2)(2x^3 + 3)$
17. $4(2x^3 + x^2 + 2x + 1)$
$= 4[x^2(2x + 1) + (2x + 1)] = 4(2x + 1)(x^2 + 1)$
18. $5(2x^3 - 2x^2 + x - 1)$
$= 5[2x^2(x - 1) + (x - 1)] = 5(x - 1)(2x^2 + 1)$
19. $x(6x^3 + 3x^2 - 10x - 5)$
$= x[3x^2(2x + 1) - 5(2x + 1)]$
$= x(2x + 1)(3x^2 - 5)$
20. $2x(x^3 + 3x^2 - 2x - 6)$
$= 2x[x^2(x + 3) - 2(x + 3)]$
$= 2x(x + 3)(x^2 - 2)$

21. $x(2x - 5)$

22. $3(x^2 + 3x - 2)$

23. $(x - 2)(x^2 - 7)$

24. $(4x + 5)(x^3 + 1)$

25. $x^2(x - 1) - 3(x - 1) = (x - 1)(x^2 - 3)$

26. $x^2(5x - 2) + (5x - 2) = (5x - 2)(x^2 + 1)$

27. $x^3(2x + 1) + 7(2x + 1) = (2x + 1)(x^3 + 7)$

28. $5x^3(x^2 + 4) - (x^2 + 4) = (x^2 + 4)(5x^3 - 1)$

29. $3(x^3 + x^2 + 2x + 2)$
$= 3[x^2(x + 1) + 2(x + 1)] = 3(x + 1)(x^2 + 2)$

30. $4(3x^3 - 15x^2 - x + 5)$
$= 4[3x^2(x - 5) - (x - 5)] = 4(x - 5)(3x^2 - 1)$

31. $3(x^3 + 2x^2 - 5x - 10)$
$= 3[x^2(x + 2) - 5(x + 2)] = 3(x + 2)(x^2 - 5)$

32. $2(7x^3 - 35x^2 - x + 5)$
$= 2[7x^2(x - 5) - (x - 5)] = 2(x - 5)(7x^2 - 1)$

33. $x^2(12x^3 - 4x^2 + 9x - 3)$
$= x^2[4x^2(3x - 1) + 3(3x - 1)]$
$= x^2(3x - 1)(4x^2 + 3)$

34. $2x(10x^3 - 4x^2 + 15x - 6)$
$= 2x[2x^2(5x - 2) + 3(5x - 2)]$
$= 2x(5x - 2)(2x^2 + 3)$

LESSON 95

1. $6 = 3n$, so $n = 2$.
$b = n + 3$, so $b = 5$.
$x^2 + 5x + 6$
$= (x + 3)(x + 2)$

2. $8 = 2n$, so $n = 4$.
$b = n + 2$, so $b = 6$.
$x^2 + 6x + 8$
$= (x + 2)(x + 4)$

3. $c = 1 \times 2 = 2$
$b = 1 + 2 = 3$
$(x + 1)(x + 2)$

4. $c = 2 \times 5 = 10$
$b = 2 + 5 = 7$
$(x + 2)(x + 5)$

5. $c = -1 \times -2 = 2$
$b = -1 + -2 = -3$
$(x - 1)(x - 2)$

6. $c = -2 \times 5 = -10$
$b = -2 + 5 = 3$
$(x - 2)(x + 5)$

7. $5 = 5n$, so $n = 1$.
$b = n + 5$, so $b = 6$.
$x^2 + 6x + 5$
$= (x + 5)(x + 1)$

8. $-6 = -2n$, so $n = 3$.
$b = n - 2$, so $b = 1$.
$x^2 + x - 6$
$= (x - 2)(x + 3)$

9. $-12 = 3n$, so $n = -4$.
$b = n + 3$, so $b = -1$.
$x^2 - x - 12$
$= (x + 3)(x - 4)$

10. $20 = -4n$, so $n = -5$.
$b = n - 4$, so $b = -9$.
$x^2 - 9x + 20$
$= (x - 4)(x - 5)$

11. $c = 1 \times -2 = -2$
$b = 1 + -2 = -1$
$(x + 1)(x - 2)$

12. $c = -1 \times 2 = -2$
$b = -1 + 2 = 1$
$(x - 1)(x + 2)$

13. $c = 1 \times 6 = 6$
$b = 1 + 6 = 7$
$(x + 1)(x + 6)$

14. $c = 1 \times 5 = 5$
$b = 1 + 5 = 6$
$(x + 1)(x + 5)$

15. $c = 3 \times -5 = -15$
$b = 3 + -5 = -2$
$(x + 3)(x - 5)$

16. $c = 2 \times 7 = 14$
$b = 2 + 7 = 9$
$(x + 2)(x + 7)$

17. $c = -4 \times -5 = 20$
$b = -4 + -5 = -9$
$(x - 4)(x - 5)$

18. $c = -2 \times 6 = -12$
$b = -2 + 6 = 4$
$(x - 2)(x + 6)$

19. $c = 4 \times 6 = 24$
$b = 4 + 6 = 10$
$(x + 4)(x + 6)$

20. $c = -5 \times -7 = 35$
$b = -5 + -7 = -12$
$(x - 5)(x - 7)$

21. $c = -2 \times 3 = -6$
$b = -2 + 3 = 1$
$(x - 2)(x + 3)$

22. $c = 2 \times -3 = -6$
$b = 2 + -3 = -1$
$(x + 2)(x - 3)$

23. $c = 1 \times 3 = 3$
$b = 1 + 3 = 4$
$(x + 1)(x + 3)$

24. $c = -1 \times 3 = -3$
$b = -1 + 3 = 2$
$(x - 1)(x + 3)$

25. $c = -1 \times -6 = 6$
$b = -1 + -6 = -7$
$(x - 1)(x - 6)$

26. $c = -2 \times -3 = 6$
$b = -2 + -3 = -5$
$(x - 2)(x - 3)$

27. $c = -2 \times 4 = -8$
$b = -2 + 4 = 2$
$(x - 2)(x + 4)$

28. $c = 2 \times -4 = -8$
$b = 2 + -4 = -2$
$(x + 2)(x - 4)$

29. $c = 3 \times 4 = 12$
$b = 3 + 4 = 7$
$(x + 3)(x + 4)$

30. $c = 2 \times -6 = -12$
$b = 2 + -6 = -4$
$(x + 2)(x - 6)$

31. $c = 3 \times 6 = 18$
$b = 3 + 6 = 9$
$(x + 3)(x + 6)$

32. $c = -3 \times -6 = 18$
$b = -3 + -6 = -9$
$(x - 3)(x - 6)$

33. $c = 5 \times 6 = 30$
$b = 5 + 6 = 11$
$(x + 5)(x + 6)$

34. $c = -5 \times -6 = 30$
$b = -5 + -6 = -11$
$(x - 5)(x - 6)$

LESSON 96

1. $2x(x - 3)$

2. $2(4x^2 + x + 5)$

3. $(x + 1)(x + 3)$

4. $(x + 2)(x - 4)$

5. $2(x^2 + 7x + 10)$
$= 2(x + 2)(x + 5)$

6. $5(x^2 + x - 12)$
$= 5(x - 3)(x + 4)$

7. $(x + 2)(x - 3)$

8. $(x - 3)(x - 4)$

9. $(x - 4)(x + 8)$

10. $(x + 4)(x - 9)$

11. $(x - 3)(x - 7)$

12. $(x + 5)(x + 8)$

13. $(x + 4)(x + 6)$

14. $(x - 5)(x + 9)$

15. $3(x^2 + x - 6)$
$= 3(x - 2)(x + 3)$

16. $2(x^2 + 6x + 8)$
$= 2(x + 2)(x + 4)$

17. $4(x^2 + x - 20)$
$= 4(x - 4)(x + 5)$

18. $7(x^2 - 7x + 10)$
$= 7(x - 2)(x - 5)$

19. $2(x^2 - 5x - 14)$
$= 2(x + 2)(x - 7)$

20. $9(x^2 + 10x + 9)$
$= 9(x + 1)(x + 9)$

21. $7(x^2 + 9x + 8)$
$= 7(x + 1)(x + 8)$

22. $4(x^2 - 8x + 15)$
$= 4(x - 3)(x - 5)$

23. $(x + 1)(x - 2)$

24. $(x - 2)(x + 3)$

25. $(x + 2)(x + 3)$

26. $(x - 1)(x + 5)$

27. $(x - 2)(x - 7)$

28. $(x - 3)(x - 4)$

29. $(x + 5)(x - 6)$

30. $(x - 7)(x + 8)$

31. $(x + 2)(x - 9)$

32. $(x - 3)(x + 8)$

33. $(x + 4)(x + 5)$

34. $(x + 6)(x + 8)$

35. $(x - 4)(x - 7)$

36. $(x - 3)(x - 9)$

37. $4(x^2 - 5x - 24)$
$= 4(x + 3)(x - 8)$

38. $3(x^2 - 4x - 12)$
$= 3(x + 2)(x - 6)$

39. $3(x^2 - 9x + 18)$
$3(x - 3)(x - 6)$

40. $2(x^2 + 2x - 35)$
$= 2(x - 5)(x + 7)$

41. $4(x^2 - 6x + 8)$
$= 4(x - 2)(x - 4)$

42. $3(x^2 + 5x + 6)$
$= 3(x + 2)(x + 3)$

43. $7x(x^2 - 5x + 6)$
$= 7x(x - 2)(x - 3)$

44. $4x(x^2 + 4x - 12)$
$= 4x(x - 2)(x + 6)$

LESSON 97

1. $(x + 3)(x + 6)$

2. $(x - 4)(x + 9)$

3. $3 = 3n$, so $n = 1$.
$b = n + 6$, so $b = 7$.

$2x^2 + 7x + 3$
$= (x + 3)(2x + 1)$

4. $-8 = -2n$, so $n = 4$.
$b = n - 6$, so $b = -2$.

$3x^2 - 2x - 8$
$= (x - 2)(3x + 4)$

5. $6 = -3n$, so $n = -2$.
$b = 2n - 9$, so $b = -13$.

$6x^2 - 13x + 6$
$= (2x - 3)(3x - 2)$

6. $-20 = 4n$, so $n = -5$.
$b = 3n + 16$, so $b = 1$.

$12x^2 + x - 20$
$= (3x + 4)(4x - 5)$

7. Set up $(x\ \ )(8x\ \ )$ and $(2x\ \ )(4x\ \ )$, then check factors of −5.

Possible factorization: Middle term:

$(x + 1)(8x - 5)$ $-5x + 8x = 3x$
$(2x + 1)(4x - 5)$ $-10x + 4x = -6x$
...
$(x - 5)(8x + 1)$ $x - 40x = -39x$
$(2x - 5)(4x + 1)$ $2x - 20x = -18x$ ✓
...

8. Set up $(x\ \ )(12x\ \ )$, $(2x\ \ )(6x\ \ )$, and $(3x\ \ )(4x\ \ )$, then check factors of −6.

Possible factorization: Middle term:

$(x + 1)(12x - 6)$ $-6x + 12x = 6x$
$(2x + 1)(6x - 6)$ $-12x + 6x = -6x$
$(3x + 1)(4x - 6)$ $-18x + 4x = -14x$
...
$(x - 2)(12x + 3)$ $3x - 24x = -21x$
$(2x - 2)(6x + 3)$ $6x - 12x = -6x$
$(3x - 2)(4x + 3)$ $9x - 8x = x$ ✓
...

9. Set up $(x\ \ )(2x\ \ )$, then check factors of 3.

Possible factorization: Middle term:

$(x + 1)(2x + 3)$ $3x + 2x = 5x$ ✓
$(x - 1)(2x - 3)$ $-3x - 2x = -5x$
$(x + 3)(2x + 1)$ $x + 6x = 7x$
$(x - 3)(2x - 1)$ $-x - 6x = -7x$

10. Set up $(x\ \ )(3x\ \ )$, then check factors of 5.

Possible factorization: Middle term:

$(x + 1)(3x + 5)$ $5x + 3x = 8x$
$(x - 1)(3x - 5)$ $-5x - 3x = -8x$
$(x + 5)(3x + 1)$ $x + 15x = 16x$
$(x - 5)(3x - 1)$ $-x - 15x = -16x$ ✓

11. Set up $(x\ \ )(7x\ \ )$, then check factors of −2.

Possible factorization: Middle term:

$(x + 1)(7x - 2)$ $-2x + 7x = 5x$
$(x - 1)(7x + 2)$ $2x - 7x = -5x$
$(x + 2)(7x - 1)$ $-x + 14x = 13x$ ✓
$(x - 2)(7x + 1)$ $x - 14x = -13x$

12. Set up $(x\ \ )(5x\ \ )$, then check factors of 3.

Possible factorization: Middle term:

$(x + 1)(5x + 3)$ $3x + 5x = 8x$
$(x - 1)(5x - 3)$ $-3x - 5x = -8x$
$(x + 3)(5x + 1)$ $x + 15x = 16x$ ✓
$(x - 3)(5x - 1)$ $-x - 15x = -16x$

13. Set up $(x\ \ )(8x\ \ )$ and $(2x\ \ )(4x\ \ )$, then check factors of 5.

Possible factorization: Middle term:

$(x + 1)(8x + 5)$ $5x + 8x = 13x$
$(2x + 1)(4x + 5)$ $10x + 4x = 14x$
...
$(x - 1)(8x - 5)$ $-5x - 8x = -13x$
$(2x - 1)(4x - 5)$ $-10x - 4x = -14x$
$(x - 5)(8x - 1)$ $-x - 40x = -41x$
$(2x - 5)(4x - 1)$ $-2x - 20x = -22x$ ✓

14. Set up $(x \quad)(4x \quad)$ and $(2x \quad)(2x \quad)$, then check factors of -12.

Possible factorization: Middle term:

...

$(x + 2)(4x - 6)$ $-6x + 8x = 2x$

$(2x + 2)(2x - 6)$ $-12x + 4x = -8x$

...

$(x + 4)(4x - 3)$ $-3x + 16x = 13x$ ✓

$(2x + 4)(2x - 3)$ $-6x + 8x = 2x$

...

15. Set up $(x \quad)(6x \quad)$ and $(2x \quad)(3x \quad)$, then check factors of 3.

$(2x + 3)(3x + 1)$

16. Set up $(x \quad)(15x \quad)$ and $(3x \quad)(5x \quad)$, then check factors of -4.

$(3x - 2)(5x + 2)$

17. Set up $(x \quad)(12x \quad)$, $(2x \quad)(6x \quad)$, and $(3x \quad)(4x \quad)$, then check factors of 3.

$(2x + 3)(6x + 1)$

18. Set up $(x \quad)(20x \quad)$, $(2x \quad)(10x \quad)$, and $(4x \quad)(5x \quad)$, then check factors of -5.

$(4x - 5)(5x + 1)$

19. Set up $(x \quad)(18x \quad)$, $(2x \quad)(9x \quad)$, and $(3x \quad)(6x \quad)$, then check factors of 4.

$(2x - 1)(9x - 4)$

20. Set up $(x \quad)(16x \quad)$, $(2x \quad)(8x \quad)$, and $(4x \quad)(4x \quad)$, then check factors of -21.

$(4x - 3)(4x + 7)$

21. $(x + 5)(x - 8)$

22. $(x - 3)(x - 4)$

23. $(x + 1)(2x - 1)$

24. $(x - 2)(5x + 1)$

25. $(x - 1)(5x + 3)$

26. $(x + 3)(3x - 2)$

27. $(x + 1)(2x + 9)$

28. $(x - 4)(3x - 2)$

29. $(2x - 3)(4x + 1)$

30. $(2x + 5)(3x - 4)$

31. $(2x + 3)(2x + 5)$

32. $(2x + 7)(5x - 2)$

33. $(3x - 2)(4x + 5)$

34. $(4x - 3)(5x - 2)$

35. $(3x + 4)(6x + 5)$

36. $(2x - 3)(8x + 5)$

LESSON 98

1. $(x + 3)(x^2 + 1)$

2. $(3x + 4)(3x^2 - 1)$

3. $x(x - 1) + 2(x - 1) = (x - 1)(x + 2)$

4. $2x(2x + 1) - 3(2x + 1) = (2x + 1)(2x - 3)$

5. $ac = 2, b = 3$
   $rs = 1 \times 2 = 2$
   $r + s = 1 + 2 = 3$
   $\Rightarrow 2x^2 + x + 2x + 1$
   $= x(2x + 1) + (2x + 1)$
   $= (2x + 1)(x + 1)$

6. $ac = -6, b = 5$
   $rs = -1 \times 6 = -6$
   $r + s = -1 + 6 = 5$
   $\Rightarrow 3x^2 - x + 6x - 2$
   $= x(3x - 1) + 2(3x - 1)$
   $= (3x - 1)(x + 2)$

7. $x^2(2x + 1) + 3(2x + 1) = (2x + 1)(x^2 + 3)$

8. $x^2(3x - 2) - 5(3x - 2) = (3x - 2)(x^2 - 5)$

9. $x(x + 4) + 3(x + 4) = (x + 4)(x + 3)$

10. $x(3x + 2) + 5(3x + 2) = (3x + 2)(x + 5)$

11. $ac = 4, b = -5$
    $rs = -1 \times -4 = 4$
    $r + s = -1 - 4 = -5$
    $\Rightarrow 2x^2 - x - 4x + 2$
    $= x(2x - 1) - 2(2x - 1)$
    $= (2x - 1)(x - 2)$

12. $ac = -12, b = 4$
    $rs = -2 \times 6 = -12$
    $r + s = -2 + 6 = 4$
    $\Rightarrow 3x^2 - 2x + 6x - 4$
    $= x(3x - 2) + 2(3x - 2)$
    $= (3x - 2)(x + 2)$

13. $ac = 15, b = 8$
    $rs = 3 \times 5 = 15$
    $r + s = 3 + 5 = 8$
    $\Rightarrow 3x^2 + 3x + 5x + 5$
    $= 3x(x + 1) + 5(x + 1)$
    $= (x + 1)(3x + 5)$

14. $ac = 10, b = -7$
    $rs = -2 \times -5 = 10$
    $r + s = -2 - 5 = -7$
    $\Rightarrow 2x^2 - 2x - 5x + 5$
    $= 2x(x - 1) - 5(x - 1)$
    $= (x - 1)(2x - 5)$

15. $ac = -12, b = -4$
    $rs = 2 \times -6 = -12$
    $r + s = 2 - 6 = -4$
    $\Rightarrow 4x^2 + 2x - 6x - 3$
    $= 2x(2x + 1) - 3(2x + 1)$
    $= (2x + 1)(2x - 3)$

16. $ac = -15, b = 14$
    $rs = -1 \times 15 = -15$
    $r + s = -1 + 15 = 14$
    $\Rightarrow 5x^2 - x + 15x - 3$
    $= x(5x - 1) + 3(5x - 1)$
    $= (5x - 1)(x + 3)$

17. $ac = 42, b = 13$
    $rs = 6 \times 7 = 42$
    $r + s = 6 + 7 = 13$
    $\Rightarrow 2x^2 + 6x + 7x + 21$
    $= 2x(x + 3) + 7(x + 3)$
    $= (x + 3)(2x + 7)$

18. $ac = -16, b = -6$
    $rs = 2 \times -8 = -16$
    $r + s = 2 - 8 = -6$
    $\Rightarrow 16x^2 + 2x - 8x - 1$
    $= 2x(8x + 1) - (8x + 1)$
    $= (8x + 1)(2x - 1)$

19. $ac = 80, b = 21$
    $rs = 5 \times 16 = 80$
    $r + s = 5 + 16 = 21$
    $\Rightarrow 4x^2 + 5x + 16x + 20$
    $= x(4x + 5) + 4(4x + 5)$
    $= (4x + 5)(x + 4)$

20. $ac = -60, b = 4$
    $rs = -6 \times 10 = -60$
    $r + s = -6 + 10 = 4$
    $\Rightarrow 12x^2 - 6x + 10x - 5$
    $= 6x(2x - 1) + 5(2x - 1)$
    $= (2x - 1)(6x + 5)$

21. $ac = 10, b = 7$
    $rs = 2 \times 5 = 10$
    $r + s = 2 + 5 = 7$
    $\Rightarrow 5x^2 + 2x + 5x + 2$
    $= x(5x + 2) + (5x + 2)$
    $= (5x + 2)(x + 1)$

22. $ac = -18, b = -3$
    $rs = 3 \times -6 = -18$
    $r + s = 3 - 6 = -3$
    $\Rightarrow 2x^2 + 3x - 6x - 9$
    $= x(2x + 3) - 3(2x + 3)$
    $= (2x + 3)(x - 3)$

23. $ac = 8, b = -9$
    $rs = -1 \times -8 = 8$
    $r + s = -1 - 8 = -9$
    $\Rightarrow 2x^2 - x - 8x + 4$
    $= x(2x - 1) - 4(2x - 1)$
    $= (2x - 1)(x - 4)$

24. $ac = 6, b = 5$ $\quad\triangleright\quad$ $6x^2 + 2x + 3x + 1$
 $rs = 2 \times 3 = 6$ $\qquad = 2x(3x + 1) + (3x + 1)$
 $r + s = 2 + 3 = 5$ $\qquad = (3x + 1)(2x + 1)$

25. $ac = 12, b = 13$ $\quad\triangleright\quad$ $6x^2 + x + 12x + 2$
 $rs = 1 \times 12 = 12$ $\qquad = x(6x + 1) + 2(6x + 1)$
 $r + s = 1 + 12 = 13$ $\qquad = (6x + 1)(x + 2)$

26. $ac = 30, b = -11$ $\quad\triangleright\quad$ $3x^2 - 5x - 6x + 10$
 $rs = -5 \times -6 = 30$ $\qquad = x(3x - 5) - 2(3x - 5)$
 $r + s = -5 - 6 = -11$ $\qquad = (3x - 5)(x - 2)$

27. $ac = 72, b = 18$ $\quad\triangleright\quad$ $8x^2 + 6x + 12x + 9$
 $rs = 6 \times 12 = 72$ $\qquad = 2x(4x + 3) + 3(4x + 3)$
 $r + s = 6 + 12 = 18$ $\qquad = (4x + 3)(2x + 3)$

28. $ac = -36, b = -9$ $\quad\triangleright\quad$ $18x^2 + 3x - 12x - 2$
 $rs = 3 \times -12 = -36$ $\qquad = 3x(6x + 1) - 2(6x + 1)$
 $r + s = 3 - 12 = -9$ $\qquad = (6x + 1)(3x - 2)$

29. $ac = -45, b = -4$ $\quad\triangleright\quad$ $15x^2 + 5x - 9x - 3$
 $rs = 5 \times -9 = -45$ $\qquad = 5x(3x + 1) - 3(3x + 1)$
 $r + s = 5 - 9 = -4$ $\qquad = (3x + 1)(5x - 3)$

30. $ac = 60, b = -19$ $\quad\triangleright\quad$ $3x^2 - 4x - 15x + 20$
 $rs = -4 \times -15 = 60$ $\qquad = x(3x - 4) - 5(3x - 4)$
 $r + s = -4 - 15 = -19$ $\qquad = (3x - 4)(x - 5)$

31. $ac = -70, b = 3$ $\quad\triangleright\quad$ $2x^2 - 7x + 10x - 35$
 $rs = -7 \times 10 = -70$ $\qquad = x(2x - 7) + 5(2x - 7)$
 $r + s = -7 + 10 = 3$ $\qquad = (2x - 7)(x + 5)$

32. $ac = -84, b = -8$ $\quad\triangleright\quad$ $4x^2 + 6x - 14x - 21$
 $rs = 6 \times -14 = -84$ $\qquad = 2x(2x + 3) - 7(2x + 3)$
 $r + s = 6 - 14 = -8$ $\qquad = (2x + 3)(2x - 7)$

33. $ac = -24, b = 5$ $\quad\triangleright\quad$ $12x^2 - 3x + 8x - 2$
 $rs = -3 \times 8 = -24$ $\qquad = 3x(4x - 1) + 2(4x - 1)$
 $r + s = -3 + 8 = 5$ $\qquad = (4x - 1)(3x + 2)$

34. $ac = 90, b = 19$ $\quad\triangleright\quad$ $15x^2 + 9x + 10x + 6$
 $rs = 9 \times 10 = 90$ $\qquad = 3x(5x + 3) + 2(5x + 3)$
 $r + s = 9 + 10 = 19$ $\qquad = (5x + 3)(3x + 2)$

LESSON 99

1. $x^2 + 2x + 1$

2. $x^2 - 4x + 4$

3. $x^2 - 9$

4. $x^2 + 2 \cdot x \cdot 2 + 2^2$
$ = (x + 2)^2$

5. $x^2 + 2 \cdot x \cdot 7 + 7^2$
$ = (x + 7)^2$

6. $(4x)^2 + 2 \cdot 4x \cdot 1 + 1^2$
$ = (4x + 1)^2$

7. $(3x)^2 + 2 \cdot 3x \cdot 5 + 5^2$
$ = (3x + 5)^2$

8. $x^2 - 2 \cdot x \cdot 1 + 1^2$
$ = (x - 1)^2$

9. $x^2 - 2 \cdot x \cdot 5 + 5^2$
$ = (x - 5)^2$

10. $(6x)^2 - 2 \cdot 6x \cdot 1 + 1^2$
$ = (6x - 1)^2$

11. $(4x)^2 - 2 \cdot 4x \cdot 3 + 3^2$
$ = (4x - 3)^2$

12. $x^2 - 4^2$
$ = (x + 4)(x - 4)$

13. $x^2 - 8^2$
$ = (x + 8)(x - 8)$

14. $(2x)^2 - 1^2$
$ = (2x + 1)(2x - 1)$

15. $(7x)^2 - 2^2$
$ = (7x - 2)(7x + 2)$

16. $x^2 - 2^2$
$ = (x + 2)(x - 2)$

17. $x^2 - 2 \cdot x \cdot 3 + 3^2$
$ = (x - 3)^2$

18. $x^2 + 2 \cdot x \cdot 4 + 4^2$
$ = (x + 4)^2$

19. $x^2 - 10^2$
$ = (x + 10)(x - 10)$

20. $x^2 - 2 \cdot x \cdot 7 + 7^2$
$ = (x - 7)^2$

21. $x^2 + 2 \cdot x \cdot 5 + 5^2$
$ = (x + 5)^2$

22. $(3x)^2 - 2 \cdot 3x \cdot 2 + 2^2$
$ = (3x - 2)^2$

23. $(2x)^2 + 2 \cdot 2x \cdot 9 + 9^2$
$ = (2x + 9)^2$

24. $(4x)^2 + 2 \cdot 4x \cdot 3 + 3^2$
$ = (4x + 3)^2$

25. $(6x)^2 - 7^2$
$ = (6x + 7)(6x - 7)$

26. $(8x)^2 - 3^2$
$ = (8x + 3)(8x - 3)$

27. $(5x)^2 - 2 \cdot 5x \cdot 6 + 6^2$
$ = (5x - 6)^2$

28. $x^2 - 2 \cdot x \cdot 2 + 2^2$
$ = (x - 2)^2$

29. $x^2 + 2 \cdot x \cdot 6 + 6^2$
$ = (x + 6)^2$

30. $x^2 - 6^2$
$ = (x + 6)(x - 6)$

31. $x^2 - 2 \cdot x \cdot 10 + 10^2$
$ = (x - 10)^2$

32. $x^2 + 2 \cdot x \cdot 9 + 9^2$
$ = (x + 9)^2$

33. $x^2 - 5^2$
$ = (x + 5)(x - 5)$

34. $x^2 - 2 \cdot x \cdot 12 + 12^2$
$ = (x - 12)^2$

35. $x^2 - 8^2$
$ = (x + 8)(x - 8)$

36. $(2x)^2 - 2 \cdot 2x \cdot 1 + 1^2$
$ = (2x - 1)^2$

37. $(8x)^2 - 2 \cdot 8x \cdot 5 + 5^2$
$ = (8x - 5)^2$

38. $(2x)^2 - 9^2$
$ = (2x + 9)(2x - 9)$

39. $(6x)^2 + 2 \cdot 6x \cdot 1 + 1^2$
$ = (6x + 1)^2$

40. $(2x)^2 - 2 \cdot 2x \cdot 7 + 7^2$
$ = (2x - 7)^2$

41. $(5x)^2 - 6^2$
$ = (5x + 6)(5x - 6)$

42. $(5x)^2 + 2 \cdot 5x \cdot 3 + 3^2$
$ = (5x + 3)^2$

43. $(3x)^2 - 2 \cdot 3x \cdot 8 + 8^2$
$ = (3x - 8)^2$

LESSON 100

1. $(x - 1)(x + 2)$

2. $(x + 2)(x + 7)$

3. $(x + 2)(2x - 5)$

4. $(4x + 3)(2x + 5)$

5. $(x + 2)^2$

6. $(6x + 7)(6x - 7)$

7. $-(x^2 + 2x - 24)$
$ = -(x - 4)(x + 6)$

8. $-5(4x^2 + 12x + 5)$
$ = -5(2x + 1)(2x + 5)$

9. $(x - 2)(x + 5)$

10. $(x - 3)(x - 4)$

11. $(x + 2)(x - 2)$

12. $(2x - 1)(x + 4)$

13. $(5x - 3)(x - 1)$

14. $(3x - 1)^2$

15. $-(x^2 - 10x + 25)$
$= -(x - 5)^2$

16. $-(16x^2 - 9)$
$= -(4x + 3)(4x - 3)$

17. $-(3x^2 + 10x + 3)$
$= -(3x + 1)(x + 3)$

18. $-(14x^2 - 17x - 6)$
$= -(7x + 2)(2x - 3)$

19. $-3(x^2 - 8x + 16)$
$= -3(x - 4)^2$

20. $-2(3x^2 - 16x - 12)$
$= -2(3x + 2)(x - 6)$

21. $(x + 2)(x + 4)$

22. $(x - 2)^2$

23. $(x + 4)(x - 7)$

24. $(x - 3)(x + 6)$

25. $(x - 5)(x - 7)$

26. $(x + 3)(x + 5)$

27. $5x^2 + 2x - 15x - 6$
$= (5x + 2)(x - 3)$

28. $3x^2 + 2x - 18x - 12$
$= (3x + 2)(x - 6)$

29. $7x^2 + 4x + 14x + 8$
$= (7x + 4)(x + 2)$

30. $(2x)^2 - 5^2$
$= (2x + 5)(2x - 5)$

31. $(4x)^2 - 2 \cdot 4x \cdot 1 + 1^2$
$(4x - 1)^2$

32. $8x^2 + 6x + 12x + 9$
$= (4x + 3)(2x + 3)$

33. $6x^2 + 4x - 15x - 10$
$= (3x + 2)(2x - 5)$

34. $15x^2 - 6x + 20x - 8$
$= (5x - 2)(3x + 4)$

35. $2(x^2 + 4x - 21)$
$= 2(x - 3)(x + 7)$

36. $6(x^2 + 2x + 1)$
$= 6(x + 1)^2$

37. $5(3x^2 + 13x + 4)$
$= 5(3x + 1)(x + 4)$

38. $7(3x^2 + 5x - 2)$
$= 7(3x - 1)(x + 2)$

39. $4(20x^2 - 9x + 1)$
$= 4(5x - 1)(4x - 1)$

40. $2(12x^2 + x - 6)$
$= 2(3x - 2)(4x + 3)$

41. $-(x^2 - 36)$
$= -(x + 6)(x - 6)$

42. $-(5x^2 + 18x - 8)$
$= -(5x - 2)(x + 4)$

43. $-(8x^2 - 30x + 25)$
$= -(4x - 5)(2x - 5)$

44. $-3(12x^2 + 16x + 5)$
$= -3(2x + 1)(6x + 5)$

LESSON 101

1. See the second example in Lesson 93.

2. See the second example in Lesson 94.

3. See the examples in Lesson 97 and in Lesson 98.

4. $(x^2 + 9)(x^2 - 9) = (x^2 + 9)(x + 3)(x - 3)$

5. $4x(x^2 - 25) = 4x(x + 5)(x - 5)$

6. $x^2(x + 1) - 9(x + 1)$
$= (x + 1)(x^2 - 9) = (x + 1)(x + 3)(x - 3)$

7. $-(2x^3 + x^2 - 8x - 4)$
$= -[x^2(2x + 1) - 4(2x + 1)]$
$= -(2x + 1)(x^2 - 4) = -(2x + 1)(x + 2)(x - 2)$

8. $2(3x^2 + 5x - 3)$

9. $5x^2(5x^2 + 2x + 3)$

10. $x^2 - 2 \cdot x \cdot 5 + 5^2$
$= (x - 5)^2$

11. $x^2 - 6^2$
$= (x + 6)(x - 6)$

12. $ac = 18, b = -9$
$rs = -3 \times -6 = 18$
$r + s = -3 - 6 = -9$

$\dashrightarrow$ $x^2 - 3x - 6x + 18$
$= x(x - 3) - 6(x - 3)$
$= (x - 3)(x - 6)$

13. $ac = 72, b = 17$
$rs = 8 \times 9 = 72$
$r + s = 8 + 9 = 17$

$\dashrightarrow$ $12x^2 + 8x + 9x + 6$
$= 4x(3x + 2) + 3(3x + 2)$
$= (3x + 2)(4x + 3)$

14. $6x^2(x - 3) - (x - 3) = (x - 3)(6x^2 - 1)$

15. $7x^2(2x + 1) - (2x + 1) = (2x + 1)(7x^2 - 1)$

16. $2(4x^2 - x - 3) = 2(4x + 3)(x - 1)$

17. $3(20x^2 - 3x - 2) = 3(4x + 1)(5x - 2)$

18. $x(x^2 - 49) = x(x + 7)(x - 7)$

19 $-2x(4x^2 + 4x + 1) = -2x(2x + 1)^2$

20. $3(x^4 - 16)$
$= 3(x^2 + 4)(x^2 - 4) = 3(x^2 + 4)(x + 2)(x - 2)$

21. $x^2(x + 4) - 9(x + 4)$
$= (x + 4)(x^2 - 9) = (x + 4)(x + 3)(x - 3)$

22. $(x - 5)(x + 8)$

23. $(2x + 1)(5x - 3)$

24. $(3x + 2)^2$

25. $(2x + 9)(2x - 9)$

26. $5(x^2 - 3x - 4) = 5(x + 1)(x - 4)$

27. $-3(6x^2 - 7x + 2) = -3(2x - 1)(3x - 2)$

28. $3x(x^2 + 4x + 4) = 3x(x + 2)^2$

29. $x^2(x - 5) - 4(x - 5)$
$= (x - 5)(x^2 - 4) = (x - 5)(x + 2)(x - 2)$

30. $x(x^2 - 25) = x(x + 5)(x - 5)$

31. $-(10x^3 - 2x^2 + 15x - 3)$
$= -[2x^2(5x - 1) + 3(5x - 1)]$
$= -(5x - 1)(2x^2 + 3)$

LESSON 102

1. $3(x^2 - 2)$

2. $2x(4x^4 + 3x + 2)$

3. $4y(x - 2)$

4. $9x^2y^2(2x + 3y)$

5. $(x - 5)(x^2 + 1)$

6. $(x - 5)(x^3 - 3)$

7. $(2x + 1)(x^2 + 4)$

8. $(4x + 3)(2x^2 - 3)$

9. $(x + 2)(x + 4)$

10. $(x - 1)(x + 6)$

11. $(x - 3)(x - 5)$

12. $(x + 2)(x - 6)$

13. $(2x - 1)(x + 1)$

14. $(3x + 2)(x - 2)$

15. $(3x + 1)(2x + 3)$

16. $(5x - 2)(4x - 3)$

17. $(x - 6)^2$

18. $(x + 5)^2$

19. $(x + 4)(x - 4)$

20. $(3x + 11)(3x - 11)$

21. $-(x + 3)(x - 5)$

22. $-(x - 7)^2$

23. $-3(2x - 1)^2$

24. $-7(3x - 1)(x + 2)$

25. $x^2(3x + 2)(3x - 2)$ **26.** $(x + 4)(2x^2 + 5)$

27. $-2(x^2 + 9)(x + 3)(x - 3)$

28. $(3x - 4)(x + 5)(x - 5)$

29. Mean = average = 4.8

30. Median = middle value = 4.5

31. Mode = most frequent value = 3

32. 27% of 200 = 0.27 × 200 = 54 students

33. Median = middle value = 1°C

LESSON 103

1. 9   **2.** 9   **3.** $2\sqrt{3}$ **4.** x

5. $x = \pm\sqrt{25}$
$x = \pm5$

6. $x = \pm\sqrt{40}$
$x = \pm2\sqrt{10}$

7. $x^2 = 6$
$x = \pm\sqrt{6}$

8. $x^2 = 32$
$x = \pm\sqrt{32}$
$x = \pm4\sqrt{2}$

9. $x^2 = 5$
$x = \pm\sqrt{5}$

10. $5x^2 = 135$
$x^2 = 27$
$x = \pm\sqrt{27}$
$x = \pm3\sqrt{3}$

11. $x = \pm\sqrt{8}$
$x = \pm2\sqrt{2}$

12. $x^2 = 16$
$x = \pm\sqrt{16}$
$x = \pm4$

13. $x^2 = 54$
$x = \pm\sqrt{54}$
$x = \pm3\sqrt{6}$

14. $x^2 = 27$
$x = \pm\sqrt{27}$
$x = \pm3\sqrt{3}$

15. $x^2 = 48$
$x = \pm\sqrt{48}$
$x = \pm4\sqrt{3}$

16. $2x^2 = 100$
$x^2 = 50$
$x = \pm\sqrt{50}$
$x = \pm5\sqrt{2}$

17. $3x^2 = 54$
$x^2 = 18$
$x = \pm\sqrt{18}$
$x = \pm3\sqrt{2}$

18. $5x^2 = 55$
$x^2 = 11$
$x = \pm\sqrt{11}$

19. $x^2 = 108$
$x = \pm\sqrt{108}$
$x = \pm6\sqrt{3}$

20. $2x^2 = 24$
$x^2 = 12$
$x = \pm\sqrt{12}$
$x = \pm2\sqrt{3}$

21. $x = \pm\sqrt{49}$
$x = \pm7$

22. $x^2 = 20$
$x = \pm\sqrt{20}$
$x = \pm2\sqrt{5}$

23. $x^2 = 43$
$x = \pm\sqrt{43}$

24. $x^2 = 121$
$x = \pm\sqrt{121}$
$x = \pm11$

25. $x^2 = 4$
$x = \pm\sqrt{4}$
$x = \pm2$

26. $6x^2 = 216$
$x^2 = 36$
$x = \pm\sqrt{36}$
$x = \pm6$

27. $2x^2 = 64$
$x^2 = 32$
$x = \pm\sqrt{32}$
$x = \pm4\sqrt{2}$

28. $7x^2 = 63$
$x^2 = 9$
$x = \pm\sqrt{9}$
$x = \pm3$

29. $-9x^2 = -9$
$x^2 = 1$
$x = \pm\sqrt{1}$
$x = \pm1$

30. $2x^2 = 162$
$x^2 = 81$
$x = \pm\sqrt{81}$
$x = \pm9$

31. $-x^2 = -51$
$x^2 = 51$
$x = \pm\sqrt{51}$

32. $-3x^2 = -6$
$x^2 = 2$
$x = \pm\sqrt{2}$

33. $x^2 - 9 = 5$
$x^2 = 14$
$x = \pm\sqrt{14}$

34. $4x^2 - 1 = 23$
$4x^2 = 24$
$x^2 = 6$
$x = \pm\sqrt{6}$

35. $3x^2 - 48 = 18$
$3x^2 = 66$
$x^2 = 22$
$x = \pm\sqrt{22}$

36. $3x^2 + 8x - 3 = 8x$
$3x^2 = 3$
$x^2 = 1$
$x = \pm1$

37. $9x^2 - 25 = x^2 - 1$
$8x^2 = 24$
$x^2 = 3$
$x = \pm\sqrt{3}$

38. $x^2 - 4 = 4x^2 - 49$
$-3x^2 = -45$
$x^2 = 15$
$x = \pm\sqrt{15}$

1. $x = 3$

2. $x = \pm 2\sqrt{2}$

3. $x - 9 = \pm\sqrt{4}$
   $x - 9 = \pm 2$
   $x = 9 \pm 2$
   $x = 11, x = 7$

4. $(x + 5)^2 = 81$
   $x + 5 = \pm\sqrt{81}$
   $x + 5 = \pm 9$
   $x = -5 \pm 9$
   $x = 4, x = -14$

5. $3x - 5 = \pm\sqrt{16}$
   $3x - 5 = \pm 4$
   $3x = 5 \pm 4$
   $3x = 9, 3x = 1$
   $x = 3, x = 1/3$

6. $(4x + 12)^2 = 32$
   $4x + 12 = \pm\sqrt{32}$
   $4x + 12 = \pm 4\sqrt{2}$
   $4x = -12 \pm 4\sqrt{2}$
   $x = -3 \pm \sqrt{2}$

7. $(5x - 1)^2 = 10$
   $5x - 1 = \pm\sqrt{10}$
   $5x = 1 \pm \sqrt{10}$
   $x = \dfrac{1 \pm \sqrt{10}}{5}$

8. $5(4x + 3)^2 = 10$
   $(4x + 3)^2 = 2$
   $4x + 3 = \pm\sqrt{2}$
   $4x = -3 \pm \sqrt{2}$
   $x = \dfrac{-3 \pm \sqrt{2}}{4}$

9. $x + 5 = \pm\sqrt{90}$
   $x + 5 = \pm 3\sqrt{10}$
   $x = -5 \pm 3\sqrt{10}$

10. $(x - 1)^2 = 5$
    $x - 1 = \pm\sqrt{5}$
    $x = 1 \pm \sqrt{5}$

11. $(x - 7)^2 = 49$
    $x - 7 = \pm\sqrt{49}$
    $x - 7 = \pm 7$
    $x = 7 \pm 7$
    $x = 14, x = 0$

12. $(x + 1)^2 = 150$
    $x + 1 = \pm\sqrt{150}$
    $x + 1 = \pm 5\sqrt{6}$
    $x = -1 \pm 5\sqrt{6}$

13. $(x - 1)^2 = 25$
    $x - 1 = \pm\sqrt{25}$
    $x - 1 = \pm 5$
    $x = 1 \pm 5$
    $x = 6, x = -4$

14. $4x - 3 = \pm\sqrt{25}$
    $4x - 3 = \pm 5$
    $4x = 3 \pm 5$
    $4x = 8, 4x = -2$
    $x = 2, x = -1/2$

15. $3(x - 4)^2 = 27$
    $(x - 4)^2 = 9$
    $x - 4 = \pm\sqrt{9}$
    $x - 4 = \pm 3$
    $x = 4 \pm 3$
    $x = 7, x = 1$

16. $5(x + 2)^2 = 65$
    $(x + 2)^2 = 13$
    $x + 2 = \pm\sqrt{13}$
    $x = -2 \pm \sqrt{13}$

17. $(2x + 3)^2 = 6$
    $2x + 3 = \pm\sqrt{6}$
    $2x = -3 \pm \sqrt{6}$
    $x = \dfrac{-3 \pm \sqrt{6}}{2}$

18. $(5x - 2)^2 = 45$
    $5x - 2 = \pm\sqrt{45}$
    $5x - 2 = \pm 3\sqrt{5}$
    $5x = 2 \pm 3\sqrt{5}$
    $x = \dfrac{2 \pm 3\sqrt{5}}{5}$

19. $2(3x - 1)^2 = 16$
    $(3x - 1)^2 = 8$
    $3x - 1 = \pm\sqrt{8}$
    $3x - 1 = \pm 2\sqrt{2}$
    $3x = 1 \pm 2\sqrt{2}$
    $x = \dfrac{1 \pm 2\sqrt{2}}{3}$

20. $6(3x + 5)^2 = 96$
    $(3x + 5)^2 = 16$
    $3x + 5 = \pm\sqrt{16}$
    $3x + 5 = \pm 4$
    $3x = -5 \pm 4$
    $3x = -1, 3x = -9$
    $x = -1/3, x = -3$

21. $x^2 = 12$
    $x = \pm\sqrt{12}$
    $x = \pm 2\sqrt{3}$

22. $3x^2 = 27$
    $x^2 = 9$
    $x = \pm 3$

23. $x - 3 = \pm\sqrt{20}$
    $x - 3 = \pm 2\sqrt{5}$
    $x = 3 \pm 2\sqrt{5}$

24. $9x - 5 = 0$
    $x = 5/9$

25. $(x + 1)^2 = 9$
    $x + 1 = \pm\sqrt{9}$
    $x + 1 = \pm 3$
    $x = -1 \pm 3$
    $x = 2, x = -4$

26. $(x - 4)^2 = 48$
    $x - 4 = \pm\sqrt{48}$
    $x - 4 = \pm 4\sqrt{3}$
    $x = 4 \pm 4\sqrt{3}$

27. $(2x + 6)^2 = 28$
    $2x + 6 = \pm\sqrt{28}$
    $2x + 6 = \pm 2\sqrt{7}$
    $2x = -6 \pm 2\sqrt{7}$
    $x = -3 \pm \sqrt{7}$

28. $3(x + 4)^2 = 90$
    $(x + 4)^2 = 30$
    $x + 4 = \pm\sqrt{30}$
    $x = -4 \pm \sqrt{30}$

29. $4(x - 7)^2 = 64$
    $(x - 7)^2 = 16$
    $x - 7 = \pm\sqrt{16}$
    $x - 7 = \pm 4$
    $x = 7 \pm 4$
    $x = 11, x = 3$

30. $2(4x + 1)^2 = 24$
    $(4x + 1)^2 = 12$
    $4x + 1 = \pm\sqrt{12}$
    $4x + 1 = \pm 2\sqrt{3}$
    $4x + 1 = -1 \pm 2\sqrt{3}$
    $x = \dfrac{-1 \pm 2\sqrt{3}}{4}$

31. $(x+1)^2 = 5$

$x + 1 = \pm\sqrt{5}$

$x = -1 \pm \sqrt{5}$

32. $(x-3)^2 = 7$

$x - 3 = \pm\sqrt{7}$

$x = 3 \pm \sqrt{7}$

33. $(x-5)^2 = 9$

$x - 5 = \pm\sqrt{9}$

$x - 5 = \pm 3$

$x = 5 \pm 3$

$x = 8, x = 2$

34. $(x+6)^2 = 8$

$x + 6 = \pm\sqrt{8}$

$x + 6 = \pm 2\sqrt{2}$

$x = -6 \pm 2\sqrt{2}$

35. $(2x+1)^2 = 49$

$2x + 1 = \pm\sqrt{49}$

$2x + 1 = \pm 7$

$2x = -1 \pm 7$

$2x = 6, 2x = -8$

$x = 3, x = -4$

36. $(2x-3)^2 = 25$

$2x - 3 = \pm\sqrt{25}$

$2x - 3 = \pm 5$

$2x = 3 \pm 5$

$2x = 8, 2x = -2$

$x = 4, x = -1$

LESSON 105

1. $x = 8$

2. $x = 8, x = 2$

3. $(x-2)(x-4)$

4. $(x+3)(x+4)$

5. $x = 0, x = 5$

6. $x = -2, x = -3$

7. $(x+1)(x+2) = 0$

$x = -1, x = -2$

8. $(x-1)(x+4) = 0$

$x = 1, x = -4$

9. $x^2 - 5x + 6 = 0$

$(x-2)(x-3) = 0$

$x = 2, x = 3$

10. $x^2 - 13x + 40 = 0$

$(x-5)(x-8) = 0$

$x = 5, x = 8$

11. $(x+1)(x-2) = 0$

$x = -1, x = 2$

12. $(x-2)(x-3) = 0$

$x = 2, x = 3$

13. $(x+2)(x+6) = 0$

$x = -2, x = -6$

14. $(x-1)(x-6) = 0$

$x = 1, x = 6$

15. $(x+1)(x+3) = 0$

$x = -1, x = -3$

16. $(x-3)(x+4) = 0$

$x = 3, x = -4$

17. $x^2 + x - 6 = 0$

$(x-2)(x+3) = 0$

$x = 2, x = -3$

18. $x^2 - 6x + 8 = 0$

$(x-2)(x-4) = 0$

$x = 2, x = 4$

19. $x^2 - 4x - 5 = 0$

$(x+1)(x-5) = 0$

$x = -1, x = 5$

20. $x^2 + 9x + 14 = 0$

$(x+2)(x+7) = 0$

$x = -2, x = -7$

21. $(x-1)(x+2) = 0$

$x = 1, x = -2$

22. $(x+2)^2 = 0$

$x = -2$

23. $(x+2)(x-3) = 0$

$x = -2, x = 3$

24. $(x-1)(x-8) = 0$

$x = 1, x = 8$

25. $(x-3)^2 = 0$

$x = 3$

26. $(x-2)(x+5) = 0$

$x = 2, x = -5$

27. $(x-2)(x-5) = 0$

$x = 2, x = 5$

28. $(x-3)(x-4) = 0$

$x = 3, x = 4$

29. $(x-4)(x+9) = 0$

$x = 4, x = -9$

30. $(x+4)(x+8) = 0$

$x = -4, x = -8$

31. $x^2 - 2x - 15 = 0$

$(x+3)(x-5) = 0$

$x = -3, x = 5$

32. $x^2 + 2x - 8 = 0$

$(x-2)(x+4) = 0$

$x = 2, x = -4$

33. $x^2 + 5x + 4 = 0$

$(x+1)(x+4) = 0$

$x = -1, x = -4$

34. $x^2 + 9x + 18 = 0$

$(x+3)(x+6) = 0$

$x = -3, x = -6$

35. $x^2 + 3x - 10 = 0$

$(x-2)(x+5) = 0$

$x = 2, x = -5$

36. $x^2 - 13x + 40 = 0$

$(x-5)(x-8) = 0$

$x = 5, x = 8$

37. $x^2 - 10x + 16 = 0$

$(x-2)(x-8) = 0$

$x = 2, x = 8$

38. $x^2 + 8x + 7 = 0$

$(x+1)(x+7) = 0$

$x = -1, x = -7$

LESSON 106

1. $x = -2, x = -5$

2. $x = -2, x = 4$

3. $(7x-2)(x+1)$

4. $(3x-1)(2x+3)$

5. $x(x+5)(x-5)$

6. $(x-5)(x+2)(x-2)$

7. $(2x+1)(x+6) = 0$

$x = -1/2, x = -6$

8. $(3x-4)(2x+5) = 0$

$x = 4/3, x = -5/2$

9. $x^2 + x - 30 = 0$

$(x-5)(x+6) = 0$

$x = 5, x = -6$

10. $4x^2 - 13x + 3 = 0$

$(4x-1)(x-3) = 0$

$x = 1/4, x = 3$

11. $x(x^2 - 3x + 2) = 0$

$x(x-1)(x-2) = 0$

$x = 0, x = 1, x = 2$

12. $2x(2x^2 + 9x - 5) = 0$

$2x(2x-1)(x+5) = 0$

$x = 0, x = 1/2, x = -5$

13. $(5x-1)(x+1) = 0$

$x = 1/5, x = -1$

14. $(4x+3)(x-4) = 0$

$x = -3/4, x = 4$

15. $(2x+7)(2x-7) = 0$

$x = 7/2, x = -7/2$

16. $(3x+1)(2x+3) = 0$

$x = -1/3, x = -3/2$

17. $x^2 - 8x + 16 = 0$

$(x-4)^2 = 0$

$x = 4$

18. $7x^2 + 43x + 6 = 0$

$(7x+1)(x+6) = 0$

$x = -1/7, x = -6$

19. $x(x^2 + 6x + 9) = 0$

$x(x+3)^2 = 0$

$x = 0, x = -3$

20. $-x(2x^2 + x - 1) = 0$

$-x(2x-1)(x+1) = 0$

$x = 0, x = 1/2, x = -1$

21. $(5x+1)(x-2) = 0$

$x = -1/5, x = 2$

22. $(3x-2)(x+3) = 0$

$x = 2/3, x = -3$

23. $(5x + 2)(3x − 2) = 0$
$x = −2/5, x = 2/3$

24. $(6x − 1)(2x − 3) = 0$
$x = 1/6, x = 3/2$

25. $(4x − 1)(2x − 5) = 0$
$x = 1/4, x = 5/2$

26. $(3x − 4)^2 = 0$
$x = 4/3$

27. $x^2 − 11x + 28 = 0$
$(x − 4)(x − 7) = 0$
$x = 4, x = 7$

28. $2x^2 − 5x − 25 = 0$
$(2x + 5)(x − 5) = 0$
$x = −5/2, x = 5$

29. $x^2 − x = 0$
$x(x − 1) = 0$
$x = 0, x = 1$

30. $x^2 − x − 20 = 0$
$(x + 4)(x − 5) = 0$
$x = −4, x = 5$

31. $x(x + 4)(x − 4) = 0$
$x = 0, x = −4, x = 4$

32. $2x(4x^2 + 4x + 1) = 0$
$2x(2x + 1)^2 = 0$
$x = 0, x = −1/2$

LESSON 107

1. $(x + 2)^2$

2. $(x − 3)^2$

3. $x = 9, x = 5$

4. $x = −3 \pm 2\sqrt{2}$

5. $d = b/2 = 2/2 = 1$
$c = d^2 = 1^2 = 1$
$x^2 + 2x + 1$
$= (x + 1)^2$

6. $d = b/2 = −4/2 = −2$
$c = d^2 = (−2)^2 = 4$
$x^2 − 4x + 4$
$= (x − 2)^2$

7. $x^2 + 2x = 3$
$x^2 + 2x + 1 = 3 + 1$
$(x + 1)^2 = 4$
$x + 1 = \pm 2$
$x = −1 \pm 2$
$x = 1, x = −3$

8. $x^2 − 6x = −4$
$x^2 − 6x + 9 = −4 + 9$
$(x − 3)^2 = 5$
$x − 3 = \pm\sqrt{5}$
$x = 3 \pm \sqrt{5}$

9. $x^2 + 6x + 9$
$= (x + 3)^2$

10. $x^2 − 10x + 25$
$= (x − 5)^2$

11. $x^2 − 4x = 6$
$x^2 − 4x + 4 = 10$
$(x − 2)^2 = 10$
$x − 2 = \pm\sqrt{10}$
$x = 2 \pm \sqrt{10}$

12. $x^2 + 2x = 8$
$x^2 + 2x + 1 = 9$
$(x + 1)^2 = 9$
$x + 1 = \pm 3$
$x = 2, x = −4$

13. $x^2 − 6x = 9$
$x^2 − 6x + 9 = 18$
$(x − 3)^2 = 18$
$x − 3 = \pm 3\sqrt{2}$
$x = 3 \pm 3\sqrt{2}$

14. $x^2 + 8x = −7$
$x^2 + 8x + 16 = 9$
$(x + 4)^2 = 9$
$x + 4 = \pm 3$
$x = −1, x = −7$

15. $x^2 − 20x = 21$
$x^2 − 20x + 100 = 121$
$(x − 10)^2 = 121$
$x − 10 = \pm 11$
$x = 21, x = −1$

16. $x^2 + 12x = −20$
$x^2 + 12x + 36 = 16$
$(x + 6)^2 = 16$
$x + 6 = \pm 4$
$x = −2, x = −10$

17. $x^2 − 18x = −74$
$x^2 − 18x + 81 = 7$
$(x − 9)^2 = 7$
$x − 9 = \pm\sqrt{7}$
$x = 9 \pm \sqrt{7}$

18. $x^2 − 10x = −15$
$x^2 − 10x + 25 = 10$
$(x − 5)^2 = 10$
$x − 5 = \pm\sqrt{10}$
$x = 5 \pm \sqrt{10}$

19. $x^2 + 4x = 5$
$x^2 + 4x + 4 = 9$
$(x + 2)^2 = 9$
$x + 2 = \pm 3$
$x = 1, x = −5$

20. $x^2 − 6x = −8$
$x^2 − 6x + 9 = 1$
$(x − 3)^2 = 1$
$x − 3 = \pm 1$
$x = 4, x = 2$

21. $x^2 + 2x = 1$
$x^2 + 2x + 1 = 2$
$(x + 1)^2 = 2$
$x + 1 = \pm\sqrt{2}$
$x = −1 \pm \sqrt{2}$

22. $x^2 − 6x = 7$
$x^2 − 6x + 9 = 16$
$(x − 3)^2 = 16$
$x − 3 = \pm 4$
$x = 7, x = −1$

23. $x^2 − 8x = 5$
$x^2 − 8x + 16 = 21$
$(x − 4)^2 = 21$
$x − 4 = \pm\sqrt{21}$
$x = 4 \pm \sqrt{21}$

24. $x^2 + 4x = 8$
$x^2 + 4x + 4 = 12$
$(x + 2)^2 = 12$
$x + 2 = \pm 2\sqrt{3}$
$x = −2 \pm 2\sqrt{3}$

25. $x^2 + 6x = −4$
$x^2 + 6x + 9 = 5$
$(x + 3)^2 = 5$
$x + 3 = \pm\sqrt{5}$
$x = −3 \pm \sqrt{5}$

26. $x^2 + 8x = −12$
$x^2 + 8x + 16 = 4$
$(x + 4)^2 = 4$
$x + 4 = \pm 2$
$x = −2, x = −6$

27. $x^2 + 10x = 56$
$x^2 + 10x + 25 = 81$
$(x + 5)^2 = 81$
$x + 5 = \pm 9$
$x = 4, x = −14$

28. $x^2 − 16x = −10$
$x^2 − 16x + 64 = 54$
$(x − 8)^2 = 54$
$x − 8 = \pm 3\sqrt{6}$
$x = 8 \pm 3\sqrt{6}$

29. $x^2 − 12x = 28$
$x^2 − 12x + 36 = 64$
$(x − 6)^2 = 64$
$x − 6 = \pm 8$
$x = 14, x = −2$

30. $x^2 + 18x = 9$
$x^2 + 18x + 81 = 90$
$(x + 9)^2 = 90$
$x + 9 = \pm 3\sqrt{10}$
$x = −9 \pm 3\sqrt{10}$

31. $x^2 − 10x = 7$
$x^2 − 10x + 25 = 32$
$(x − 5)^2 = 32$
$x − 5 = \pm 4\sqrt{2}$
$x = 5 \pm 4\sqrt{2}$

32. $x^2 − 14x = 32$
$x^2 − 14x + 49 = 81$
$(x − 7)^2 = 81$
$x − 7 = \pm 9$
$x = 16, x = −2$

33. $x^2 + 2x = 3$
$x^2 + 2x + 1 = 4$
$(x + 1)^2 = 4$
$x + 1 = \pm 2$
$x = 1, x = −3$

34. $x^2 − 6x = 18$
$x^2 − 6x + 9 = 27$
$(x − 3)^2 = 27$
$x − 3 = \pm 3\sqrt{3}$
$x = 3 \pm 3\sqrt{3}$

35. $x^2 - 8x = 9$
$x^2 - 8x + 16 = 25$
$(x - 4)^2 = 25$
$x - 4 = \pm 5$
$x = 9, x = -1$

36. $x^2 + 16x = -40$
$x^2 + 16x + 64 = 24$
$(x + 8)^2 = 24$
$x + 8 = \pm 2\sqrt{6}$
$x = -8 \pm 2\sqrt{6}$

LESSON 108 ·······························

1. $x^2 + 2x + 1$
$= (x + 1)^2$

2. $x^2 - 8x + 16$
$= (x - 4)^2$

3. $x = -2 \pm \sqrt{11}$

4. $x = 3 \pm 2\sqrt{6}$

5. $x^2 - 3x = 1$

$x^2 - 3x + \dfrac{9}{4} = 1 + \dfrac{9}{4}$ $\quad \Rightarrow \quad$ $x - \dfrac{3}{2} = \pm \dfrac{\sqrt{13}}{2}$

$\left(x - \dfrac{3}{2}\right)^2 = \dfrac{13}{4}$ $\quad \quad$ $x = \dfrac{3 \pm \sqrt{13}}{2}$

6. $x^2 + 5x = -2$

$x^2 + 5x + \dfrac{25}{4} = -2 + \dfrac{25}{4}$ $\quad \Rightarrow \quad$ $x + \dfrac{5}{2} = \pm \dfrac{\sqrt{17}}{2}$

$\left(x + \dfrac{5}{2}\right)^2 = \dfrac{17}{4}$ $\quad \quad$ $x = \dfrac{-5 \pm \sqrt{17}}{2}$

7. $x^2 + x - \dfrac{1}{2} = 0$ $\quad \Rightarrow \quad$ $\left(x + \dfrac{1}{2}\right)^2 = \dfrac{3}{4}$

$x^2 + x = \dfrac{1}{2}$ $\quad \quad$ $x + \dfrac{1}{2} = \pm \dfrac{\sqrt{3}}{2}$

$x^2 + x + \dfrac{1}{4} = \dfrac{1}{2} + \dfrac{1}{4}$ $\quad \quad$ $x = \dfrac{-1 \pm \sqrt{3}}{2}$

8. $x^2 + \dfrac{6}{5}x - \dfrac{7}{5} = 0$ $\quad \Rightarrow \quad$ $\left(x + \dfrac{3}{5}\right)^2 = \dfrac{44}{25}$

$x^2 + \dfrac{6}{5}x = \dfrac{7}{5}$ $\quad \quad$ $x + \dfrac{3}{5} = \pm \dfrac{2\sqrt{11}}{5}$

$x^2 + \dfrac{6}{5}x + \dfrac{9}{25} = \dfrac{7}{5} + \dfrac{9}{25}$ $\quad \quad$ $x = \dfrac{-3 \pm 2\sqrt{11}}{5}$

9. $x^2 - x + \dfrac{1}{4} = \left(x - \dfrac{1}{2}\right)^2$

10. $x^2 + \dfrac{2}{3}x + \dfrac{1}{9} = \left(x + \dfrac{1}{3}\right)^2$

11. $x^2 - x = 1$

$x^2 - x + \dfrac{1}{4} = 1 + \dfrac{1}{4}$ $\quad \Rightarrow \quad$ $x - \dfrac{1}{2} = \pm \dfrac{\sqrt{5}}{2}$

$\left(x - \dfrac{1}{2}\right)^2 = \dfrac{5}{4}$ $\quad \quad$ $x = \dfrac{1 \pm \sqrt{5}}{2}$

12. $x^2 + 3x = 3$

$x^2 + 3x + \dfrac{9}{4} = 3 + \dfrac{9}{4}$ $\quad \Rightarrow \quad$ $x + \dfrac{3}{2} = \pm \dfrac{\sqrt{21}}{2}$

$\left(x + \dfrac{3}{2}\right)^2 = \dfrac{21}{4}$ $\quad \quad$ $x = \dfrac{-3 \pm \sqrt{21}}{2}$

13. $x^2 + 7x = -10$

$x^2 + 7x + \dfrac{49}{4} = -10 + \dfrac{49}{4}$ $\quad \Rightarrow \quad$ $x + \dfrac{7}{2} = \pm \dfrac{3}{2}$

$\left(x + \dfrac{7}{2}\right)^2 = \dfrac{9}{4}$ $\quad \quad$ $x = -2, x = -5$

14. $x^2 + 9x = -15$

$x^2 + 9x + \dfrac{81}{4} = -15 + \dfrac{81}{4}$ $\quad \Rightarrow \quad$ $x + \dfrac{9}{2} = \pm \dfrac{\sqrt{21}}{2}$

$\left(x + \dfrac{9}{2}\right)^2 = \dfrac{21}{4}$ $\quad \quad$ $x = \dfrac{-9 \pm \sqrt{21}}{2}$

15. $x^2 + 2x - \dfrac{3}{4} = 0$ $\quad \Rightarrow \quad$ $(x + 1)^2 = \dfrac{7}{4}$

$x^2 + 2x = \dfrac{3}{4}$ $\quad \quad$ $x + 1 = \pm \dfrac{\sqrt{7}}{2}$

$x^2 + 2x + 1 = \dfrac{3}{4} + 1$ $\quad \quad$ $x = \dfrac{-2 \pm \sqrt{7}}{2}$

16. $x^2 + 5x - 6 = 0$
$x^2 + 5x = 6$

$x^2 + 5x + \dfrac{25}{4} = 6 + \dfrac{25}{4}$ $\quad \Rightarrow \quad$ $x + \dfrac{5}{2} = \pm \dfrac{7}{2}$

$\left(x + \dfrac{5}{2}\right)^2 = \dfrac{49}{4}$ $\quad \quad$ $x = 1, x = -6$

17. $x^2 - x - 6 = 0$
$x^2 - x = 6$

$x^2 - x + \dfrac{1}{4} = 6 + \dfrac{1}{4}$ $\quad \Rightarrow \quad$ $x - \dfrac{1}{2} = \pm \dfrac{5}{2}$

$\left(x - \dfrac{1}{2}\right)^2 = \dfrac{25}{4}$ $\quad \quad$ $x = 3, x = -2$

18. $x^2 + \dfrac{2}{3}x - 2 = 0$ $\quad \Rightarrow \quad$ $\left(x + \dfrac{1}{3}\right)^2 = \dfrac{19}{9}$

$x^2 + \dfrac{2}{3}x = 2$ $\quad \quad$ $x + \dfrac{1}{3} = \pm \dfrac{\sqrt{19}}{3}$

$x^2 + \dfrac{2}{3}x + \dfrac{1}{9} = 2 + \dfrac{1}{9}$ $\quad \quad$ $x = \dfrac{-1 \pm \sqrt{19}}{3}$

19. $x^2 - 2x - 3 = 0$ $\quad \Rightarrow \quad$ $(x - 1)^2 = 4$
$x^2 - 2x = 3$ $\quad \quad$ $x - 1 = \pm 2$
$x^2 - 2x + 1 = 3 + 1$ $\quad \quad$ $x = 3, x = -1$

20. $x^2 - \dfrac{6}{5}x - \dfrac{3}{5} = 0$ $\quad\dashrightarrow\quad$ $\left(x - \dfrac{3}{5}\right)^2 = \dfrac{24}{25}$

$\quad x^2 - \dfrac{6}{5}x = \dfrac{3}{5}$ $\qquad\qquad\quad x - \dfrac{3}{5} = \pm\dfrac{2\sqrt{6}}{5}$

$\quad x^2 - \dfrac{6}{5}x + \dfrac{9}{25} = \dfrac{3}{5} + \dfrac{9}{25}$ $\quad x = \dfrac{3 \pm 2\sqrt{6}}{5}$

21. $x^2 - 4x = 6$ $\qquad\dashrightarrow\quad x - 2 = \pm\sqrt{10}$

$\quad x^2 - 4x + 4 = 10$ $\qquad\qquad x = 2 \pm \sqrt{10}$

$\quad (x - 2)^2 = 10$

22. $x^2 + 2x = 8$ $\qquad\dashrightarrow\quad x + 1 = \pm 3$

$\quad x^2 + 2x + 1 = 9$ $\qquad\qquad x = 2, x = -4$

$\quad (x + 1)^2 = 9$

23. $x^2 + x = 1$

$\quad x^2 + x + \dfrac{1}{4} = 1 + \dfrac{1}{4}$ $\quad\dashrightarrow\quad x + \dfrac{1}{2} = \pm\dfrac{\sqrt{5}}{2}$

$\quad \left(x + \dfrac{1}{2}\right)^2 = \dfrac{5}{4}$ $\qquad\qquad x = \dfrac{-1 \pm \sqrt{5}}{2}$

24. $x^2 - 5x = 4$

$\quad x^2 - 5x + \dfrac{25}{4} = 4 + \dfrac{25}{4}$ $\quad\dashrightarrow\quad x - \dfrac{5}{2} = \pm\dfrac{\sqrt{41}}{2}$

$\quad \left(x - \dfrac{5}{2}\right)^2 = \dfrac{41}{4}$ $\qquad\qquad x = \dfrac{5 \pm \sqrt{41}}{2}$

25. $x^2 - x - 3 = 0$

$\quad x^2 - x = 3$

$\quad x^2 - x + \dfrac{1}{4} = 3 + \dfrac{1}{4}$ $\quad\dashrightarrow\quad x - \dfrac{1}{2} = \pm\dfrac{\sqrt{13}}{2}$

$\quad \left(x - \dfrac{1}{2}\right)^2 = \dfrac{13}{4}$ $\qquad\qquad x = \dfrac{1 \pm \sqrt{13}}{2}$

26. $x^2 - 2x + \dfrac{1}{4} = 0$ $\quad\dashrightarrow\quad (x - 1)^2 = \dfrac{3}{4}$

$\quad x^2 - 2x = -\dfrac{1}{4}$ $\qquad\qquad x - 1 = \pm\dfrac{\sqrt{3}}{2}$

$\quad x^2 - 2x + 1 = -\dfrac{1}{4} + 1$ $\quad\; x = \dfrac{2 \pm \sqrt{3}}{2}$

27. $x^2 - \dfrac{2}{5}x - \dfrac{3}{5} = 0$ $\quad\dashrightarrow\quad \left(x - \dfrac{1}{5}\right)^2 = \dfrac{16}{25}$

$\quad x^2 - \dfrac{2}{5}x = \dfrac{3}{5}$ $\qquad\qquad x - \dfrac{1}{5} = \pm\dfrac{4}{5}$

$\quad x^2 - \dfrac{2}{5}x + \dfrac{1}{25} = \dfrac{3}{5} + \dfrac{1}{25}$ $\quad x = 1, x = -\dfrac{3}{5}$

28. $x^2 - \dfrac{3}{2}x - 1 = 0$ $\quad\dashrightarrow\quad \left(x - \dfrac{3}{4}\right)^2 = \dfrac{25}{16}$

$\quad x^2 - \dfrac{3}{2}x = 1$ $\qquad\qquad\quad x - \dfrac{3}{4} = \pm\dfrac{5}{4}$

$\quad x^2 - \dfrac{3}{2}x + \dfrac{9}{16} = 1 + \dfrac{9}{16}$ $\quad x = 2, x = -\dfrac{1}{2}$

29. $x^2 + \dfrac{1}{2}x - 2 = 0$ $\quad\dashrightarrow\quad \left(x + \dfrac{1}{4}\right)^2 = \dfrac{33}{16}$

$\quad x^2 + \dfrac{1}{2}x = 2$ $\qquad\qquad\quad x + \dfrac{1}{4} = \pm\dfrac{\sqrt{33}}{4}$

$\quad x^2 + \dfrac{1}{2}x + \dfrac{1}{16} = 2 + \dfrac{1}{16}$ $\quad x = \dfrac{-1 \pm \sqrt{33}}{4}$

30. $x^2 - \dfrac{1}{2}x - \dfrac{3}{4} = 0$ $\quad\dashrightarrow\quad \left(x - \dfrac{1}{4}\right)^2 = \dfrac{13}{16}$

$\quad x^2 - \dfrac{1}{2}x = \dfrac{3}{4}$ $\qquad\qquad\quad x - \dfrac{1}{4} = \pm\dfrac{\sqrt{13}}{4}$

$\quad x^2 - \dfrac{1}{2}x + \dfrac{1}{16} = \dfrac{3}{4} + \dfrac{1}{16}$ $\quad x = \dfrac{1 \pm \sqrt{13}}{4}$

31. $x^2 - x = 5$

$\quad x^2 - x + \dfrac{1}{4} = 5 + \dfrac{1}{4}$ $\quad\dashrightarrow\quad x - \dfrac{1}{2} = \pm\dfrac{\sqrt{21}}{2}$

$\quad \left(x - \dfrac{1}{2}\right)^2 = \dfrac{21}{4}$ $\qquad\qquad x = \dfrac{1 \pm \sqrt{21}}{2}$

32. $x^2 - 9x = -9$

$\quad x^2 - 9x + \dfrac{81}{4} = -9 + \dfrac{81}{4}$ $\quad\dashrightarrow\quad x - \dfrac{9}{2} = \pm\dfrac{3\sqrt{5}}{2}$

$\quad \left(x - \dfrac{9}{2}\right)^2 = \dfrac{45}{4}$ $\qquad\qquad x = \dfrac{9 \pm 3\sqrt{5}}{2}$

33. $6x^2 - 12x = -3$

$\quad x^2 - 2x = -\dfrac{1}{2}$ $\quad\dashrightarrow\quad x - 1 = \pm\dfrac{1}{\sqrt{2}} \cdot \dfrac{\sqrt{2}}{\sqrt{2}}$

$\quad x^2 - 2x + 1 = -\dfrac{1}{2} + 1$ $\qquad x - 1 = \pm\dfrac{\sqrt{2}}{2}$

$\quad (x - 1)^2 = \dfrac{1}{2}$ $\qquad\qquad\quad x = \dfrac{2 \pm \sqrt{2}}{2}$

34. $9x^2 - 6x = 5$

$\quad x^2 - \dfrac{2}{3}x = \dfrac{5}{9}$ $\quad\dashrightarrow\quad x - \dfrac{1}{3} = \pm\dfrac{\sqrt{2}}{\sqrt{3}} \cdot \dfrac{\sqrt{3}}{\sqrt{3}}$

$\quad x^2 - \dfrac{2}{3}x + \dfrac{1}{9} = \dfrac{5}{9} + \dfrac{1}{9}$ $\qquad x - \dfrac{1}{3} = \pm\dfrac{\sqrt{6}}{3}$

$\quad \left(x - \dfrac{1}{3}\right)^2 = \dfrac{2}{3}$ $\qquad\qquad\quad x = \dfrac{1 \pm \sqrt{6}}{3}$

1. $x = 2 \pm \sqrt{14}$

2. $x = (-5 \pm \sqrt{5})/2$

3. $x = (2 \pm \sqrt{3})/2$

4. $x = 3 \pm 2\sqrt{3}$

5. $a = 1, b = -1, c = -2$

$$x = \frac{-(-1) \pm \sqrt{(-1)^2 - 4(1)(-2)}}{2(1)} = \frac{1 \pm \sqrt{9}}{2} = \frac{1 \pm 3}{2}$$

$$x = 2, x = -1$$

6. $a = 1, b = 7, c = 9$

$$x = \frac{-7 \pm \sqrt{7^2 - 4(1)(9)}}{2(1)} = \frac{-7 \pm \sqrt{13}}{2}$$

7. $a = 4, b = -9, c = 5$

$$x = \frac{-(-9) \pm \sqrt{(-9)^2 - 4(4)(5)}}{2(4)} = \frac{9 \pm \sqrt{1}}{8} = \frac{9 \pm 1}{8}$$

$$x = 5/4, x = 1$$

8. $a = 1, b = 0, c = -7$

$$x = \frac{-0 \pm \sqrt{0^2 - 4(1)(-7)}}{2(1)} = \frac{\pm\sqrt{28}}{2} = \frac{\pm 2\sqrt{7}}{2} = \pm\sqrt{7}$$

9. $a = 4, b = -3, c = 0$

$$x = \frac{-(-3) \pm \sqrt{(-3)^2 - 4(4)(0)}}{2(4)} = \frac{3 \pm \sqrt{9}}{8} = \frac{3 \pm 3}{8}$$

$$x = 3/4, x = 0$$

10. $a = 1, b = 0, c = -8$

$$x = \frac{0 \pm \sqrt{32}}{2}$$

$$x = \pm 2\sqrt{2}$$

11. $a = 1, b = -5, c = 2$

$$x = \frac{5 \pm \sqrt{17}}{2}$$

12. $a = 1, b = 4, c = 2$

$$x = \frac{-4 \pm \sqrt{8}}{2}$$

$$x = -2 \pm \sqrt{2}$$

13. $a = 1, b = -2, c = -3$

$$x = \frac{2 \pm \sqrt{16}}{2}$$

$$x = 3, x = -1$$

14. $a = 1, b = 8, c = 6$

$$x = \frac{-8 \pm \sqrt{40}}{2}$$

$$x = -4 \pm \sqrt{10}$$

15. $a = 1, b = -6, c = 9$

$$x = \frac{6 \pm \sqrt{0}}{2}$$

$$x = 3$$

16. $a = 7, b = -3, c = 0$

$$x = \frac{3 \pm \sqrt{9}}{14}$$

$$x = 3/7, x = 0$$

17. $a = 6, b = -7, c = 2$

$$x = \frac{7 \pm \sqrt{1}}{12}$$

$$x = 2/3, x = 1/2$$

18. $a = 5, b = -5, c = -1$

$$x = \frac{5 \pm \sqrt{45}}{10}$$

$$x = \frac{5 \pm 3\sqrt{5}}{10}$$

19. $a = 4, b = 6, c = 1$

$$x = \frac{-6 \pm \sqrt{20}}{8}$$

$$x = \frac{-3 \pm \sqrt{5}}{4}$$

20. $a = 1, b = -9, c = 0$

$$x = \frac{9 \pm \sqrt{81}}{2}$$

$$x = 9, x = 0$$

21. $a = 1, b = 7, c = 6$

$$x = \frac{-7 \pm \sqrt{25}}{2}$$

$$x = -1, x = -6$$

22. $a = 1, b = -1, c = -4$

$$x = \frac{1 \pm \sqrt{17}}{2}$$

23. $a = 1, b = -3, c = -5$

$$x = \frac{3 \pm \sqrt{29}}{2}$$

24. $a = 1, b = 5, c = 6$

$$x = \frac{-5 \pm \sqrt{1}}{2}$$

$$x = -2, x = -3$$

25. $a = 1, b = 6, c = 4$

$$x = \frac{-6 \pm \sqrt{20}}{2}$$

$$x = -3 \pm \sqrt{5}$$

26. $a = 1, b = -7, c = 4$

$$x = \frac{7 \pm \sqrt{33}}{2}$$

27. $a = 1, b = -3, c = -3$

$$x = \frac{3 \pm \sqrt{21}}{2}$$

28. $a = 1, b = 2, c = -6$

$$x = \frac{-2 \pm \sqrt{28}}{2}$$

$$x = -1 \pm \sqrt{7}$$

29. $a = 1, b = -9, c = 8$

$$x = \frac{9 \pm \sqrt{49}}{2}$$

$$x = 8, x = 1$$

30. $a = 5, b = 0, c = -25$

$$x = \frac{0 \pm \sqrt{500}}{10}$$

$$x = \pm\sqrt{5}$$

31. $a = 2, b = 8, c = 8$

$$x = \frac{-8 \pm \sqrt{0}}{4}$$

$$x = -2$$

32. $a = 2, b = -9, c = 7$

$$x = \frac{9 \pm \sqrt{25}}{4}$$

$$x = 7/2, x = 1$$

33. $a = 3, b = 7, c = -6$

$$x = \frac{-7 \pm \sqrt{121}}{6}$$

$$x = 2/3, x = -3$$

34. $a = 5, b = -11, c = 6$

$$x = \frac{11 \pm \sqrt{1}}{10}$$

$$x = 6/5, x = 1$$

35. $a = 12, b = -20, c = 3$

$$x = \frac{20 \pm \sqrt{256}}{24}$$

$$x = 3/2, x = 1/6$$

36. $a = 3, b = 12, c = 10$

$$x = \frac{-12 \pm \sqrt{24}}{6}$$

$$x = \frac{-6 \pm \sqrt{6}}{3}$$

37. $a = 2, b = 13, c = 15$

$$x = \frac{-13 \pm \sqrt{49}}{4}$$

$$x = -3/2, x = -5$$

LESSON 110

1. $x = 1, x = -3$

2. $x = -4 \pm \sqrt{6}$

3. $x = (-3 \pm \sqrt{13})/2$

4. $x = 1, x = -3/5$

5. $x = 1 \pm \sqrt{5}$

6. $x = (-5 \pm \sqrt{13})/2$

7. $x = 2, x = -1/2$

8. $x = (1 \pm \sqrt{5})/4$

9. $a = 1, b = -1, c = -5$
$$x = \frac{1 \pm \sqrt{21}}{2}$$

10. $a = 1, b = -2, c = -1$
$$x = \frac{2 \pm \sqrt{8}}{2}$$
$$x = 1 \pm \sqrt{2}$$

11. $a = 1, b = -9, c = 14$
$$x = \frac{9 \pm \sqrt{25}}{2}$$
$$x = 7, x = 2$$

12. $a = 1, b = 4, c = -2$
$$x = \frac{-4 \pm \sqrt{24}}{2}$$
$$x = -2 \pm \sqrt{6}$$

13. $a = 5, b = -2, c = -3$
$$x = \frac{2 \pm \sqrt{64}}{10}$$
$$x = 1, x = -3/5$$

14. $a = 2, b = 1, c = -2$
$$x = \frac{-1 \pm \sqrt{17}}{4}$$

15. $a = 3, b = 6, c = -5$
$$x = \frac{-6 \pm \sqrt{96}}{6}$$
$$x = \frac{-3 \pm 2\sqrt{6}}{3}$$

16. $a = 4, b = 10, c = 5$
$$x = \frac{-10 \pm \sqrt{20}}{8}$$
$$x = \frac{-5 \pm \sqrt{5}}{4}$$

17. $x^2 + 5x - 5 = 0$
$a = 1, b = 5, c = -5$
$$x = \frac{-5 \pm \sqrt{45}}{2}$$
$$x = \frac{-5 \pm 3\sqrt{5}}{2}$$

18. $-5x^2 + 5x - 1 = 0$
$a = -5, b = 5, c = -1$
$$x = \frac{-5 \pm \sqrt{5}}{-10}$$
$$x = \frac{5 \pm \sqrt{5}}{10}$$

19. $x^2 + 4x - 12 = 0$
$a = 1, b = 4, c = -12$
$$x = \frac{-4 \pm \sqrt{64}}{2}$$
$$x = 2, x = -6$$

20. $3x^2 + 8x + 5 = 0$
$a = 3, b = 8, c = 5$
$$x = \frac{-8 \pm \sqrt{4}}{6}$$
$$x = -1, x = -5/3$$

21. $a = 1, b = 8, c = 2$
$$x = \frac{-8 \pm \sqrt{56}}{2}$$
$$x = -4 \pm \sqrt{14}$$

22. $a = 1, b = -1, c = -10$
$$x = \frac{1 \pm \sqrt{41}}{2}$$

23. $a = 1, b = 6, c = 4$
$$x = \frac{-6 \pm \sqrt{20}}{2}$$
$$x = -3 \pm \sqrt{5}$$

24. $a = 1, b = -6, c = -16$
$$x = \frac{6 \pm \sqrt{100}}{2}$$
$$x = 8, x = -2$$

25. $a = 5, b = -5, c = 1$
$$x = \frac{5 \pm \sqrt{5}}{10}$$

26. $a = 4, b = -11, c = 6$
$$x = \frac{11 \pm \sqrt{25}}{8}$$
$$x = 2, x = 3/4$$

27. $a = 3, b = 2, c = -2$
$$x = \frac{-2 \pm \sqrt{28}}{6}$$
$$x = \frac{-1 \pm \sqrt{7}}{3}$$

28. $a = 4, b = 8, c = -1$
$$x = \frac{-8 \pm \sqrt{80}}{8}$$
$$x = \frac{-2 \pm \sqrt{5}}{2}$$

29. $a = 6, b = -7, c = -3$
$$x = \frac{7 \pm \sqrt{121}}{12}$$
$$x = 3/2, x = -1/3$$

30. $a = 2, b = -13, c = -7$
$$x = \frac{13 \pm \sqrt{225}}{4}$$
$$x = 7, x = -1/2$$

31. $x^2 + 2x - 8 = 0$
$a = 1, b = 2, c = -8$
$$x = \frac{-2 \pm \sqrt{36}}{2}$$
$$x = 2, x = -4$$

32. $x^2 - 2x - 7 = 0$
$a = 1, b = -2, c = -7$
$$x = \frac{2 \pm \sqrt{32}}{2}$$
$$x = 1 \pm 2\sqrt{2}$$

33. $3x^2 + 4x - 4 = 0$
$a = 3, b = 4, c = -4$
$$x = \frac{-4 \pm \sqrt{64}}{6}$$
$$x = 2/3, x = -2$$

34. $9x^2 + 3x - 2 = 0$
$a = 9, b = 3, c = -2$
$$x = \frac{-3 \pm \sqrt{81}}{18}$$
$$x = 1/3, x = -2/3$$

35. $2x^2 - 8x + 5 = 0$
$a = 2, b = -8, c = 5$
$$x = \frac{8 \pm \sqrt{24}}{4}$$
$$x = \frac{4 \pm \sqrt{6}}{2}$$

36. $4x^2 - 12x + 1 = 0$
$a = 4, b = -12, c = 1$
$$x = \frac{12 \pm \sqrt{128}}{8}$$
$$x = \frac{3 \pm 2\sqrt{2}}{2}$$

LESSON 111

1. See the first example in Lesson 104.

2. See the second example in Lesson 105.

3. See the second example in Lesson 107.

4. See the first example in Lesson 109.

5. By the quad. formula:
$a = 1, b = 3, c = 1$
$x = (-3 \pm \sqrt{5})/2$

6. By factoring:
$(x + 1)(x - 2) = 0$
$x = -1, x = 2$

7. By comp. the square:
$$x^2 + 2x = 4$$
$$x^2 + 2x + 1 = 4 + 1$$
$$(x + 1)^2 = 5$$
$$x + 1 = \pm\sqrt{5}$$
$$x = -1 \pm \sqrt{5}$$

8. By taking square roots:
$$3x^2 = 12$$
$$x^2 = 4$$
$$x = \pm 2$$

9. By factoring:
$$(3x + 1)(x - 2) = 0$$
$$x = -1/3, x = 2$$

10. By the quad. formula:
$$a = 4, b = 4, c = -5$$
$$x = (-1 \pm \sqrt{6})/2$$

11. $2x^2 = 16$
$$x^2 = 8$$
$$x = \pm 2\sqrt{2}$$

12. $(x + 2)^2 = 11$
$$x + 2 = \pm\sqrt{11}$$
$$x = -2 \pm \sqrt{11}$$

13. $(x - 2)(x + 3) = 0$
$$x = 2, x = -3$$

14. $(2x - 1)(x - 2) = 0$
$$x = 1/2, x = 2$$

15. $x^2 - 4x = 4$
$$x^2 - 4x + 4 = 8$$
$$(x - 2)^2 = 8$$
$$x - 2 = \pm 2\sqrt{2}$$
$$x = 2 \pm 2\sqrt{2}$$

16. $x^2 + 12x = -16$
$$x^2 + 12x + 36 = 20$$
$$(x + 6)^2 = 20$$
$$x + 6 = \pm 2\sqrt{5}$$
$$x = -6 \pm 2\sqrt{5}$$

17. $a = 1, b = -7, c = 5$
$$x = (7 \pm \sqrt{29})/2$$

18. $a = 9, b = 6, c = -1$
$$x = (-1 \pm \sqrt{2})/3$$

19. $x^2 + 8x = 2$
$$x^2 + 8x + 16 = 18$$
$$(x + 4)^2 = 18$$
$$x + 4 = \pm 3\sqrt{2}$$
$$x = -4 \pm 3\sqrt{2}$$

20. $(x - 2)^2 = 12$
$$x - 2 = \pm 2\sqrt{3}$$
$$x = 2 \pm 2\sqrt{3}$$

21. $(x + 3)(x + 4) = 0$
$$x = -3, x = -4$$

22. $a = 5, b = -10, c = -4$
$$x = (5 \pm 3\sqrt{5})/5$$

23. $x^2 = 6$
$$x = \pm\sqrt{6}$$

24. $a = 1, b = 3, c = -9$
$$x = (-3 \pm 3\sqrt{5})/2$$

25. $(x - 1)(x + 4) = 0$
$$x = 1, x = -4$$

26. $x^2 = 20$
$$x = \pm 2\sqrt{5}$$

27. $a = 1, b = -7, c = 9$
$$x = (7 \pm \sqrt{13})/2$$

28. $(x + 3)(x - 5) = 0$
$$x = -3, x = 5$$

29. $x^2 - 4x = 3$
$$x^2 - 4x + 4 = 7$$
$$(x - 2)^2 = 7$$
$$x - 2 = \pm\sqrt{7}$$
$$x = 2 \pm \sqrt{7}$$

30. $x^2 + 10x = 2$
$$x^2 + 10x + 25 = 27$$
$$(x + 5)^2 = 27$$
$$x + 5 = \pm 3\sqrt{3}$$
$$x = -5 \pm 3\sqrt{3}$$

31. $a = 2, b = 8, c = 7$
$$x = (-4 \pm \sqrt{2})/2$$

32. $4(2x - 1)^2 = 36$
$$(2x - 1)^2 = 9$$
$$2x - 1 = \pm 3$$
$$2x = 4, 2x = -2$$
$$x = 2, x = -1$$

LESSON 112

1. $x = -1, x = -2$

2. $x = 1/2, x = -2$

3. $x = 1, x = -3$

4. $x = (-1 \pm \sqrt{6})/5$

5. $x = (5 \pm \sqrt{17})/2$

6. $x = -1/3, x = -2$

7. $D = (-4)^2 - 4(1)(7) = -12 < 0 \Rightarrow$ No solution

8. $D = 3^2 - 4(1)(-5) = 29 > 0 \Rightarrow$ Two solutions

9. $D = 3^2 - 4(4)(1) = -7 < 0 \Rightarrow$ No solution

10. $D = 12^2 - 4(9)(4) = 0 \Rightarrow$ One solution

11. $D = (-4)^2 - 4 \cdot 1 \cdot 4 = 0 \Rightarrow$ One solution

12. $D = (-6)^2 - 4 \cdot 1 \cdot 11 = -8 < 0 \Rightarrow$ No solution

13. $D = (-5)^2 - 4 \cdot 7 \cdot 2 = -31 < 0 \Rightarrow$ No solution

14. $D = 7^2 - 4 \cdot 5 \cdot (-6) = 169 > 0 \Rightarrow$ Two solutions

15. $x^2 + 2x = 1$
$$(x + 1)^2 = 2$$
$$x = -1 \pm \sqrt{2}$$

16. $a = 1, b = 3, c = 9$
No solution ($D = -27$)

17. $a = 1, b = 5, c = 2$
$$x = (-5 \pm \sqrt{17})/2$$

18. $(x - 4)^2 = 0$
$$x = 4$$

19. $a = 2, b = -5, c = 7$
No solution ($D = -31$)

20. $(3x - 4)(x + 2) = 0$
$$x = 4/3, x = -2$$

21. $16x^2 = 49$
$$x^2 = 49/16$$
$$x = 7/4, x = -7/4$$

22. $a = 2, b = 6, c = 5$
No solution ($D = -4$)

23. $(x - 2)(x + 4) = 0$
$$x = 2, x = -4$$

24. $a = 1, b = -5, c = 10$
No solution ($D = -15$)

25. $(x + 3)^2 = 0$
$$x = -3$$

26. $x^2 = 20$
$$x = \pm 2\sqrt{5}$$

27. $(x - 3)(x - 5) = 0$
$$x = 3, x = 5$$

28. $x^2 + 10x = -4$
$$(x + 5)^2 = 21$$
$$x = -5 \pm \sqrt{21}$$

29. $a = 1, b = -4, c = 13$
No solution ($D = -36$)

30. $(x - 7)^2 = 0$
$$x = 7$$

31. $a = 7, b = -2, c = -1$
$$x = (1 \pm 2\sqrt{2})/7$$

32. $a = 4, b = -4, c = 3$
No solution ($D = -32$)

33. $4x^2 = 28$
$$x^2 = 7$$
$$x = \pm\sqrt{7}$$

34. $a = 5, b = 8, c = 2$
$$x = (-4 \pm \sqrt{6})/5$$

35. $(3x - 2)(x - 2) = 0$
$$x = 2/3, x = 2$$

36. $a = 4, b = 9, c = 3$
$$x = (-9 \pm \sqrt{33})/8$$

37. $(7x - 1)(2x - 1) = 0$
$$x = 1/7, x = 1/2$$

38. $(5x + 2)^2 = 0$
$$x = -2/5$$

LESSON 113 ···

1–2. See the first and fourth examples in Lesson 9.

3. $6^2 + 8^2 = x^2$
    $x^2 = 100$
    $x = \pm 10$
    $x > 0$, so $x = 10$

4. $x^2 + 5^2 = 10^2$
    $x^2 = 75$
    $x = \pm 5\sqrt{3}$
    $x > 0$, so $x = 5\sqrt{3}$

5. x = the first even integer
    $x + 2$ = the second even integer
    The product is 168, so $x(x + 2) = 168$.
    $x^2 + 2x - 168 = 0$; $(x - 12)(x + 14) = 0$; $x = 12$, $x = -14$
    The two positive integers are 12 and 14.

6. x = the first integer
    $x + 5$ = the second integer
    The product is 84, so $x(x + 5) = 84$.
    $x^2 + 5x - 84 = 0$; $(x - 7)(x + 12) = 0$; $x = 7$, $x = -12$
    The two positive integers are 7 and 12.

7. x = the side length of the square
    The Pythagorean Theorem gives $x^2 + x^2 = (9\sqrt{2})^2$.
    $2x^2 = 162$; $x^2 = 81$; $x = 9$, $x = -9$
    The length of each side is 9 cm.

8. x = the hypotenuse of the triangle
    $x - 2$ and $x - 4$ = the legs of the triangle
    The Pythagorean Theorem gives $(x - 2)^2 + (x - 4)^2 = x^2$.
    $x^2 - 12x + 20 = 0$; $(x - 2)(x - 10) = 0$; $x = 2$, $x = 10$
    The dimensions are 10 in, 8 in, and 6 in.

9. x = the width of the rectangle
    $x + 4$ = the length of the rectangle
    The area is 96, so $x(x + 4) = 96$.
    $x^2 + 4x - 96 = 0$; $(x - 8)(x + 12) = 0$; $x = 8$, $x = -12$
    The dimensions are 8 cm and 12 cm.

10. x = the width of the rectangle
    $3x - 3$ = the length of the rectangle
    The area is 90, so $x(3x - 3) = 90$.
    $3x^2 - 3x - 90 = 0$; $3(x + 5)(x - 6) = 0$; $x = -5$, $x = 6$
    The dimensions are 6 cm and 15 cm.

11. x = the first integer
    $x + 1$ = the second integer
    The sum of the squares = 61, so $x^2 + (x + 1)^2 = 61$.
    $2x^2 + 2x - 60 = 0$; $2(x - 5)(x + 6) = 0$; $x = 5$, $x = -6$
    The two positive integers are 5 and 6.

12. x = the first integer;
    $10 - x$ = the second integer
    The sum of the squares = 58, so $x^2 + (10 - x)^2 = 58$.
    $2x^2 - 20x + 42 = 0$; $2(x - 3)(x - 7) = 0$; $x = 3$, $x = 7$
    The two positive integers are 3 and 7.

13. x = the smaller integer
    $x + 3$ = the larger integer
    The smaller + the square of the larger = 39,
    so $x + (x + 3)^2 = 39$.
    $x^2 + 7x - 30 = 0$; $(x - 3)(x + 10) = 0$; $x = 3$, $x = -10$
    The two positive integers are 3 and 6.

14. x = the height of the rectangle
    The Pythagorean Theorem gives $x^2 + 5^2 = 13^2$.
    $x^2 = 144$; $x = 12$, $x = -12$
    The height of the rectangle is 12 cm.

15. x = the hypotenuse of the triangle
    $x - 1$ and $x - 2$ = the legs of the triangle
    The Pythagorean Theorem gives $(x - 1)^2 + (x - 2)^2 = x^2$.
    $x^2 - 6x + 5 = 0$; $(x - 1)(x - 5) = 0$; $x = 1$, $x = 5$
    The dimensions are 5 cm, 4 cm, and 3 cm.

16. x = the width of the rectangle
    $3x - 2$ = the length of the rectangle
    The area is 65, so $x(3x - 2) = 65$.
    $3x^2 - 2x - 65 = 0$; $(3x + 13)(x - 5) = 0$; $x = -13/3$, $x = 5$
    The dimensions are 5 cm and 13 cm.

17. x = the width of the rectangle
    $18 - x$ = the length of the rectangle
    The area is 80, so $x(18 - x) = 80$.
    $-x^2 + 18x - 80 = 0$; $-(x - 8)(x - 10) = 0$; $x = 8$, $x = 10$
    The dimensions are 8 in and 10 in.

18. x = the legs of the triangle
    The Pythagorean Theorem gives $x^2 + x^2 = (4\sqrt{2})^2$.
    $2x^2 = 32$; $x^2 = 16$; $x = 4$, $x = -4$
    The perimeter is $4 + 4 + 4\sqrt{2} = 8 + 4\sqrt{2}$ ft.

19. x = the width of the strip
    $x + 5$ and $x + 4$ = the dimensions of the new rectangle
    The new area = the original area + 36,
    so $(x + 5)(x + 4) = 5 \times 4 + 36$.
    $x^2 + 9x - 36 = 0$; $(x - 3)(x + 12) = 0$; $x = 3$, $x = -12$
    The width of the strip is 3 cm.

20. x = the distance traveled by car B
    $x + 10$ = the distance between
    the two cars
    The Pythagorean Theorem gives
    $20^2 + x^2 = (x + 10)^2$.
    $-20x = -300$; $x = 15$
    Car B traveled 15 miles.

LESSON 114

1. $x = \pm 3\sqrt{5}$
2. $x = 5, x = -3$
3. $x = (5 \pm 2\sqrt{2})/9$
4. $x = (1 \pm \sqrt{6})/2$
5. $x = 2, x = 3$
6. $x = 5, x = -5$
7. $x = -1/2, x = -3/2$
8. $x = -1/5, x = 2$
9. $x = 2 \pm \sqrt{14}$
10. $x = -3 \pm 2\sqrt{5}$
11. $x = (-1 \pm \sqrt{10})/3$
12. $x = -1, x = -5$
13. $x = (1 \pm \sqrt{33})/2$
14. $x = (-3 \pm \sqrt{5})/2$
15. $x = (-1 \pm \sqrt{11})/5$
16. $x = 4/3, x = -1$
17. $x = -6$
18. $x = 4, x = -4$
19. $x = (-4 \pm \sqrt{2})/2$
20. No solution
21. 6 and 8
22. 3 cm
23. 5 feet by 12 feet

24. A ∪ B 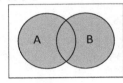   A ∩ B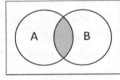

A^C 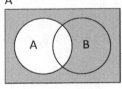   A − B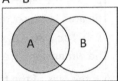

25. A ∩ B = {3, 4}, so A − (A ∩ B) = {1, 2}.

26. False; 1 is not an element of {2, 3, 5}.

27. True

28. H1, H2, H3, H4, H5, H6, T1, T2, T3, T4, T5, T6

29. 5 × 4 = 20 outfits are possible.

LESSON 115

1–2. See the third example in Lesson 14.

3.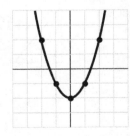

Points:
(−2, 2), (−1, −1), (0, −2)
(1, −1), (2, 2)

4. Vertex: (2, 0)
Axis of symmetry: $x = 2$
y-intercept: 4
x-intercept(s): 2

5. Vertex: (0, 0)
Axis of symmetry: $x = 0$
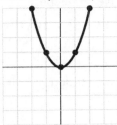

6. Vertex: (0, −3)
Axis of symmetry: $x = 0$
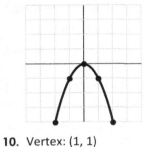

7. Vertex: (−1, −1)
Axis of symmetry: $x = -1$
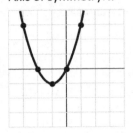

8. Vertex: (0, 0)
Axis of symmetry: $x = 0$

9. Vertex: (0, 2)
Axis of symmetry: $x = 0$
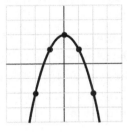

10. Vertex: (1, 1)
Axis of symmetry: $x = 1$
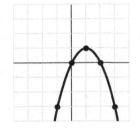

11. Vertex: (1, 0)
Axis of symmetry: $x = 1$
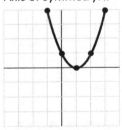

12. Vertex: (0, 0)
Axis of symmetry: $x = 0$
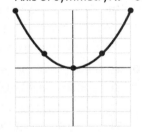

13. Vertex: (0, 4)
Axis of symmetry: $x = 0$

LESSON 116

1. See the first example in Lesson 115.

2. Vertex: $(2, -3)$, axis of symmetry: $x = 2$

3. $x = -\dfrac{-2}{2(1)} = 1$

   $y = 1^2 - 2(1) + 1 = 0$

   Vertex: $(1, 0)$

4. $x = -\dfrac{6}{2(-1)} = 3$

   $y = -3^2 + 6(3) - 5 = 4$

   Vertex: $(3, 4)$

5. $x = -\dfrac{4}{2(1/2)} = -4$

   $y = \dfrac{1}{2}(-4)^2 + 4(-4) - 2 = -10$

   Vertex: $(-4, -10)$

6. Vertex: $(3, -1)$
   Axis of symmetry: $x = 3$
   Points: $(1, 3), (2, 0)$
   Reflected: $(5, 3), (4, 0)$

   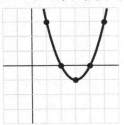

7. Vertex: $(-2, 1)$,
   Axis of symmetry: $x = -2$
   Points: $(-6, -3), (-4, 0)$
   Reflected: $(2, -3), (0, 0)$

   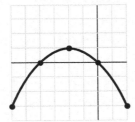

8. $x = -\dfrac{8}{2(1)} = -4$

   Axis of symmetry: $x = -4$

   $y = -16$ at $x = -4$
   Vertex: $(-4, -16)$

   $y = 0$ at $x = 0$
   y-intercept: 0

9. $x = -\dfrac{6}{2(1)} = -3$

   Axis of symmetry: $x = -3$

   $y = -4$ at $x = -3$
   Vertex: $(-3, -4)$

   $y = 5$ at $x = 0$
   y-intercept: 5

10. $x = -\dfrac{0}{2(-1)} = 0$

    Axis of symmetry: $x = 0$

    $y = 4$ at $x = 0$
    Vertex: $(0, 4)$

    $y = 4$ at $x = 0$
    y-intercept: 4

11. $x = -\dfrac{8}{2(-1)} = 4$

    Axis of symmetry: $x = 4$

    $y = 9$ at $x = 4$
    Vertex: $(4, 9)$

    $y = -7$ at $x = 0$
    y-intercept: -7

12. $x = -\dfrac{-6}{2(3)} = 1$

    Axis of symmetry: $x = 1$

    $y = -2$ at $x = 1$
    Vertex: $(1, -2)$

    $y = 1$ at $x = 0$
    y-intercept: 1

13. $x = -\dfrac{-2}{2(-1/2)} = -2$

    Axis of symmetry: $x = -2$

    $y = 4$ at $x = -2$
    Vertex: $(-2, 4)$

    $y = 2$ at $x = 0$
    y-intercept: 2

14.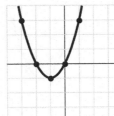

15.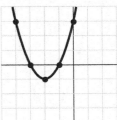

16.

17.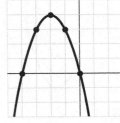

18.

19.

LESSON 117

1–2. See the first and second examples in Lesson 116.

3. $h = 0$ and $k = 3$, so the vertex is $(0, 3)$.

4. $h = 1$ and $k = 0$, so the vertex is $(1, 0)$.

5. $h = -4$ and $k = -2$, so the vertex is $(-4, -2)$.

6.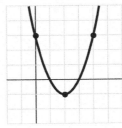

   Vertex: $(2, -1)$
   Axis of symmetry: $x = 2$
   Point: $(0, 3)$
   Reflected: $(4, 3)$

7. $h = 0$ and $k = 5$
   Axis of symmetry: $x = 0$
   Vertex: $(0, 5)$
   y-intercept: 5

8. $h = 0$ and $k = -7$
   Axis of symmetry: $x = 0$
   Vertex: $(0, -7)$
   y-intercept: -7

9. $h = 4$ and $k = 0$
Axis of symmetry: $x = 4$
Vertex: (4, 0)
y-intercept: 16

10. $h = -3$ and $k = 0$
Axis of symmetry: $x = -3$
Vertex: (−3, 0)
y-intercept: −9

11. $h = -1$ and $k = -5$
Axis of symmetry: $x = -1$
Vertex: (−1, −5)
y-intercept: −2

12. $h = 2$ and $k = 3$
Axis of symmetry: $x = 2$
Vertex: (2, 3)
y-intercept: 2

13.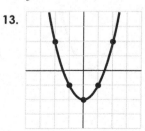

14.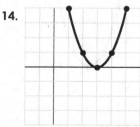

15.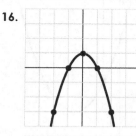

16.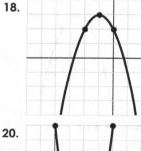

17.

18.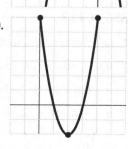

19.

20.

21.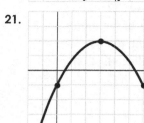

1–2. See the first and second examples in Lesson 117.

3. $p = 0$ and $q = 2$
$x = (0 + 2)/2 = 1$
$y = -1$ at $x = 1$
Vertex: (1, −1)

4. $p = -1$ and $q = 3$
$x = (-1 + 3)/2 = 1$
$y = -4$ at $x = 1$
Vertex: (1, −4)

5. $p = -4$ and $q = 4$
$x = (-4 + 4)/2 = 0$
$y = 4$ at $x = 0$
Vertex: (0, 4)

6.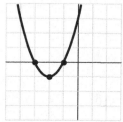

x-intercepts: −1, −3
Vertex: (−2, −1)

7. $p = 0$ and $q = 4$
x-intercept(s): 0, 4
$x = (0 + 4)/2 = 2$
$y = -4$ at $x = 2$
Vertex: (2, −4)
$y = 0$ at $x = 0$
y-intercept: 0

8. $p = 0$ and $q = -2$
x-intercept(s): 0, −2
$x = (0 - 2)/2 = -1$
$y = 1$ at $x = -1$
Vertex: (−1, 1)
$y = 0$ at $x = 0$
y-intercept: 0

9. $p = -1$ and $q = 5$
x-intercept(s): −1, 5
$x = (-1 + 5)/2 = 2$
$y = -9$ at $x = 2$
Vertex: (2, −9)
$y = -5$ at $x = 0$
y-intercept: −5

10. $p = 1$ and $q = 7$
x-intercept(s): 1, 7
$x = (1 + 7)/2 = 4$
$y = 9$ at $x = 4$
Vertex: (4, 9)
$y = -7$ at $x = 0$
y-intercept: −7

11. $p = 1$ and $q = -3$
x-intercept(s): 1, −3
$x = (1 - 3)/2 = -1$
$y = -8$ at $x = -1$
Vertex: (−1, −8)
$y = -6$ at $x = 0$
y-intercept: −6

12. $p = -2$ and $q = -6$
x-intercept(s): −2, −6
$x = (-2 - 6)/2 = -4$
$y = 2$ at $x = -4$
Vertex: (−4, 2)
$y = -6$ at $x = 0$
y-intercept: −6

13.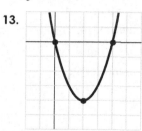

14.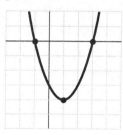

15.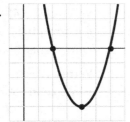

16.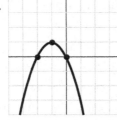

17.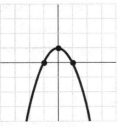

18.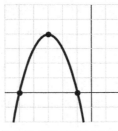

19.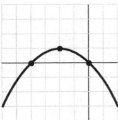

20.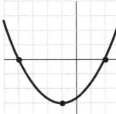

21.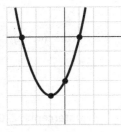

LESSON 119 ·····················

1–2. See the first and second examples in Lesson 118.

3. $y = x^2 + 2x + 1 - 1 - 3$
   $= (x + 1)^2 - 4$

4. $y = -2(x^2 + 4x) - 3$
   $= -2(x^2 + 4x + 4 - 4) - 3$
   $= -2(x^2 + 4x + 4) + 8 - 3$
   $= -2(x + 2)^2 + 5$

5. $y = (x - 1)(x + 3)$

6. $y = -2(x^2 - x - 6)$
   $= -2(x + 2)(x - 3)$

7.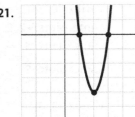

See Problems 3 and 5.
Vertex: (−1, −4)
x-intercepts: −3, 1
y-intercept: −3

8. Vertex form: $y = x^2 - 9$
   Intercept form: $y = (x + 3)(x - 3)$

9. Vertex form: $y = (x - 3)^2$
   Intercept form: $y = (x - 3)^2$

10. Vertex form: $y = x^2 - 2x + 1 - 1 - 8$
   $= (x - 1)^2 - 9$
   Intercept form: $y = (x + 2)(x - 4)$

11. Vertex form: $y = -(x^2 + 4x) + 5$
   $= -(x^2 + 4x + 4 - 4) + 5$
   $= -(x^2 + 4x + 4) + 4 + 5$
   $= -(x + 2)^2 + 9$
   Intercept form: $y = -(x^2 + 4x - 5)$
   $= -(x - 1)(x + 5)$

12. Vertex form: $y = 3(x^2 + 2x) - 9$
   $= 3(x^2 + 2x + 1 - 1) - 9$
   $= 3(x^2 + 2x + 1) - 3 - 9$
   $= 3(x + 1)^2 - 12$
   Intercept form: $y = 3(x^2 + 2x - 3)$
   $= 3(x - 1)(x + 3)$

13. Vertex form: $y = -2(x^2 - 6x) - 10$
   $= -2(x^2 - 6x + 9 - 9) - 10$
   $= -2(x^2 - 6x + 9) + 18 - 10$
   $= -2(x - 3)^2 + 8$
   Intercept form: $y = -2(x^2 - 6x + 5)$
   $= -2(x - 1)(x - 5)$

14. Vertex form: $y = \dfrac{1}{5}(x^2 - 10x)$

   $= \dfrac{1}{5}(x^2 - 10x + 25 - 25)$

   $= \dfrac{1}{5}(x^2 - 10x + 25) - 5$

   $= \dfrac{1}{5}(x - 5)^2 - 5$

   Intercept form: $y = \dfrac{1}{5}x(x - 10)$

15. Vertex form: $y = -\dfrac{1}{2}(x^2 - 4x) + 16$

   $= -\dfrac{1}{2}(x^2 - 4x + 4 - 4) + 16$

   $= -\dfrac{1}{2}(x^2 - 4x + 4) + 2 + 16$

   $= -\dfrac{1}{2}(x - 2)^2 + 18$

   Intercept form: $y = -\dfrac{1}{2}(x^2 - 4x - 32)$

   $= -\dfrac{1}{2}(x + 4)(x - 8)$

16. $y = (x + 3)^2 - 1$
$y = (x + 2)(x + 4)$

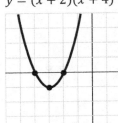

17. $y = 2(x - 2)^2 - 2$
$y = 2(x - 1)(x - 3)$

18. $y = -\dfrac{1}{2}(x + 2)(x - 2)$

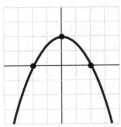

LESSON 120 ·····································

1–2. See the examples in Lesson 119.

3. $y = x^2 - 2x - 3$ y-intercept: –3
$= (x + 1)(x - 3)$ x-intercepts: –1, 3
$y = x^2 - 2x + 1 - 1 - 3$
$= (x - 1)^2 - 4$ Vertex: (1, –4)

4. $y = -x^2 + 8x - 7$ y-intercept: –7
$= -(x^2 - 8x + 7)$
$= -(x - 1)(x - 7)$ x-intercepts: 1, 7
$y = -(x^2 - 8x) - 7$
$= -(x^2 - 8x + 16 - 16) - 7$
$= -(x^2 - 8x + 16) + 16 - 7$
$= -(x - 4)^2 + 9$ Vertex: (4, 9)

5. $(x + 3)^2 - 9 = 0$
$(x + 3)^2 = 9$
$x + 3 = \pm 3$
$x = 0, x = -6$
x-intercepts: 0, –6

6. $-2(x - 1)^2 + 8 = 0$
$(x - 1)^2 = 4$
$x - 1 = \pm 2$
$x = 3, x = -1$
x-intercepts: 3, –1

7. $y = -(x^2 - 2x) - 2$
$= -(x^2 - 2x + 1 - 1) - 2$
$= -(x^2 - 2x + 1) + 1 - 2$
$= -(x - 1)^2 - 1$

Vertex form:
$y = -(x - 1)^2 - 1$
Vertex: (1, –1)
x-intercepts: none
y-intercept: –2

8. $y = (x + 2)^2 - 4$ Vertex: (–2, –4)
$= x^2 + 4x$ y-intercept: 0
$= x(x + 4)$ x-intercepts: 0, –4

9. $y = -2(x - 1)^2 - 3$ Vertex: (1, –3)
$= -2x^2 + 4x - 5$ y-intercept: –5
$-2(x - 1)^2 - 3 = 0$
$(x - 1)^2 = -3/2 < 0$ x-intercepts: none

10. $y = 4(x + 1)(x + 3)$ x-intercepts: –1, –3
$= 4x^2 + 16x + 12$ y-intercept: 12
$= 4(x^2 + 4x) + 12$
$= 4(x^2 + 4x + 4 - 4) + 12$
$= 4(x^2 + 4x + 4) - 16 + 12$
$= 4(x + 2)^2 - 4$ Vertex: (–2, –4)

11. $y = -(x + 1)(x - 5)$ x-intercepts: –1, 5
$= -x^2 + 4x + 5$ y-intercept: 5
$= -(x^2 - 4x) + 5$
$= -(x^2 - 4x + 4 - 4) + 5$
$= -(x^2 - 4x + 4) + 4 + 5$
$= -(x - 2)^2 + 9$ Vertex: (2, 9)

12. $y = x^2 - 4$ Vertex: (0, –4)
$= (x + 2)(x - 2)$ x-intercepts: –2, 2
    y-intercept: –4

13. $y = -x^2 + 6x - 9$ y-intercept: –9
$= -(x^2 - 6x + 9)$
$= -(x - 3)^2$ Vertex: (3, 0)
    x-intercept: 3

14. $y = 3x^2 + 6x + 4$ y-intercept: 4
$= 3(x^2 + 2x) + 4$
$= 3(x^2 + 2x + 1 - 1) + 4$
$= 3(x^2 + 2x + 1) - 3 + 4$
$= 3(x + 1)^2 + 1$ Vertex: (–1, 1)
$3(x + 1)^2 + 1 = 0$
$(x + 1)^2 = -1/3 < 0$ x-intercepts: none

15. $y = \dfrac{1}{2}x^2 - 4x + 6$ y-intercept: 6

$= \dfrac{1}{2}(x^2 - 8x + 16 - 16) + 6$

$= \dfrac{1}{2}(x^2 - 8x + 16) - 8 + 6$

$= \dfrac{1}{2}(x - 4)^2 - 2$ Vertex: (4, –2)

$y = \dfrac{1}{2}(x^2 - 8x + 12)$

$= \dfrac{1}{2}(x - 2)(x - 6)$ x-intercepts: 2, 6

16. $y = x^2 - 2x - 3$
$y = (x + 1)(x - 3)$

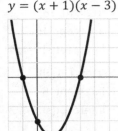

17. $y = -x^2 + 2x$
$y = -(x - 1)^2 + 1$

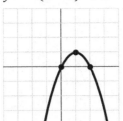

18. $y = (x - 3)^2 - 4$
$y = (x - 1)(x - 5)$

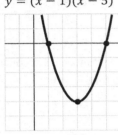

LESSON 121 ···

1. Vertex: $(-3, -1)$
y-intercept: 8
x-intercept(s): $-2, -4$

2. Vertex: $(5, 0)$
y-intercept: -25
x-intercept(s): 5

3. Vertex: $(1, -4)$
y-intercept: -3
x-intercept(s): $-1, 3$

4. Vertex: $(1, 3)$
y-intercept: 0
x-intercept(s): 0, 2

5. Vertex: $(2, -2)$
y-intercept: 6
x-intercept(s): 1, 3

6. Vertex: $(-1, 2)$
y-intercept: 5
x-intercept(s): none

7. $y = a(x - 1)^2 + 1$
$2 = a(2 - 1)^2 + 1$
$2 = a + 1$
$a = 1$
$y = (x - 1)^2 + 1$
$y = x^2 - 2x + 2$

8. $y = a(x - 3)^2 - 9$
$-1 = a(5 - 3)^2 - 9$
$-1 = 4a - 9$
$a = 2$
$y = 2(x - 3)^2 - 9$
$y = 2x^2 - 12x + 9$

9. $y = a(x - 3)(x - 7)$
$-3 = a(4 - 3)(4 - 7)$
$-3 = -3a$
$a = 1$
$y = (x - 3)(x - 7)$
$y = x^2 - 10x + 21$

10. $y = ax(x - 4)$
$9 = a(3)(3 - 4)$
$9 = -3a$
$a = -3$
$y = -3x(x - 4)$
$y = -3x^2 + 12x$

11. Using vertex form: OR   Using intercept form:
Vertex: $(2, -2)$ x-intercepts: 0, 4
Point: $(0, 0)$ Point: $(2, -2)$
$y = a(x - 2)^2 - 2$ $y = ax(x - 4)$
$0 = a(0 - 2)^2 - 2$ $-2 = a(2)(2 - 4)$
$0 = 4a - 2$ $-2 = -4a$
$a = 1/2$ $a = 1/2$
$y = \dfrac{1}{2}(x - 2)^2 - 2$ $y = \dfrac{1}{2}x(x - 4)$

12. $y = a(x + 2)^2 + 3$
$7 = a(0 + 2)^2 + 3$
$7 = 4a + 3$
$a = 1$
$y = (x + 2)^2 + 3$
$y = x^2 + 4x + 7$

13. $y = ax^2 + 9$
$5 = a \cdot 2^2 + 9$
$5 = 4a + 9$
$a = -1$
$y = -x^2 + 9$

14. $y = ax^2 - 6$
$-3 = a \cdot 3^2 - 6$
$-3 = 9a - 6$
$a = 1/3$
$y = \dfrac{1}{3}x^2 - 6$

15. $y = a(x - 1)(x - 5)$
$5 = a(0 - 1)(0 - 5)$
$5 = 5a$
$a = 1$
$y = (x - 1)(x - 5)$
$y = x^2 - 6x + 5$

16. $y = ax(x - 3)$
$4 = a(1)(1 - 3)$
$4 = -2a$
$a = -2$
$y = -2x(x - 3)$
$y = -2x^2 + 6x$

17. $y = a(x + 4)(x - 4)$
$7 = a(3 + 4)(3 - 4)$
$7 = -7a$
$a = -1$
$y = -(x + 4)(x - 4)$
$y = -x^2 + 16$

18. $y = a(x - 4)(x + 8)$
$-5 = a(2 - 4)(2 + 8)$
$-5 = -20a$
$a = 1/4$
$y = \dfrac{1}{4}(x - 4)(x + 8)$
$y = \dfrac{1}{4}x^2 + x - 8$

19. Vertex: $(3, 1)$
Point: $(2, 2)$
$y = a(x - 3)^2 + 1$
$2 = a(2 - 3)^2 + 1$
$2 = a + 1$
$a = 1$
$y = (x - 3)^2 + 1$
$y = x^2 - 6x + 10$

20. Vertex: $(1, 2)$
Point: $(0, 0)$
$y = a(x - 1)^2 + 2$
$0 = a(0 - 1)^2 + 2$
$0 = a + 2$
$a = -2$
$y = -2(x - 1)^2 + 2$
$y = -2x^2 + 4x$

21. x-intercepts: 0, -4
Point: $(-2, 1)$
$y = ax(x + 4)$
$1 = a(-2)(-2 + 4)$
$1 = -4a$
$a = -1/4$
$y = -\dfrac{1}{4}x(x + 4)$
$y = -\dfrac{1}{4}x^2 - x$

LESSON 122 ·······································

1. Shift $y = x^2$ up 3 units.

2. Shift $y = x^2$ left 2 units.

3. Shift $y = x^2$ right 1 unit and down 4 units.

4. Flip $y = x^2$ over the x-axis, then shift up 1 unit.

5. Flip $y = x^2$ over the x-axis, then shift right 3 units.

6. Flip $y = x^2$ over the x-axis, shift left 2 units, then shift down 5 units.

7. Scale $y = x^2$ by 3.

8. Scale $y = x^2$ by 1/2, then shift up 4 units.

9. Scale $y = x^2$ by 4, flip over the x-axis, shift right 1 unit, then shift up 2 units.

10. The graph is flipped over the x-axis, so $a = -1$.
    The vertex is at (1, –4) after shifting, so $h = 1$ and $k = -4$.
    $y = -(x - 1)^2 - 4$

11. The graph is scaled by 3, so $a = 3$.
    The vertex is at (–2, 3) after shifting, so $h = -2$ and $k = 3$.
    $y = 3(x + 2)^2 + 3$

12. Shift up 1 unit.

13. Shift left 5 units and down 3 units.

14. Flip over the x-axis, then shift right 3 units.

15. Scale by 2, shift right 1 unit, then shift up 5 units.

16. Flip over the x-axis, then shift up 2 units.

17. Scale by 1/2, then shift left 2 units.

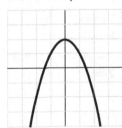
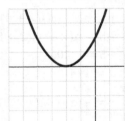

18. Scale by 4, then shift right 3 units and down 2 units.

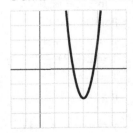

19. $a = 1, h = 4, k = 2$
    $y = (x - 4)^2 + 2$

20. $a = -1, h = 0, k = 4$
    $y = -x^2 + 4$

21. $a = 2, h = 3, k = 0$
    $y = 2(x - 3)^2$

22. $a = -3, h = 0, k = 0$
    $y = -3x^2$

LESSON 123 ·······································

1. Vertex: (0, –9)
   y-intercept: –9
   x-intercept(s): –3, 3

2. Vertex: (0, 16)
   y-intercept: 16
   x-intercept(s): –4, 4

3. Vertex: (–2, 0)
   y-intercept: 4
   x-intercept(s): –2

4. Vertex: (–1, 9)
   y-intercept: 8
   x-intercept(s): –4, 2

5. Vertex: (1, –8)
   y-intercept: –6
   x-intercept(s): –1, 3

6. Vertex: (2, 20)
   y-intercept: 0
   x-intercept(s): 0, 4

7. a. $h(t) = -16\left(t - \dfrac{3}{2}\right)^2 + 196$
   It reaches the maximum height after 1.5 seconds.

   b. The maximum height is 196 feet.

   c. $-16t^2 + 48t + 160 = 0$
   $-16(t + 2)(t - 5) = 0; \; t = -2, t = 5$
   It will hit the ground after 5 seconds.

   d. $-16t^2 + 48t + 160 = 160$
   $-16t(t - 3) = 0; \; t = 0, t = 3$
   It will reach a height of 160 feet after 3 seconds.

8. a. $-16t^2 + 64 = 0$
   $-16t^2 = -64; \; t^2 = 4; \; t = 2, t = -2$
   It will hit the ground after 2 seconds.

   b. $-16t^2 + 64 = 48$
   $-16t^2 = -16; \; t^2 = 1; \; t = 1, t = -1$
   It will reach a height of 48 feet after 1 second.

9. a. $h(t) = -4.9(t - 2)^2 + 44.1$
   It reaches the maximum height after 2 seconds.

   b. The maximum height is 44.1 meters, so it rises $44.1 - 24.5 = 19.6$ meters above the top of the building.

   c. $-4.9t^2 + 19.6t + 24.5 = 0$
   $-4.9(t + 1)(t - 5) = 0; \; t = -1, t = 5$
   It will hit the ground after 5 seconds.

10. a. $h(t) = -16(t - 3)^2 + 144$
    It reaches the maximum height after 3 seconds.

    b. The maximum height is 144 feet.

    c. $-16t^2 + 96t = 0$
    $-16t(t - 6) = 0; \; t = 0, t = 6$
    It will take 6 seconds for the ball to hit the ground.

    d. $-16t^2 + 96t = 80$
    $-16(t - 1)(t - 5) = 0; \; t = 1, t = 5$
    It will reach a height of 80 feet after 1 second and after 5 seconds.

11. a. $f(t) = -(t-4)^2 + 20$

    $f(t)$ is maximum when $t = 4$, which is 4 hours since 9.
    The computer room most crowded at 1 p.m.

    b. 3 p.m. is 6 hours since 9, so we need to find $f(6)$.

    $f(6) = -6^2 + 8(6) + 4 = 16$

    On average, 16 patrons are using the computer room at 3 p.m.

LESSON 124

1.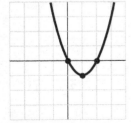

2.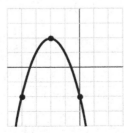

3.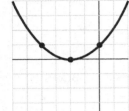

4.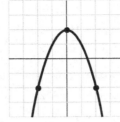

5.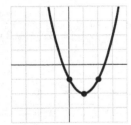

6.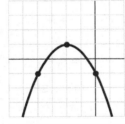

7.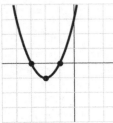

8.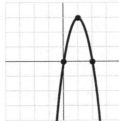

9.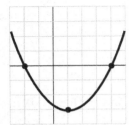

10. Vertex: $(-1, 3)$
    y-intercept: 4
    x-intercept(s): none

11. Vertex: $(1, 9)$
    y-intercept: 8
    x-intercept(s): $-2, 4$

12. Vertex: $(3, 0)$
    y-intercept: 9
    x-intercept(s): 3

13. Vertex: $(2, -1)$
    y-intercept: -5
    x-intercept(s): none

14. $y = x^2 + 6x + 8$

15. $y = 2x^2 - 8x + 6$

16. $y = -\dfrac{1}{3}x^2 + \dfrac{4}{3}x + \dfrac{5}{3}$

17. $y = (x + 3)^2 + 4$

18. $y = (x - 2)^2 - 5$

19. $y = 4(x - 1)^2$

20. $y = -x^2 + 6$

21. 256 feet

22. $\dfrac{10!}{8!} = \dfrac{10 \cdot 9 \cdot 8!}{8!} = 10 \cdot 9 = 90$

23. It is a combination because order does not matter.

24. $4 \times 3 \times 2 \times 1 = 24$ ways

LESSON 125

1. $(x + 2)(x - 5)$

2. $(3x - 2)(x + 3)$

3. $x(x + 9)(x - 9)$

4. $(x + 4)(x + 2)(x - 2)$

5. $x^2 - 9 = 0$
    $x^2 = 9$
    $x = 3, x = -3$
    Excluded values: 3, -3

6. $x^2 + 4x - 12 = 0$
    $(x - 2)(x + 6) = 0$
    $x = 2, x = -6$
    Excluded values: 2, -6

7. $\dfrac{(x - 2)(x - 6)}{(x - 2)(x + 7)} = \dfrac{x - 6}{x + 7}$ $for\ x \neq 2, -7$

8. $\dfrac{x(2x + 1)}{(2x + 1)(x + 5)} = \dfrac{x}{x + 5}$ $for\ x \neq -\dfrac{1}{2}, -5$

9. $2x^2 - 8x = 0$
    $2x(x - 4) = 0$
    $x = 0, x = 4$
    Excluded values: 0, 4

10. $x^2 - x - 6 = 0$
    $(x + 2)(x - 3) = 0$
    $x = -2, x = 3$
    Excluded values: $-2, 3$

11. $\dfrac{x^2}{4}$ $for\ x \neq 0$

12. $\dfrac{5x}{5x(x + 2)} = \dfrac{1}{x + 2}$ $for\ x \neq 0, -2$

13. $\dfrac{-(x - 9)}{x(x - 9)} = -\dfrac{1}{x}$ $for\ x \neq 0, 9$

14. $\dfrac{x - 5}{-2x(x - 5)} = -\dfrac{1}{2x}$ $for\ x \neq 0, 5$

15. $\dfrac{x + 4}{(x + 1)(x + 4)} = \dfrac{1}{x + 1}$ $for\ x \neq -1, -4$

16. $\dfrac{x + 3}{(2x - 5)(x + 3)} = \dfrac{1}{2x - 5}$ $for\ x \neq \dfrac{5}{2}, -3$

17. $\dfrac{(x-2)(x+5)}{(x-3)(x+5)} = \dfrac{x-2}{x-3}$ for $x \neq 3, -5$

18. $\dfrac{(4x+1)(x-1)}{(x-1)(x+8)} = \dfrac{4x+1}{x+8}$ for $x \neq 1, -8$

19. $\dfrac{3x}{4}$ for $x \neq 0$

20. $\dfrac{x+5}{(x+5)(x-5)} = \dfrac{1}{x-5}$ for $x \neq 5, -5$

21. $\dfrac{x^2}{x(x+4)} = \dfrac{x}{x+4}$ for $x \neq 0, -4$

22. $\dfrac{x+4}{(x+4)(x-5)} = \dfrac{1}{x-5}$ for $x \neq -4, 5$

23. $\dfrac{(x-2)^2}{(x-2)(x+6)} = \dfrac{x-2}{x+6}$ for $x \neq 2, -6$

24. $\dfrac{(x+4)(x-4)}{(x-1)(x+4)} = \dfrac{x-4}{x-1}$ for $x \neq 1, -4$

25. $\dfrac{(2x+1)(x+2)}{(3x-2)(x+2)} = \dfrac{2x+1}{3x-2}$ for $x \neq \dfrac{2}{3}, -2$

26. $\dfrac{-x(x+2)(x+7)}{3(x-2)(x+7)} = -\dfrac{x(x+2)}{3(x-2)}$ for $x \neq 2, -7$

LESSON 126 ·······························

1. $1/3$ 2. $3/4$ 3. $5/6$ 4. $1/10$

5. $\dfrac{(x-1)(x+5)}{x(x+5)} \cdot \dfrac{x^2}{(x+1)(x-1)} = \dfrac{x}{x+1}$

    for $x \neq 0, -5, -1, 1$

6. $\dfrac{(2x-1)(x+7)}{x-5} \cdot \dfrac{x-5}{x+7} = 2x-1$ for $x \neq 5, -7$

7. $\dfrac{x^2-6x}{x+9} \cdot \dfrac{2x+18}{x-6} = \dfrac{x(x-6)}{x+9} \cdot \dfrac{2(x+9)}{x-6} = 2x$

    for $x \neq -9, 6$

8. $\dfrac{x}{x^2-9} \cdot \dfrac{5x^2+12x-9}{5x-3}$

    $= \dfrac{x}{(x+3)(x-3)} \cdot \dfrac{(x+3)(5x-3)}{5x-3} = \dfrac{x}{x-3}$

    for $x \neq -3, 3, \dfrac{3}{5}$

9. $\dfrac{2x}{3}$ for $x \neq 0$

10. $\dfrac{x+1}{x-5} \cdot \dfrac{-(x-5)}{5(x+1)} = -\dfrac{1}{5}$ for $x \neq 5, -1$

11. $\dfrac{(x-3)^2}{x(x+3)} \cdot \dfrac{2x}{x-3} = \dfrac{2(x-3)}{x+3}$ for $x \neq 0, -3, 3$

12. $\dfrac{(x+2)(x-8)}{x(2x+5)} \cdot \dfrac{2x+5}{6(x+2)} = \dfrac{x-8}{6x}$ for $x \neq 0, -\dfrac{5}{2}, -2$

13. $\dfrac{x-4}{(x+3)(x-3)} \cdot \dfrac{(5x+1)(x+3)}{(5x+1)(x-4)} = \dfrac{1}{x-3}$

    for $x \neq -3, 3, -\dfrac{1}{5}, 4$

14. $\dfrac{(2x-3)(x-2)}{(2x-3)(x+1)(x-1)} \cdot \dfrac{x(x-1)}{7(x-2)} = \dfrac{x}{7(x+1)}$

    for $x \neq \dfrac{3}{2}, -1, 1, 2$

15. $\dfrac{12x}{5} \cdot \dfrac{10}{6x^2} = \dfrac{4}{x}$ for $x \neq 0$

16. $\dfrac{x+2}{x+5} \cdot \dfrac{3x+15}{x-2} = \dfrac{x+2}{x+5} \cdot \dfrac{3(x+5)}{x-2} = \dfrac{3(x+2)}{x-2}$

    for $x \neq -5, 2$

17. $\dfrac{x^2+6x+9}{8x} \cdot \dfrac{24x^2}{x+3} = \dfrac{(x+3)^2}{8x} \cdot \dfrac{24x^2}{x+3} = 3x(x+3)$

    for $x \neq 0, -3$

18. $\dfrac{x^2+11x+28}{x^2+3x-28} \cdot \dfrac{1}{x+4} = \dfrac{(x+4)(x+7)}{(x-4)(x+7)} \cdot \dfrac{1}{x+4}$

    $= \dfrac{1}{x-4}$ for $x \neq 4, -7, -4$

19. $\dfrac{2x^2+x-21}{2x+7} \cdot \dfrac{1}{x^2+4x-21}$

    $= \dfrac{(x-3)(2x+7)}{2x+7} \cdot \dfrac{1}{(x-3)(x+7)} = \dfrac{1}{x+7}$

    for $x \neq -\dfrac{7}{2}, 3, -7$

20. $\dfrac{x-8}{3x^2+20x+25} \cdot \dfrac{9x^2-25}{40-5x}$

    $= \dfrac{x-8}{(3x+5)(x+5)} \cdot \dfrac{(3x+5)(3x-5)}{-5(x-8)} = -\dfrac{3x-5}{5(x+5)}$

    for $x \neq -\dfrac{5}{3}, -5, \dfrac{5}{3}, 8$

21. $\dfrac{1}{6x}$ for $x \neq 0$

22. $\dfrac{7}{2x^2} \cdot \dfrac{5x^3}{14} = \dfrac{5x}{4}$ $for\ x \neq 0$

23. $\dfrac{(x+2)(x-2)}{x+2} \cdot \dfrac{x+1}{x-2} = x+1$ $for\ x \neq -2, 2$

24. $\dfrac{x^2+2x-8}{x+4} \cdot \dfrac{1}{x^2+3x-10}$

$= \dfrac{(x-2)(x+4)}{x+4} \cdot \dfrac{1}{(x-2)(x+5)} = \dfrac{1}{x+5}$

$for\ x \neq -4, 2, -5$

25. $\dfrac{(x-3)^2}{(x-1)^2} \cdot \dfrac{x-1}{x-3} = \dfrac{x-3}{x-1}$ $for\ x \neq 1, 3$

26. $\dfrac{x^2-3x-10}{2x^2-4x-30} \cdot \dfrac{4x^2-36}{x-3}$

$= \dfrac{(x+2)(x-5)}{2(x+3)(x-5)} \cdot \dfrac{4(x+3)(x-3)}{(x-3)} = 2(x+2)$

$for\ x \neq -3, 5, 3$

LESSON 127

1. 1   **2.** 2/3   **3.** 5/6   **4.** 7/18

5. $\dfrac{x+1+3x+5}{2x+3} = \dfrac{4x+6}{2x+3} == \dfrac{2(2x+3)}{2x+3} = 2$

$for\ x \neq -3/2$

6. $\dfrac{2x+5-x-7}{x^2+3x-10} = \dfrac{x-2}{(x-2)(x+5)} = \dfrac{1}{x+5}$

$for\ x \neq 2, -5$

7. $LCM = (x+1)(x-5)$

8. $x(x+1)$ and $(x+1)^2$
$LCM = x(x+1)^2$

9. $(x+4)(x-4)$ and $(3x-2)(x+4)$
$LCM = (x+4)(x-4)(3x-2)$

10. $\dfrac{(x+2)(x+4)}{x(x+4)} - \dfrac{(x+6)x}{(x+4)x}$

$= \dfrac{x^2+6x+8}{x(x+4)} - \dfrac{x^2+6x}{(x+4)x} = \dfrac{8}{x(x+4)}$ $for\ x \neq 0, -4$

11. $\dfrac{x^2-9x}{(x-1)(x+3)} + \dfrac{9}{x+3}$

$= \dfrac{x^2-9x}{(x-1)(x+3)} + \dfrac{9(x-1)}{(x+3)(x-1)} = \dfrac{x^2-9}{(x-1)(x+3)}$

$= \dfrac{(x+3)(x-3)}{(x-1)(x+3)} = \dfrac{x-3}{x-1}$ $for\ x \neq 1, -3$

12. $\dfrac{x^2-4}{x+2} = \dfrac{(x+2)(x-2)}{x+2} = x-2$ $for\ x \neq -2$

13. $\dfrac{2x-5+x-1}{x^2+5x-14} = \dfrac{3(x-2)}{(x-2)(x+7)} = \dfrac{3}{x+7}$

$for\ x \neq 2, -7$

14. $\dfrac{(x+4)x}{(x+5)x} - \dfrac{(x-1)(x+5)}{x(x+5)}$

$= \dfrac{x^2+4x}{(x+5)x} - \dfrac{x^2+4x-5}{x(x+5)} = \dfrac{5}{x(x+5)}$ $for\ x \neq -5, 0$

15. $\dfrac{x^2+8}{(x+2)(x-4)} + \dfrac{2}{x+2}$

$= \dfrac{x^2+8}{(x+2)(x-4)} + \dfrac{2(x-4)}{(x+2)(x-4)}$

$= \dfrac{x^2+2x}{(x+2)(x-4)} = \dfrac{x(x+2)}{(x+2)(x-4)} = \dfrac{x}{x-4}$

$for\ x \neq -2, 4$

16. $\dfrac{x}{x-3} - \dfrac{5x+6}{(x-3)(x+4)}$

$= \dfrac{x(x+4)}{(x-3)(x+4)} - \dfrac{5x+6}{(x-3)(x+4)}$

$= \dfrac{x^2-x-6}{(x-3)(x+4)} = \dfrac{(x-3)(x+2)}{(x-3)(x+4)} = \dfrac{x+2}{x+4}$

$for\ x \neq 3, -4$

17. $\dfrac{x^2+5x+1}{(3x-1)(2x+1)} + \dfrac{x}{2x+1}$

$= \dfrac{x^2+5x+1}{(3x-1)(2x+1)} + \dfrac{x(3x-1)}{(2x+1)(3x-1)}$

$= \dfrac{4x^2+4x+1}{(3x-1)(2x+1)} = \dfrac{(2x+1)^2}{(3x-1)(2x+1)} = \dfrac{2x+1}{3x-1}$

$for\ x \neq \dfrac{1}{3}, -\dfrac{1}{2}$

18. $\dfrac{2x+4}{x+2} = \dfrac{2(x+2)}{x+2} = 2$ $for\ x \neq -2$

19. $\dfrac{x^3-4x}{x^4-16} = \dfrac{x(x+2)(x-2)}{(x^2+4)(x+2)(x-2)} = \dfrac{x}{x^2+4}$

$for\ x \neq 2, -2$

20. $\dfrac{x}{(x+5)^2} - \dfrac{1}{x+5} = \dfrac{x}{(x+5)^2} - \dfrac{x+5}{(x+5)(x+5)}$

$= -\dfrac{5}{(x+5)^2}$ $for\ x \neq -5$

21. $\dfrac{x-5}{x-6} + \dfrac{x-15}{(x+3)(x-6)}$

$= \dfrac{(x-5)(x+3)}{(x-6)(x+3)} + \dfrac{x-15}{(x+3)(x-6)}$

$= \dfrac{x^2-x-30}{(x+3)(x-6)} = \dfrac{(x+5)(x-6)}{(x+3)(x-6)} = \dfrac{x+5}{x+3}$

$for\ x \neq -3, 6$

22. $\dfrac{-(x-5)}{(x+3)(x-5)} + \dfrac{x-2}{x+3}$

$= \dfrac{-1}{x+3} + \dfrac{x-2}{x+3} = \dfrac{x-3}{x+3}\ for\ x \neq -3, 5$

23. $\dfrac{1}{2x+1} + \dfrac{x-2}{(2x+1)(x+3)}$

$= \dfrac{x+3}{(2x+1)(x+3)} + \dfrac{x-2}{(2x+1)(x+3)}$

$= \dfrac{2x+1}{(2x+1)(x+3)} = \dfrac{1}{x+3}\ for\ x \neq -\dfrac{1}{2}, -3$

LESSON 128 ···

1. $x = 1$

2. $x = 1/3$

3. Excluded: $x \neq 0$; LCD $= x^2$
Multiply by the LCD: $\quad 5 + 4x = 9x$
Solve for x: $\quad\quad\quad -5x = -5$
$\quad\quad\quad\quad\quad\quad\quad\quad x = 1$

4. Excluded: $x \neq 5, 3$; LCD $= (x-5)(x-3)$
Multiply by the LCD: $\quad 7(x-3) = 5(x-5)$
Solve for x: $\quad\quad\quad 7x - 21 = 5x - 25$
$\quad\quad\quad\quad\quad\quad\quad\quad 2x = -4$
$\quad\quad\quad\quad\quad\quad\quad\quad x = -2$

5. Excluded: $x \neq 0$; LCD $= 12x$
Multiply by the LCD: $\quad 3 - 2 = 4x^2$
Solve for x: $\quad\quad\quad 4x^2 = 1$
$\quad\quad\quad\quad\quad\quad\quad\quad x^2 = 1/4$
$\quad\quad\quad\quad\quad\quad\quad\quad x = -1/2, x = 1/2$

6. Excluded: $x \neq -5, 0$; LCD $= x(x+5)$
Multiply by the LCD: $\quad x^2 = 2(x+5) - 5x$
Solve for x: $\quad\quad\quad x^2 + 3x - 10 = 0$
$\quad\quad\quad\quad\quad\quad\quad\quad (x-2)(x+5) = 0$
$\quad\quad\quad\quad\quad\quad\quad\quad x = 2, x = -5$
$\quad\quad\quad\quad\quad\quad\quad\quad x \neq -5, so\ x = 2$

7. Excluded: $x \neq 0$; LCD $= 4x$
Multiply by the LCD, then solve for x.
$2 + x = 8$
$x = 6$

8. Excluded: $x \neq -6, 0$; LCD $= x(x+6)$
Multiply by the LCD, then solve for x.
$5x - 2(x+6) = 0 \quad\quad 3x = 12$
$3x - 12 = 0 \quad\quad\quad\quad x = 4$

9. Excluded: $x \neq 5/2, 0$; LCD $= x(2x-5)$
Multiply by the LCD, then solve for x.
$x = 3(2x-5) \quad\quad\quad -5x = -15$
$x = 6x - 15 \quad\quad\quad\quad x = 3$

10. Excluded: $x \neq 7, 9$; LCD $= (x-7)(x-9)$
Multiply by the LCD, then solve for x.
$4(x-9) = 2(x-7) \quad\quad 2x = 22$
$4x - 36 = 2x - 14 \quad\quad x = 11$

11. Excluded: $x \neq 0$; LCD $= 5x^2$
Multiply by the LCD, then solve for x.
$10x = x + 45 \quad\quad\quad x = 5$
$9x = 45$

12. Excluded: $x \neq 2, -3$; LCD $= (x-2)(x+3)$
Multiply by the LCD, then solve for x.
$x(x+3) - (x-2)^2 = x - 2$
$7x - 4 = x - 2 \quad\quad\quad x = 1/3$
$6x = 2$

13. Excluded: $x \neq 0, 8$; LCD $= x(x-8)$
Multiply by the LCD, then solve for x.
$5(x-8) + x^2 = x - 8 \quad (x-4)(x+8) = 0$
$x^2 + 4x - 32 = 0 \quad\quad x = 4, x = -8$

14. $\dfrac{x}{x-1} - \dfrac{5}{x} = \dfrac{1}{x(x-1)}$

Excluded: $x \neq 1, 0$; LCD $= x(x-1)$
Multiply by the LCD, then solve for x.
$x^2 - 5(x-1) = 1 \quad\quad x = 1, x = 4$
$x^2 - 5x + 4 = 0 \quad\quad x \neq 1, so\ x = 4$
$(x-1)(x-4) = 0$

15. Excluded: $x \neq 0$; LCD $= 4x$
Multiply by the LCD, then solve for x.
$2x - 4 = x$
$x = 4$

16. Excluded: $x \neq -2, 4$; LCD $= (x+2)(x-4)$
Multiply by the LCD, then solve for x.
$x - 4 = 2(x+2) \quad\quad -x = 8$
$x - 4 = 2x + 4 \quad\quad\quad x = -8$

17. Excluded: $x \neq 2/3, 2$; LCD $= (3x-2)(x-2)$
Multiply by the LCD, then solve for x.
$5(x-2) = 3(3x-2) \quad\quad -4x = 4$
$5x - 10 = 9x - 6 \quad\quad\quad x = -1$

18. $\dfrac{x+7}{(x+3)(x-3)} = \dfrac{1}{x-3} + \dfrac{2}{x+3}$

Excluded: $x \neq 3, -3$; LCD $= (x+3)(x-3)$
Multiply by the LCD, then solve for x.

$x + 7 = x + 3 + 2(x - 3)$ ⟹ $-2x = -10$
$x + 7 = 3x - 3$ ⟶ $x = 5$

19. Excluded: $x \neq 0$; LCD $= 3x$
Multiply by the LCD, then solve for x.

$x^2 - 3 = 2x$ ⟹ $(x + 1)(x - 3) = 0$
$x^2 - 2x - 3 = 0$ ⟶ $x = -1, x = 3$

20. Excluded: $x \neq -6, 0$; LCD $= x(x+6)$
Multiply by the LCD, then solve for x.

$x^2 - (x + 6) = 2(x + 6)$ ⟹ $(x + 3)(x - 6) = 0$
$x^2 - 3x - 18 = 0$ ⟶ $x = -3, x = 6$

21. Excluded: $x \neq 0$; LCD $= 2x$
Multiply by the LCD, then solve for x.

$x^2 - 6 = 2(x + 9)$ ⟹ $(x + 4)(x - 6) = 0$
$x^2 - 2x - 24 = 0$ ⟶ $x = -4, x = 6$

22. Excluded: $x \neq -1/2, -3$; LCD $= 3(2x+1)(x+3)$
Multiply by the LCD, then solve for x.

$3x(x + 3) + 3(2x + 1) = (2x + 1)(x + 3)$
$x^2 + 8x = 0$ ⟹ $x = 0, x = -8$
$x(x + 8) = 0$ ⟶

LESSON 129 ··

1. $0x = 6$
No solution

2. $0x = 0$
Infinitely many solutions

3. $D = b^2 - 4ac = 5$
Two solutions

4. $D = b^2 - 4ac = -7$
No solution

5. LCD $= (x - 3)(x + 1)$
$x = -5$

6. LCD $= x(x + 3)$
$x = -1, x = 2$

7. Excluded: $x \neq 2, 0$; LCD $= x(x - 2)$
Multiply by the LCD, then solve for x.

$x = x - 2$ ⟹ No solution (no
$0x = -2$ ⟶ potential solution)

8. Excluded: $x \neq 0$; LCD $= 6x$
Multiply by the LCD, then solve for x.

$6 = 2 + x + 4$ ⟹ No solution (0 is an
$x = 0$ ⟶ excluded value.)

9. Excluded: $x \neq 0$; LCD $= 2x$
Multiply by the LCD, then solve for x.

$2(x + 1) - 3 = 2x - 1$ ⟹ $0x = 0$
$2x - 1 = 2x - 1$ ⟶ All x but 0

10. Excluded: $x \neq 2, -1$; LCD $= (x - 2)(x + 1)$
Multiply by the LCD, then solve for x.

$x + 1 + 2(x - 2) = x(x + 1)$
$x^2 - 2x + 3 = 0$ ⟹ No solution (no
$D = b^2 - 4ac = -8 < 0$ ⟶ potential solution)

11. Excluded: $x \neq -5/3, 0$; LCD $= x(3x + 5)$
Multiply by the LCD, then solve for x.

$x = 2(3x + 5)$ ⟹ $-5x = 10$
$x = 6x + 10$ ⟶ $x = -2$

12. Excluded: $x \neq 0$; LCD $= 2x$
Multiply by the LCD, then solve for x.

$x^2 + 16 = 2(x + 6)$ ⟹ $D = b^2 - 4ac = -12$
$x^2 - 2x + 4 = 0$ ⟶ No solution ($D < 0$)

13. Excluded: $x \neq 2/3, 2$; LCD $= (3x - 2)(x - 2)$
Multiply by the LCD, then solve for x.

$5(x - 2) = 3(3x - 2)$ ⟹ $-4x = 4$
$5x - 10 = 9x - 6$ ⟶ $x = -1$

14. Excluded: $x \neq 0$; LCD $= x^2$
Multiply by the LCD, then solve for x.

$x^2 + 8 = 6x - 1$ ⟹ $(x - 3)^2 = 0$
$x^2 - 6x + 9 = 0$ ⟶ $x = 3$

15. Excluded: $x \neq -3, 2$; LCD $= (x + 3)(x - 2)$
Multiply by the LCD, then solve for x.

$(x - 2)^2 = 2(x + 3) - 5(x - 2)$
$x^2 - x - 12 = 0$ ⟹ $x = -3, x = 4$
$(x + 3)(x - 4) = 0$ ⟶ $x \neq -3$, so $x = 4$

16. $\dfrac{x-7}{(x+1)(x+4)} = \dfrac{4}{x+1} - \dfrac{5}{x+4}$

Excluded: $x \neq -1, -4$; LCD $= (x + 1)(x + 4)$
Multiply by the LCD, then solve for x.

$x - 7 = 4(x + 4) - 5(x + 1)$
$x - 7 = -x + 11$ ⟹ $x = 9$
$2x = 18$ ⟶

17. $\dfrac{1}{x+4} = \dfrac{2x-3}{(2x-1)(x+4)}$

Excluded: $x \neq -4, 1/2$; LCD $= (x + 4)(2x - 1)$
Multiply by the LCD, then solve for x.

$2x - 1 = 2x - 3$ ⟹ No solution
$0x = -2$ ⟶

18. Excluded: $x \neq -4, 1$; LCD $= (x + 4)(x - 1)$
Multiply by the LCD, then solve for x.

$(x - 1)^2 = x - 1 + 6(x + 4)$
$x^2 - 9x - 22 = 0$ ⟹ $x = -2, x = 11$
$(x + 2)(x - 11) = 0$ ⟶

19. Excluded: $x \neq 5, 3$; LCD $= (x - 5)(x - 3)$

Multiply by the LCD, then solve for x.

$4(x - 3) = 5(x - 5)$ $\Rightarrow$ $-x = -13$

$4x - 12 = 5x - 25$ $x = 13$

20. Excluded: $x \neq -2, -4$; LCD $= 2(x + 2)(x + 4)$

Multiply by the LCD, then solve for x.

$8(x + 4) - (x + 2)(x + 4) = 6(x + 2)$

$x^2 + 4x - 12 = 0$ $\Rightarrow$ $x = 2, x = -6$

$(x - 2)(x + 6) = 0$

21. Excluded: $x \neq 8/5, 0$; LCD $= x(5x - 8)$

Multiply by the LCD, then solve for x.

$x^2 - 2(5x - 8) = 0$ $\Rightarrow$ $(x - 2)(x - 8) = 0$

$x^2 - 10 + 16 = 0$ $x = 2, x = 8$

22. $\dfrac{1}{x(x + 5)} + \dfrac{2}{x} = \dfrac{x + 6}{x(x + 5)}$

Excluded: $x \neq 0, -5$; LCD $= x(x + 5)$

Multiply by the LCD, then solve for x.

$1 + 2(x + 5) = x + 6$ $\Rightarrow$ $x = -5$

$2x + 11 = x + 6$ No solution ($x \neq -5$)

23. Excluded: $x \neq -1/2, -3$; LCD $= 3(2x + 1)(x + 3)$

Multiply by the LCD, then solve for x.

$3x(x + 3) = (x + 3)(2x + 1) - 3(2x + 1)$

$x^2 + 8x = 0$ $\Rightarrow$ $x = 0, x = -8$

$x(x + 8) = 0$

24. $\dfrac{x}{x + 2} = \dfrac{1}{x + 5} - \dfrac{6}{(x + 2)(x + 5)}$

Excluded: $x \neq -2, -5$; LCD $= (x + 2)(x + 5)$

Multiply by the LCD, then solve for x.

$x(x + 5) = x + 2 - 6$ $\Rightarrow$ $x = -2$

$x^2 + 4x + 4 = 0$ No solution ($x \neq -2$)

$(x + 2)^2 = 0$

LESSON 130

1. $x = -2$

2. $x = 6$

3. $x = 11$

4. $x = 1, x = -2$

5. x = time together

$\dfrac{1}{2} + \dfrac{1}{3} = \dfrac{1}{x}$

LCD $= 6x$; $x = 6/5 = 1.2$

It will take 1.2 hours.

6. x = time together

$\dfrac{1}{30} + \dfrac{1}{45} = \dfrac{1}{x}$

LCD $= 90x$; $x = 18$

It will take 18 minutes.

7. x = Julie's time alone

$\dfrac{1}{3} + \dfrac{1}{x} = \dfrac{1}{1}$

LCD $= 3x$; $x = 3/2 = 1.5$

It will take 1.5 hours.

8. x = Pipe B's time alone

$\dfrac{1}{4} + \dfrac{1}{x} = \dfrac{1}{2}$

LCD $= 4x$; $x = 4$

It will take 4 hours.

9. x = Brian's time alone

$x - 6$ = Laura's time alone

$\dfrac{1}{x} + \dfrac{1}{x - 6} = \dfrac{1}{4}$

LCD $= 4x(x - 6)$; $x = 2, 12$

$x - 6 > 0$, so $x = 12$.

It will take 12 hours.

10. x = Liam's time alone

$3x$ = Alex's time alone

$\dfrac{1}{x} + \dfrac{1}{3x} = \dfrac{1}{6}$

LCD $= 6x$; $x = 8$

It will take 8 hours.

11. x = time together

$\dfrac{1}{8} + \dfrac{1}{12} = \dfrac{1}{x}$

LCD $= 24x$; $x = 24/5 = 4.8$

It will take 4.8 hours.

12. x = time together

$\dfrac{1}{40} + \dfrac{1}{60} + \dfrac{1}{120} = \dfrac{1}{x}$

LCD $= 120x$; $x = 20$

It will take 20 minutes.

13. x = Jerry's time alone

$\dfrac{1}{3} + \dfrac{1}{x} = \dfrac{1}{2}$

LCD $= 6x$; $x = 6$

It will take 6 hours.

14. x = Jennifer's time alone

$\dfrac{1}{60} + \dfrac{1}{x} = \dfrac{1}{20}$

LCD $= 60x$; $x = 30$

It will take 30 minutes.

15. x = Pipe A's time alone

$2x$ = Pipe B's time alone

$\dfrac{1}{x} + \dfrac{1}{2x} = \dfrac{1}{2}$

LCD $= 2x$; $x = 3$

It will take 3 hours.

LESSON 131

1. $(x - 2)(x + 4)$

2. $(2x - 1)(x - 4)$

3. $x(x + 5)(x - 5)$

4. $(x - 5)(x + 2)(x - 2)$

5. $\dfrac{x^3}{3}$; $x \neq 0$

6. $\dfrac{2}{x}$; $x \neq 0, -4$

7. $\dfrac{2x + 5}{x + 9}$; $x \neq 3, -9$

8. $\dfrac{x + 3}{x}$; $x \neq 0, \dfrac{1}{2}, 3$

9. $\dfrac{x - 3}{4}$; $x \neq -5, -2$

10. $\dfrac{3x}{4(x - 1)}$; $x \neq 0, 8, 1$

11. $\dfrac{1}{x + 1}$; $x \neq 1, -1, -5$

12. $2(x + 2)$; $x \neq 5, -3, 3$

13. $\dfrac{3}{x}$; $x \neq 0$

14. $-\dfrac{5}{x(x + 5)}$; $x = 0, -5$

15. $\dfrac{x + 2}{x + 4}$; $x \neq 3, -4$

16. $\dfrac{x - 3}{x + 3}$; $x \neq 5, -3$

17. $x = -1/5$

18. No solution

19. $x = 1, x = -2$

20. $x = -7, x = 1$

21. 12 minutes

22. 7.5 hours

23. Sunny: 30 minutes
Adam: 1 hour

24. 1

25. 1, 2, 3, 4, 5, 6

26. 8 possible outcomes:
HHH, HHT, HTH, HTT, THH, THT, TTH, TTT
1 favorable outcome: HHH
P(three heads) = 1/8

27. 36 possible outcomes: 11, 12, 13, …, 66
6 favorable outcomes: 11, 22, 33, 44, 55, 66
P(same numbers) = 1/6

28. 36 possible outcomes: 11, 12, 13, …, 66
5 favorable outcomes: 26, 35, 44, 53, 62
P(sum of 8) = 5/36

LESSON 132

1. $x = 1$

2. $x \geq -3$

3. $x = -2$

4. $-1 \leq x < 4$

5. $x = 0, x = 2/3$

6. $x < 2$ or $x > 6$

7. $22

8. 4 feet by 8 feet

9. 7.5 miles

10. 8 ounces

11. $3.80 per pound

12. $(2, -3)$

13. $(3, 5)$

14. Boat: 21 km/h
Current: 3 km/h

15. 10% solution: 6 gallons
30% solution: 4 gallons

16. Almonds: 3 pounds
Cereal: 5 pounds

17.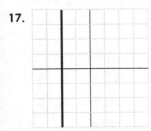

18.

19.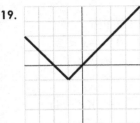

20.

21. $y = -2x + 5$
$2x + y = 5$

22. $y = 5x - 1$
$5x - y = 1$

LESSON 133

1. True
Input 3 has two outputs.

2. False
Range: $0 \leq y < 4$

3. False
$f(0) + g(-1) = 1 + 0 = 1$

4. True
Slope = 2

5. False
Avg. rate of change = -1

6. True

7. $y = 0.05x$
$4

8. $xy = 30000$
$6,000

9. $a_n = 7n - 5$
$a_1 = 2, a_n = a_{n-1} + 7$

10. $a_n = -3n + 6$
$a_1 = 3, a_n = a_{n-1} - 3$

11. $a_n = 6(3)^{n-1}$
$a_1 = 6, a_n = 3a_{n-1}$

12. $a_n = 2(5)^{n-1}$
$a_1 = 2, a_n = 5a_{n-1}$

13. $5,800

14. About 0.93 meter

15. $6\sqrt{3}$

16. $3y\sqrt{x}$

17. No solution

18. $x = 3$

19. 4√5 feet

20. $6/x^2$

21. $4x$

22. $y = 5000(1.03)^x$
About $5796.37

23. $2x^3 + 7x^2 - x - 2$

24. $x + 3 + \dfrac{5}{3x - 1}$

LESSON 134

1. $4(x^2 - 2x - 1)$

2. $2x(6x^2 + 3x - 4)$

3. $(x - 4)(x^2 + 1)$

4. $(x + 2)(x^2 - 3)$

5. $(2x - 1)(x^2 + 3)$

6. $(3x - 2)(2x^2 - 1)$

7. $(x + 1)(x + 2)$

8. $(x + 2)(x - 4)$

9. $(x + 1)(2x + 3)$

10. $(4x - 1)(x + 4)$

11. $(x + 2)^2$

12. $(x - 3)^2$

13. $(5x - 1)^2$

14. $(3x + 4)(3x - 4)$

15. $2(2x - 1)(x + 3)$

16. $(x^2 + 4)(x + 2)(x - 2)$

17. $2x(x + 5)(x - 5)$

18. $2x(4x + 1)(x^2 + 5)$

19. $x = \pm 3\sqrt{2}$

20. $x = 1/3, x = -1$

21. $x = 2, x = -5$

22. $x = 1/3, x = 2$

23. $x = 2 \pm 2\sqrt{3}$

24. $x = -1 \pm \sqrt{5}$

25. $x = (-5 \pm \sqrt{5})/2$

26. $x = (4 \pm \sqrt{10})/3$

27. $x = 3, x = -1$

28. $x = -4 \pm 2\sqrt{3}$

29. $x = 3/5, x = -3/5$

30. No solution

31. 5 and 9

32. 10 cm, 24 cm, 26 cm

33. 5 cm by 13 cm

LESSON 135

1.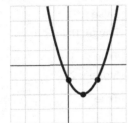

2.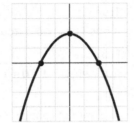

3.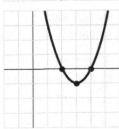

4. Vertex: (2, 3)
y-intercept: 7
x-intercept(s): none

5. Vertex: (2, 4)
y-intercept: –12
x-intercept(s): 1, 3

6. Vertex: (–4, 25)
y-intercept: 9
x-intercept(s): 1, –9

7. Vertex: (–2, 0)
y-intercept: 8
x-intercept(s): –2

8. $y = x^2 - 4x + 1$

9. $y = \frac{1}{2}x^2 - 4x + 6$

10. $y = (x + 5)^2 - 2$

11. $y = -3x^2$

12. 76 – 60 = 16 feet

13. $\frac{1}{2x + 5}; \; x \neq 0, -\frac{5}{2}$

14. $\frac{x + 5}{x(x - 4)}; \; x \neq 0, 4, -4$

15. $1; \; x \neq -1, -2, 2$

16. $\frac{x - 5}{2}; \; x \neq -1, -4, 0$

17. $2x; \; x \neq -\frac{5}{3}$

18. $\frac{x - 1}{x + 3}; \; x \neq 3, -3$

19. $x = -9$

20. $x = -4$

21. $x = 2$

22. $x = 2/5$

23. 2 hours

24. 36 minutes

25. 30 minutes

LESSON 136

1. D **2.** C **3.** A **4.** B **5.** D **6.** B

7. A **8.** A **9.** B **10.** B **11.** C **12.** D

13. D **14.** D **15.** A **16.** D **17.** B

Worked-out solutions to selected problems:

1. $m = 4/3$ and $n = 5$, so $3m + 2n = 4 + 10 = 14$.

2. $(2^5)^2 \cdot (2^2)^{-3} = 2^{10} \cdot 2^{-6} = 2^4$

5. $3/p = 1/3$, so $p = 9$.

6. $(x - 2)(x + 5) = 0$
$x = 2, x = -5$

7. $x^2 - 2x = 1$
$x^2 - 2x + 1 = 1 + 1$ $\;\Rightarrow\;$ $(x - 1)^2 = 2$
$x = 1 \pm \sqrt{2}$

8. $\frac{(x + 2)(x - 2)}{x + 2} \cdot \frac{x + 1}{x - 2} = x + 1 \; for \; x \neq 2, -2$

9. Excluded: $x \neq 0, -5$; LCD $= x(x + 5)$
Multiply both sides by the LCD, then solve for x.
$x^2 = 2(x + 5) - 5x$ $\;\Rightarrow\;$ $x = 2, x = -5$
$x^2 + 3x - 10 = 0$ $\quad\;$ $x \neq -5$, so $x = 2$
$(x - 2)(x + 5) = 0$

10. Plug (0, –2) into $y = mx + b$, and you get $b = -2$.
Plug (2, 4) into $y = mx - 2$, and you get $m = 3$.
So the linear function is $y = 3x - 2$.

11. Let's try the elimination strategy:
The parabola is upward, so eliminate D.
The parabola passes through (0, 0), so eliminate A.
The parabola passes through (2, 0), so the answer is C.

12. Got 4/5 correct = Missed 1/5 = Missed 5 problems
Let x = the number of problems in the test.
$(1/5)x = 5; \; x = 25$

13. Set up a proportion, then solve.
$5:75 = 3:x; \; x = 45$

14. x = width
$2x - 3$ = length
$x(2x - 3) = 35$
$x = 5, x = -7/2$
The garden is 5 ft by 7 ft,
so the perimeter is 24 ft.

17. x = time together
$\frac{1}{2} + \frac{1}{3} = \frac{1}{x}$
$x = 6/5 = 1.2$
It will take 1.2 hours.

LESSON 137

1. B **2.** C **3.** D **4.** C **5.** C **6.** B

7. A **8.** D **9.** D **10.** A **11.** B **12.** D

13. B **14.** C **15.** C **16.** C **17.** B

Worked-out solutions to selected problems:

1. $2x + 3 = 7$ or
$2x + 3 = -7$
$x = 2, x = -5$

2. $-3 \leq -x < 2$
$-2 < x \leq 3$

4. $x = 4, y = -2$

5. $(x + 2)(x - 4)$
$= x^2 - 2x - 8$

6. $(3x + 1)(x - 3) = 0$
$x = -1/3, x = 3$

7. $2^x \cdot (2^3)^3 = 2^{x+9}$
$\sqrt[3]{(3^3)^2} = \sqrt[3]{3^6} = 3^2$
$x = 1, y = 2$

8. $\dfrac{2}{(x+1)(x-1)} + \dfrac{x}{x-1} + \dfrac{1}{x+1}$

$= \dfrac{2 + x(x+1) + x - 1}{(x+1)(x-1)} = \dfrac{x^2 + 2x + 1}{(x+1)(x-1)}$

$= \dfrac{(x+1)^2}{(x+1)(x-1)} = \dfrac{x+1}{x-1}$

9. Excluded: $x \neq 0, 3$; LCD $= x(x-3)$
Multiply both sides by the LCD, then solve for x.
$5(x-3) + x^2 = x - 3 \quad \Rightarrow \quad (x-2)(x+6) = 0$
$x^2 + 4x - 12 = 0 \quad \qquad x = 2, x = -6$

11. $0.002 \times 1000 = 2$

12. $60/2 = 30$ miles/gallon
$210/30 = 7$ gallons

13. $p = (-1+3)/2 = 1$

14. $3 = 4a + 2 + 5; a = -1$
$f(-2) = -1(4) -2 + 5 = -1$

16. The parabola is downward, so $a < 0$.
The y-intercept is positive, so $c > 0$.

17. $\dfrac{1}{60} + \dfrac{1}{x} = \dfrac{1}{20}; x = 30$

LESSON 138

1. Mean = 4

2. Mean = 5.5

3. Mean = 5   Median = 4.5

4. Mean = 7   Median = 7

5. Mean = 2   Median = 1.5   Mode(s) = 1, 4

6. Mean = 15   Median = 15   Mode(s) = none

7. The outlier is 39. When the outlier is removed, the mean decreases from 11 to 7. The median remains the same at 8.

8. The outlier is 10. When the outlier is removed, the mean increases from 48.5 to 54. The median also increases from 53 to 54.

9. Mean = 2   Median = 2   Mode(s) = 0

10. Mean = 4.5   Median = 4.5   Mode(s) = none

11. Mean = 6   Median = 6.5   Mode(s) = 8, 7

12. Mean = 4.2   Median = 5   Mode(s) = 5

13. Mean = 14   Median = 14.5   Mode(s) = 15

14. Mean = 13   Median = 13   Mode(s) = 10, 14

15. Mean = 105   Median = 105   Mode(s) = none

16. Mean = 212   Median = 210.5   Mode(s) = 312

17. The outlier is 72. When the outlier is removed, the mean decreases from 12 to 6. The median also decreases from 7 to 6.5.

18. The outlier is 5. When the outlier is removed, the mean increases from 54 to 61. The median also increases from 58 to 60.

19. Mode = 5, so at least two numbers are 5.
Mean = $(5 + 5 + x)/3 = 6$, so $x = 8$.
The numbers are 5, 5, and 8.

20. Suppose you have a, b, c, and d in an ascending order.
Median = 4.5, so a and b are less than 4.5 and c and d are greater than 4.5.
Mode = 4, so a and b are 4.
Median = 4.5, so c is 5.
Mean = $(4 + 4 + 5 + d)/4 = 5$, so $d = 7$.
The numbers are 4, 4, 5, and 7.

21. Modes = 8 and 9, so two numbers are 8 and two numbers are 9.
Mean = $(8 + 8 + 9 + 9 + x)/5 = 8$, so $x = 6$.
The numbers are 6, 8, 8, 9, and 9.

22. Suppose you have a, b, c, and d in an ascending order.
Median = 4 and mode = 4, so $b = 4$ and $c = 4$.
Range = 4, so $d = a + 4$.
Mean = $(a + 4 + 4 + a + 4)/4 = 4$, so $a = 2$.
The numbers are 2, 4, 4, and 6.

LESSON 139

1. Mean = 2.8   Median = 2   Mode(s) = 2

2. Mean = 5.5   Median = 5   Mode(s) = 4, 5

3. Range = 5

4. Range = 25

5. Mean = 5   Variance = 0   S. Deviation = 0

6. Mean = 5   Variance = 3   S. Deviation = 1.7

7. Mean = 5   Variance = 9.7   S. Deviation = 3.1

8. Mean = 5   Variance = 20.7   S. Deviation = 4.5

9. Mark's scores have a standard deviation of 3.7.
Alex's scores have a standard deviation of 10.3.

10. Mean = 5   Median = 5.5   Mode(s) = 6
Range = 6   Variance = 4   S. Deviation = 2

11. Mean = 8   Median = 8   Mode(s) = 8, 10
Range = 5   Variance = 3   S. Deviation = 1.7

12. Mean = 7   Median = 7.5   Mode(s) = 2, 7
Range = 9   Variance = 10   S. Deviation = 3.2

13. Mean = 9   Median = 8.5   Mode(s) = 8
Range = 13   Variance = 14   S. Deviation = 3.7

14. Mean = 32   Median = 30   Mode(s) = none
Range = 25   Variance = 86   S. Deviation = 9.3

15. Mean = 45 Median = 45 Mode(s) = 45, 47

Range = 5 Variance = 3 S. Deviation = 1.7

16. Logan: mean = 88, range = 30, s. deviation = 11.7

Grace: mean = 83, range = 15, s. deviation = 6

Emma: mean = 84, range = 10, s. deviation = 4.9

Joshua: mean = 80, range = 50, s. deviation = 21

Logan has the highest mean score. Joshua has the lowest mean score.

17. Joshua has the highest range. Emma has the smallest range.

18. Joshua has the highest standard deviation, and Emma has the lowest standard deviation.

19. Answers will vary. There is no right or wrong answer, as long as you can give reasoning for your answer.

LESSON 140

1. 0, 1, 4.5, 6, 7

IQR = 6 − 1 = 5

2. 2, 4, 5, 8, 9

IQR = 8 − 4 = 4

3. 2, 2.5, 4, 6.5, 8

IQR = 6.5 − 2.5 = 4

4. 10, 12, 13.5, 15, 19

IQR = 15 − 12 = 3

5. 4, 6, 7, 9, 10; IQR = 3

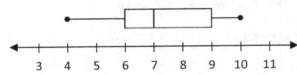

6. 30, 33, 37, 42, 44; IQR = 9

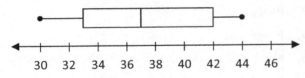

7. The second and fourth statements are correct.

8. 0, 2, 4, 6, 7; IQR = 4

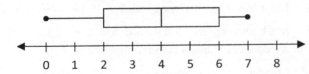

9. 2, 3, 4.5, 6, 8; IQR = 3

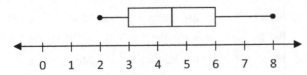

10. 1, 3, 4, 6, 7; IQR = 3

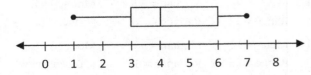

11. 4, 5, 7, 9, 10; IQR = 4

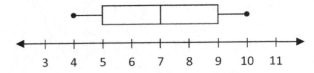

12. 8, 9, 10, 12, 14; IQR = 3

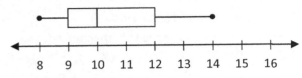

13. 14, 16, 17, 19, 20; IQR = 3

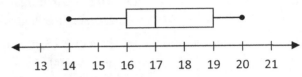

14. 20, 23, 24, 25, 26; IQR = 2

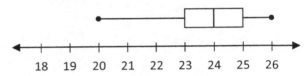

15. 30, 32, 38, 42, 44; IQR = 10

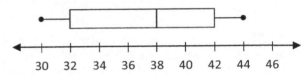

16. Store M's median = $6

Store N's median = $4

17. Store M's IQR = 7 − 4 = 3

Store N's IQR = 5 − 3 = 2

18. 75%

19. 50%

20. 25%

LESSON 141

1. 7 + 9 + 4 = 20 children

2. 9/20 = 45%

3. 2 + 1 + 3 = 6 times

4. Median = 3.5; Mode(s) = 2, 6; Range = 5

5. 4 members

6. Median = 17; Mode(s) = 10, 23; Range = 22

7. 30 seventh graders

8. 290 students

9. 290/6 = 48.33333...

About 48 students

10. 240 children

11. 130 children

12. 30/240 = 0.125 = 12.5%

13. Answers will vary.

14. Answers will vary.

15. Answers will vary.

16. Answers will vary.

17. 20 ~ 29: 8 members, 30 ~ 39: 10 members,
40 ~ 49: 7 members, 50 ~ 59: 5 members

18. 30 members

19. 10 members

20. 12/30 = 0.4 = 40%

21. 3 + 1 + 2 = 6 students

22. Median = 3
Mode = 3

23. Mean = 58/20 = 2.9
2.9 hours/student

24. 20 students

25. Median = 85
Range = 100 − 67 = 33

26. 14 students

27. 13 students

28. 16 members

29. 8 members

30. 12/16 = 0.75 = 75%

LESSON 142

1. Mean = 9   Median = 3.5   IQR = 2   SD = 12.6

Without the outlier 37:
Mean = 3.4   Median = 3   IQR = 2   SD = 1

2. Mean = 94.5   Median = 110   IQR = 5   SD = 37.2

Without the outlier 12:
Mean = 111   Median = 110   IQR = 7.5   SD = 4.9

3. True

4. False

5. The distribution for team A is skewed left, and the distribution for team B is symmetric.

Team A

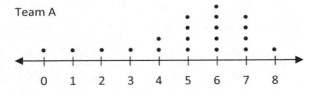

Team B

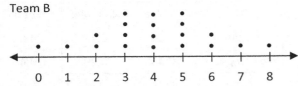

6. The median and interquartile range are better for team A because the distribution is skewed.

The mean and standard deviation are better for team B because the distribution is symmetric.

7. Runner B has the higher center and the bigger spread.

8. The distribution for runner A is symmetric, so the mean and standard deviation are better.

The distribution for runner B is skewed left, so the median and interquartile range are better.

9. Symmetric

10. Skewed right

11. Skewed left

12. Skewed left

13. Symmetric

14. Skewed right

15. a. See the stem-and-leaf plot for Problems 24 through 27 in Lesson 141.

b. The distribution is symmetric.

c. The mean and standard deviation are better.

16. a. See the histogram for Problems 28 through 30 in Lesson 141.

b. The distribution is skewed right.

c. The median and interquartile range are better.

17. The distribution for group A is symmetric, and the distribution for group B is skewed right.

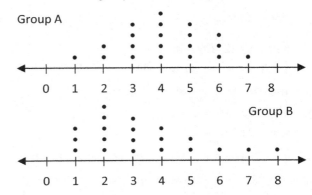

18. Group A appears to have the higher mean. Group B appears to have the higher standard deviation.

The mean and standard deviation are better for group A because the distribution is symmetric.

The median and interquartile range are better for group B because the distribution is skewed.

19. Group A: 1, 3, 4, 5, 7

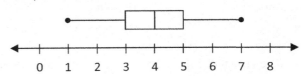

Group B: 1, 2, 3, 4, 5, 8

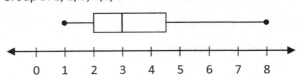

20. Group A: Mean = 4.1   Median = 4   Mode = 4
Range = 6   IQR = 2

Group B: Mean = 3.4   Median = 3   Mode = 2
Range = 7   IQR = 2.5

LESSON 143

1. Line p: $\quad\quad\quad\quad\quad$ Line q:

$$y = \frac{4}{3}x - \frac{2}{3} \quad\quad\quad y = -\frac{2}{3}x + 1$$

2. $y = 34/3$ when $x = 9$. $\quad$ $y = -5$ when $x = 9$.

3. The plot shows a positive correlation, which means that the hourly pay rate increases as experience increases.

4. *If your answers are close, you are correct.*
   (0, 2), (2, 3), (4, 4), (6, 5)

   About $y = \frac{1}{2}x + 2$

5. If you use (2, 30) and (7, 50), you get $y = 4x + 22$.
   $y = 70$ when $x = 12$, so it will be about $70 per hour.

6. The plot shows a negative correlation.

7. If you use (10, 4.5) and (50, 1.5), you get
   $y = -0.075x + 5.25$.

8. $y = 3.75$ when $x = 20$, so it will be about $3,750.

9. The colder it gets, the more jackets the store sells.

10. Positive correlation $\quad$ 11. No correlation

12. Negative correlation $\quad$ 13. Positive correlation

14. About $y = 2x - 2$ $\quad\quad$ 15. About $y = -\frac{2}{3}x + 6$

16. About $y = \frac{1}{2}x + 2$

17. About 58 $\quad\quad\quad\quad$ 18. About −14

19. About 17 $\quad\quad\quad\quad$ 20. Positive correlation

21. If you use (40, 40) and (90, 80), you get $y = \frac{4}{5}x + 8$.

22. $y = 64$ when $x = 70$, so it will be about 64%.

23. Students good at math tend to do well in physics also.

24–27. Answers will vary.

LESSON 144

1. 48 female students $\quad$ 2. 120 male students

3. 24% $\quad\quad\quad\quad\quad\quad$ 4. 64%

5. 40%

6.

	Tablet	No tablet	Total
Computer	10	5	15
No computer	8	2	10
Total	18	7	25

7.

	Cat(s)	No cat	Total
Dog(s)	0.16	0.34	0.5
No dog	0.24	0.26	0.5
Total	0.4	0.6	1.0

8.

	Cat(s)	No cat	Total
Dog(s)	0.4	0.57	0.5
No dog	0.6	0.43	0.5
Total	1.0	1.0	1.0

9.

	Cat(s)	No cat	Total
Dog(s)	0.32	0.68	1.0
No dog	0.48	0.52	1.0
Total	0.4	0.6	1.0

10.

	Tablet	No tablet	Total
Computer	0.4	0.2	0.6
No computer	0.32	0.08	0.4
Total	0.72	0.28	1.0

	Tablet	No tablet	Total
Computer	0.67	0.33	1.0
No computer	0.8	0.2	1.0
Total	0.72	0.28	1.0

	Tablet	No tablet	Total
Computer	0.56	0.71	0.6
No computer	0.44	0.29	0.4
Total	1.0	1.0	1.0

11.

	Online	In-store	Total
Teens	18	9	27
Adults	12	21	33
Total	30	30	60

12.

	Online	In-store	Total
Teens	0.3	0.15	0.45
Adults	0.2	0.35	0.55
Total	0.5	0.5	1.0

13.

	Online	In-store	Total
Teens	0.67	0.33	1.0
Adults	0.36	0.64	1.0
Total	0.5	0.5	1.0

14.

	Online	In-store	Total
Teens	0.6	0.3	0.45
Adults	0.4	0.7	0.55
Total	1.0	1.0	1.0

15. 60 people

16. 27 teens

17. 21 adults

18. 30 people

19. 45%

20. 67%

21. 64%

22. 60%

23. 30%

LESSON 145

1. Mean = 3   Median = 3   Mode(s) = none

2. Mean = 15   Median = 15   Mode(s) = 15

3. Mean = 3   Range = 4   S. deviation = 1.4

4. Mean = 4.5   Range = 8   S. deviation = 2.4

5. 8, 9, 10, 12, 15; IQR = 3

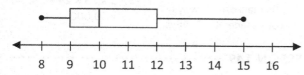

6. 30, 33, 34, 35, 36; IQR = 2

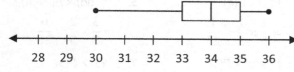

7.

Ryan

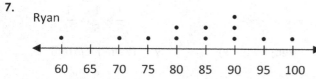

8.

Logan

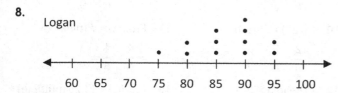

9. The distribution is skewed left, so the median and interquartile range are better.

10. The distribution is also skewed left, so the median and interquartile range are better.

Ryan's scores appear to have the greater standard deviation because they are spread out more.

11. About $y = x - 1$

12. About $y = -\frac{1}{2}x + 5$

13.

	Steak	Pasta	Total
Soup	40	32	72
Salad	68	60	128
Total	108	92	200

14.

	Steak	Pasta	Total
Soup	0.2	0.16	0.36
Salad	0.34	0.3	0.64
Total	0.54	0.46	1.0

15. Circle graph

16. Line graph

17. Bar graph

18. Dot graph

19. Scatter plot

LESSON 146

1. $P = 1/6$
Favorable: 6

2. $P = 4/6 = 2/3$
Favorable: 1, 2, 3, 4

3. $P = 2/6 = 1/3$
Favorable: 3, 6

4. $P = 3/6 = 1/2$
Favorable: 2, 3, 5

5. $P = 2/8 = 1/4$

6. $P = 6/20 = 3/10$

7. $P = (8 - 2)/8 = 3/4$

8. $P = (20 - 4)/20 = 4/5$

9. $P = (2 + 4)/8 = 3/4$

10. $P = (4 + 10)/20 = 7/10$

11. $P = 5/26$
Favorable: 5 vowels

12. $P = 5/12$
Jan, Jun, Jul, Mar, May

13. $P = 11/100 = 11\%$
9, 18, 27, 36, 45, 54, 63, 72, 81, 90, 99

14. $P = 5/100 = 5\%$
11, 31, 41, 61, 71

15. $P = 13/100 = 13\%$
1, 4, 9, 16, 25, 36, 49, 64, 81, 100 / 1, 8, 27, 64 / 1 is both.

16. $P = 0/100 = 0\%$
The cube root of a negative number is negative.

17. $P = 20/30 = 2/3$

18. $P = 0/30 = 0$

19. $P = (30 - 6)/30 = 4/5$

20. $P = (4 + 6)/30 = 1/3$

21. $P = 18/36 = 1/2$

22. $P = 2/36 = 1/18$

23. $P = (36 - 10)/36 = 13/18$

24. $P = (6 + 10)/36 = 4/9$

LESSON 147

1. 1, 2, 3, 4, 5, 6

2. HHH, HHT, HTH, HTT, THH, THT, TTH, TTT

3. H1, H2, H3, H4, H5, H6, T1, T2, T3, T4, T5, T6

4. 1st toss   2nd toss   3rd toss   Outcomes

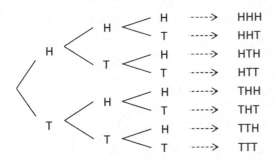

5.

	1	2	3	4	5	6
H	H1	H2	H3	H4	H5	H6
T	T1	T2	T3	T4	T5	T6

6. 26 alphabet letters
   26 possible outcomes

7. 16, 25, 36, 49, 64, 81
   6 possible outcomes

8. H1, H2, H3, … , H12, T1, T2, T3, … , T12
   24 possible outcomes

9. 1C, 1A, 1T, 2C, 2A, 2T, 3C, 3A, 3T
   9 possible outcomes

10. red-tan, red-green, red-navy,
    blue-tan, blue-green, blue-navy
    6 possible outcomes

11. 11, 12, 13, …, 65, 66
    36 possible outcomes

12. 11, 12, 13, 21, 22, 23, 31, 32, 33
    9 possible outcomes

13. 12, 13, 14, 21, 23, 24, 31, 32, 34, 41, 42, 43
    12 possible outcomes

14. TTT, TTF, TFT, TFF, FTT, FTF, FFT, FFF
    8 possible outcomes

15. 123, 132, 213, 231, 312, 321
    6 possible outcomes

16. $P = 5/26$
    Favorable: 5 vowels

17. $P = 0/6 = 0$
    Favorable: none

18. $P = 3/9 = 1/3$
    Favorable: 12, 22, 32

19. $P = 6/12 = 1/2$
    Favorable: 12, 14, 24,
    32, 34, 42

20. $P = 1/8$
    Favorable: FFF

21. 365

22. 52

23. $6 \times 7 = 42$

24. $4 \times 2 = 8$

LESSON 148

1. $2 \times 2 \times 2 \times 2 \times 2 = 32$

2. $6 \times 3 = 18$
   10s place: 1 to 6
   1s place: 1, 3, 5

3. $2 \times 6 = 12$
   10s place: 5, 6
   1s place: 1 to 6

4. $3 \times 3 = 9$
   10s place: 1, 2, 3
   1s place: 2, 4, 6

5. $6 \times 5 = 30$
   10s place: 1 to 6
   1s place: $6 - 1 = 5$ ways

6. $3 \times 5 \times 4 = 60$
   100s place: 4, 5, 6
   10s place: $6 - 1 = 5$ ways
   1s place: $6 - 2 = 4$ ways

7. $2 \times 2 \times 6 = 24$

9. $4 \times 3 \times 6 = 72$

9. $6 \times 7 \times 12 = 504$

10. $4 \times 4 \times 4 \times 4 = 256$

11. $9 \times 8 = 72$
    10s place: 1 to 9
    1s place: $9 - 1 = 8$ ways

12. $4 \times 4 \times 1 = 16$
    100s place: 2, 3, 5, 7
    10s place: 2, 3, 5, 7
    1s place: 2

13. $1 \times 3 \times 2 = 6$
    1s place: 2
    10s place: $4 - 1$ ways
    100s place: $4 - 2$ ways

14. $9 \times 9 \times 9 \times 9 = 6,561$

15. $5 \times 25 \times 24 \times 23$
    $= 69,000$

LESSON 149

1. 1/2

2. 25

3. 10

4. $P(2) \times P(4)$
   $= \dfrac{1}{5} \times \dfrac{1}{5} = \dfrac{1}{25}$

5. $P(\text{odd}) \times P(\text{even})$
   $= \dfrac{3}{5} \times \dfrac{2}{5} = \dfrac{6}{25}$

6. $P(\text{odd}) \times P(\text{odd})$
   $= \dfrac{3}{5} \times \dfrac{3}{5} = \dfrac{9}{25}$

7. $P(5) \times P(5)$
   $= \dfrac{1}{5} \times \dfrac{1}{5} = \dfrac{1}{25}$

8. $P(\text{red}) \times P(\text{pink})$
   $= \dfrac{2}{6} \times \dfrac{4}{6} = \dfrac{2}{9}$

9. $P(\text{pink}) \times P(\text{red})$
   $= \dfrac{4}{6} \times \dfrac{2}{6} = \dfrac{2}{9}$

10. $P(\text{red}) \times P(\text{red})$
    $= \dfrac{2}{6} \times \dfrac{2}{6} = \dfrac{1}{9}$

11. $P(\text{pink}) \times P(\text{pink})$
    $= \dfrac{4}{6} \times \dfrac{4}{6} = \dfrac{4}{9}$

12. $P(\text{heads}) \times P(5)$
    $= \dfrac{1}{2} \times \dfrac{1}{6} = \dfrac{1}{12}$

13. $P(\text{tails}) \times P(\text{3's multiple})$
    $= \dfrac{1}{2} \times \dfrac{2}{6} = \dfrac{1}{6}$

14. $P(\text{heads}) \times P(\text{prime})$

$= \dfrac{1}{2} \times \dfrac{3}{6} = \dfrac{1}{4}$

15. $P(\text{tails}) \times P(\text{negative})$

$= \dfrac{1}{2} \times \dfrac{0}{6} = 0$

16. $P(\text{red}) \times P(\text{pink})$

$= \dfrac{2}{8} \times \dfrac{6}{8} = \dfrac{3}{16}$

17. $P(\text{pink}) \times P(\text{red})$

$= \dfrac{6}{8} \times \dfrac{2}{8} = \dfrac{3}{16}$

18. $P(\text{red}) \times P(\text{red})$

$= \dfrac{2}{8} \times \dfrac{2}{8} = \dfrac{1}{16}$

19. $P(\text{pink}) \times P(\text{pink})$

$= \dfrac{6}{8} \times \dfrac{6}{8} = \dfrac{9}{16}$

20. $P(\text{odd}) \times P(\text{odd})$

$= \dfrac{3}{6} \times \dfrac{3}{6} = \dfrac{1}{4}$

21. $P(\text{prime}) \times P(\text{prime})$

$= \dfrac{3}{6} \times \dfrac{3}{6} = \dfrac{1}{4}$

22. $P(\text{H}) \times P(\text{H}) \times P(\text{H})$

$= \dfrac{1}{2} \times \dfrac{1}{2} \times \dfrac{1}{2} = \dfrac{1}{8}$

23. $P(\text{odd}) \times P(\text{Mon or Tue})$

$= \dfrac{3}{6} \times \dfrac{2}{7} = \dfrac{1}{7}$

24. $P(\text{correct}) \times P(\text{correct}) \times P(\text{correct}) \times P(\text{correct})$

$= \dfrac{1}{2} \times \dfrac{1}{2} \times \dfrac{1}{2} \times \dfrac{1}{2} = \dfrac{1}{16}$

LESSON 150

1. 1/12 **2.** 4/25 **3.** 3/16

4. $P(2) \times P(4\,|\,2)$

$= \dfrac{1}{5} \times \dfrac{1}{4} = \dfrac{1}{20}$

5. $P(\text{odd}) \times P(\text{even}\,|\,\text{odd})$

$= \dfrac{3}{5} \times \dfrac{2}{4} = \dfrac{3}{10}$

6. $P(\text{odd}) \times P(\text{odd}\,|\,\text{odd})$

$= \dfrac{3}{5} \times \dfrac{2}{4} = \dfrac{3}{10}$

7. $P(5) \times P(5\,|\,5)$

$= \dfrac{1}{5} \times \dfrac{0}{4} = 0$

8. $P(\text{red}) \times P(\text{pink}\,|\,\text{red})$

$= \dfrac{2}{6} \times \dfrac{4}{5} = \dfrac{4}{15}$

9. $P(\text{pink}) \times P(\text{red}\,|\,\text{pink})$

$= \dfrac{4}{6} \times \dfrac{2}{5} = \dfrac{4}{15}$

10. $P(\text{red}) \times P(\text{red}\,|\,\text{red})$

$= \dfrac{2}{6} \times \dfrac{1}{5} = \dfrac{1}{15}$

11. $P(\text{pink}) \times P(\text{pink}\,|\,\text{pink})$

$= \dfrac{4}{6} \times \dfrac{3}{5} = \dfrac{2}{5}$

12. $P = 6/36 = 1/6$

6 favorable outcomes:
11, 22, 33, 44, 55, 66

13. $P = 3/36 = 1/12$

3 favorable outcomes:
46, 55, 64

14. $P(\text{red}) \times P(\text{red}\,|\,\text{red})$

$= \dfrac{3}{6} \times \dfrac{2}{5} = \dfrac{1}{5}$

15. $P(\text{even}) \times P(\text{even}\,|\,\text{even})$

$= \dfrac{4}{9} \times \dfrac{3}{8} = \dfrac{1}{6}$

16. $P(\text{vowel}) \times$ $P(\text{vowel}\,|\,\text{vowel})$

$= \dfrac{2}{5} \times \dfrac{1}{4} = \dfrac{1}{10}$

17. $P(\text{grn}) \times P(\text{grn}\,|\,\text{grn}) \times$ $P(\text{grn}\,|\,\text{grn and grn})$

$= \dfrac{4}{10} \times \dfrac{3}{9} \times \dfrac{2}{8} = \dfrac{1}{30}$

18. $P = 3/36 = 1/12$

3 favorable outcomes:
11, 12, 21

19. $P = 15/36 = 5/12$

15 favorable outcomes:
12, 13, 14, 15, 16 /
23, 24, 25, 26 /
34, 35, 36 / 45, 46 / 56

20. $P = 4/24 = 1/6$

$6 \times 4 = 24$ possible outcomes
4 favorable outcomes: 11, 22, 33, 44

LESSON 151

1. $P(\text{odd}) \times P(\text{odd})$

$= \dfrac{3}{6} \times \dfrac{3}{6} = \dfrac{1}{4}$

2. $P = 2/36 = 1/18$

2 favorable outcomes:
12, 21

3. $P(\text{red}) + P(\text{spade})$

$= \dfrac{26}{52} + \dfrac{13}{52} = \dfrac{3}{4}$

4. $P(\text{heart}) + P(\text{diamond})$

$= \dfrac{13}{52} + \dfrac{13}{52} = \dfrac{1}{2}$

5. $P(\text{ace}) + P(\text{face})$

$= \dfrac{4}{52} + \dfrac{12}{52} = \dfrac{4}{13}$

6. $P(\text{face}) + P(\text{number} < 5)$

$= \dfrac{12}{52} + \dfrac{12}{52} = \dfrac{6}{13}$

7. $P(\text{heart}) + P(\text{face}) - P(\text{heart and face})$

$= \dfrac{13}{52} + \dfrac{12}{52} - \dfrac{3}{52} = \dfrac{11}{26}$

8. $P(\text{red}) + P(\text{number}) - P(\text{red and number})$

$= \dfrac{26}{52} + \dfrac{36}{52} - \dfrac{18}{52} = \dfrac{11}{13}$

9. $P(\text{face}) + P(\text{king}) - P(\text{face and king})$

$= \dfrac{12}{52} + \dfrac{4}{52} - \dfrac{4}{52} = \dfrac{3}{13}$

10. $P(\text{spade}) + P(\text{number} < 5) - P(\text{spade and number} < 5)$

$= \dfrac{13}{52} + \dfrac{12}{52} - \dfrac{3}{52} = \dfrac{11}{26}$

11. $P(\text{odd}) + P(\text{prime}) - P(\text{odd and prime})$

$= \dfrac{3}{6} + \dfrac{3}{6} - \dfrac{2}{6} = \dfrac{2}{3}$

12. $P(\text{odd}) + P(\text{2's multiple}) - P(\text{odd and 2's multiple})$

$= \dfrac{3}{6} + \dfrac{3}{6} - \dfrac{0}{6} = 1$

13. $P(\text{even}) + P(\text{less than 4}) - P(\text{even and less than 4})$

$= \dfrac{3}{6} + \dfrac{3}{6} - \dfrac{1}{6} = \dfrac{5}{6}$

14. $P(\text{even}) + P(\text{at least 4}) - P(\text{even and at least 4})$

$= \dfrac{3}{6} + \dfrac{3}{6} - \dfrac{2}{6} = \dfrac{2}{3}$

15. $P(\text{king}) + P(\text{queen}) - P(\text{king and queen})$

$$= \frac{4}{52} + \frac{4}{52} - \frac{0}{52} = \frac{2}{13}$$

16. $P(\text{ace}) + P(\text{club}) - P(\text{ace and club})$

$$= \frac{4}{52} + \frac{13}{52} - \frac{1}{52} = \frac{4}{13}$$

17. $P(\text{jack}) + P(\text{black}) - P(\text{jack and black})$

$$= \frac{4}{52} + \frac{26}{52} - \frac{2}{52} = \frac{7}{13}$$

18. $P(\text{red}) + P(\text{face}) - P(\text{red and face})$

$$= \frac{26}{52} + \frac{12}{52} - \frac{6}{52} = \frac{8}{13}$$

19. $P(\text{both even or both odd})$

$= P(\text{both even}) + P(\text{both odd})$

$$= \left(\frac{3}{6} \times \frac{3}{6}\right) + \left(\frac{3}{6} \times \frac{3}{6}\right) = \frac{1}{2}$$

20. $P(\text{sum is 5 or sum is 10})$

$= P(\text{sum is 5}) + P(\text{sum is 10})$

$= P(14, 23, 32, \text{ or } 41) + P(46, 55, \text{ or } 64)$

$$= \frac{4}{36} + \frac{3}{36} = \frac{7}{36}$$

LESSON 152

1. $3 \times 2 \times 1 = 6$ passwords

2. ABC, ACB, BAC, BCA, CAB, CBA

3. Order matters, so it is a permutation problem.

4. Order does not matter, so it is a combination problem.

5. $4 \times 3 \times 2 \times 1 = 24$ ways

6. $5 \times 4 \times 3 \times 2 \times 1 = 120$ ways

7. $6 \times 5 \times 4 = 120$ ways

8. $7 \times 6 = 42$ ways

9. $(9 \times 8 \times 7 \times 6)/(4 \times 3 \times 2 \times 1) = 126$ teams

10. $(10 \times 9 \times 8)/(3 \times 2 \times 1) = 120$ committees

11. Permutation, $5 \times 4 \times 3 \times 2 \times 1 = 120$ ways

12. Combination
$(15 \times 14 \times 13 \times 12)/(4 \times 3 \times 2 \times 1) = 1{,}365$ committees

13. Permutation, $6 \times 5 \times 4 \times 3 \times 2 \times 1 = 720$ ways

14. Permutation, $6 \times 5 \times 4 = 120$ ways

15. Combination, $(52 \times 51 \times 50)/(3 \times 2 \times 1) = 22{,}100$ ways

16. Permutation, $11 \times 10 \times 9 = 990$ ways

17. Permutation, $20 \times 19 \times 18 \times 17 = 116{,}280$ ways

18. Combination, $(25 \times 24 \times 23)/(3 \times 2 \times 1) = 2{,}300$ ways

LESSON 153

1. $5 \times 4 \times 3 = 60$ ways   2. $60/6 = 10$ teams

3. $\dfrac{8 \times 7 \times 6 \times 5!}{5!} = 8 \times 7 \times 6 = 336$

4. $\dfrac{7 \times 6 \times 5 \times 4!}{3! \, 4!} = \dfrac{7 \times 6 \times 5}{3!} = \dfrac{7 \times 6 \times 5}{3 \times 2} = 7 \times 5 = 35$

5. $P(5, 5) = \dfrac{5!}{(5-5)!} = \dfrac{5!}{1} = 5 \times 4 \times 3 \times 2 \times 1 = 120$

6. $P(8, 2) = \dfrac{8!}{(8-2)!} = \dfrac{8!}{6!} = \dfrac{8 \times 7 \times 6!}{6!} = 8 \times 7 = 56$

7. $C(8, 2) = \dfrac{8!}{(8-2)! \, 2!} = \dfrac{8!}{6! \, 2!} = 28$

8. $C(10, 4) = \dfrac{10!}{(10-4)! \, 4!} = \dfrac{10!}{6! \, 4!} = 210$

9. $P(4, 2) = \dfrac{4!}{(4-2)!} = \dfrac{4!}{2!} = \dfrac{4 \times 3 \times 2!}{2!} = 4 \times 3 = 12$

10. $P(9, 3) = \dfrac{9!}{(9-3)!} = \dfrac{9!}{6!} = \dfrac{9 \times 8 \times 7 \times 6!}{6!} = 504$

11. $C(8, 3) = \dfrac{8!}{(8-3)! \, 3!} = \dfrac{8!}{5! \, 3!} = 56$

12. $C(10, 7) = \dfrac{10!}{(10-7)! \, 7!} = \dfrac{10!}{3! \, 7!} = 120$

13. $C(22, 5) = 26{,}334$ ways   14. $P(8, 8) = 40{,}320$ ways

15. $C(15, 5) = 3{,}003$ teams   16. $P(9, 4) = 3{,}024$ words

17. $C(12, 6) = 924$ ways   18. $P(18, 3) = 4{,}896$ ways

19. $P(30, 3) = 24{,}360$ ways   20. $C(40, 2) = 780$ ways

LESSON 154

1. $P(\text{odd}) \times P(\text{odd}|\text{odd})$

$$= \frac{3}{5} \times \frac{2}{4} = \frac{3}{10}$$

2. $P(\text{pink}) \times P(\text{pink}|\text{pink})$

$$= \frac{4}{6} \times \frac{3}{5} = \frac{2}{5}$$

3a. Total possible outcomes $= P(6, 6)$

Favorable outcomes = permutations of 5 remaining people after seating Emma in the first seat $= P(5, 5)$

Probability $= \dfrac{P(5, 5)}{P(6, 6)} = \dfrac{5!}{6!} = \dfrac{1}{6}$

3b. Favorable outcomes = permutations of 4 remaining people after seating Emma first and Brian last $= P(4, 4)$

Probability $= \dfrac{P(4, 4)}{P(6, 6)} = \dfrac{4!}{6!} = \dfrac{1}{30}$

3c. Favorable outcomes = Emma first and Brian last + Brian first and Emma last $= P(4, 4) + P(4, 4) = 2 \times P(4, 4)$

Probability $= \dfrac{2 \cdot P(4, 4)}{P(6, 6)} = \dfrac{2 \cdot 4!}{6!} = \dfrac{1}{15}$

4a. Total possible outcomes = $C(7, 2)$

Favorable outcomes = combinations of choosing 2 balls from 3 white balls = $C(3, 2)$

Probability $= \dfrac{C(3,2)}{C(7,2)} = \dfrac{3}{21} = \dfrac{1}{7}$

4b. Favorable outcomes = combinations of choosing 2 balls from 4 black balls = $C(4, 2)$

Probability $= \dfrac{C(4,2)}{C(7,2)} = \dfrac{6}{21} = \dfrac{2}{7}$

4c. Favorable outcomes = 3 ways to choose a white ball × 4 ways to choose a black ball = 3×4

Probability $= \dfrac{3 \times 4}{C(7,2)} = \dfrac{12}{21} = \dfrac{4}{7}$

5a. Total possible outcomes = $P(8, 8)$

Favorable outcomes = permutations of 7 remaining people after seating Emma in the first seat = $P(7, 7)$

Probability $= \dfrac{P(7,7)}{P(8,8)} = \dfrac{7!}{8!} = \dfrac{1}{8}$

5b. Favorable outcomes = permutations of 6 remaining people after seating Emma first and Brian last = $P(6, 6)$

Probability $= \dfrac{P(6,6)}{P(8,8)} = \dfrac{6!}{8!} = \dfrac{1}{56}$

5c. Favorable outcomes = Emma first and Brian last + Brian first and Emma last = $P(6, 6) + P(6, 6) = 2 \times P(6, 6)$

Probability $= \dfrac{2 \cdot P(6,6)}{P(8,8)} = \dfrac{2 \cdot 6!}{8!} = \dfrac{1}{28}$

6a. Total possible outcomes = $P(5, 5)$

Favorable outcomes = 1

Probability $= \dfrac{1}{P(5,5)} = \dfrac{1}{5!} = \dfrac{1}{120}$

6b. Favorable outcomes = permutations of 4 remaining letters after placing A or E first = $2 \times P(4, 4)$

Probability $= \dfrac{2 \cdot P(4,4)}{P(5,5)} = \dfrac{2 \cdot 4!}{5!} = \dfrac{2}{5}$

6c. Favorable outcomes = A first and E last + E first and A last = $2 \times P(3, 3)$

Probability $= \dfrac{2 \cdot P(3,3)}{P(5,5)} = \dfrac{2 \cdot 3!}{5!} = \dfrac{1}{10}$

7a. Total possible outcomes = $P(9, 3)$

Favorable outcomes = permutations of choosing 3 boys out of 5 = $P(5, 3)$

Probability $= \dfrac{P(5,3)}{P(9,3)} = \dfrac{60}{504} = \dfrac{5}{42}$

7b. Favorable outcomes = permutations of choosing 3 girls out of 4 = $P(4, 3)$

Probability $= \dfrac{P(4,3)}{P(9,3)} = \dfrac{24}{504} = \dfrac{1}{21}$

7c. Favorable outcomes = ways of choosing 1 girl out of 4 × permutations of choosing 2 boys out of 5 = $4 \times P(5, 2)$

Probability $= \dfrac{4 \cdot P(5,2)}{P(9,3)} = \dfrac{4 \cdot 20}{504} = \dfrac{10}{63}$

8a. Total possible outcomes = $C(12, 3)$

Favorable outcomes = combinations of choosing 3 balls from 3 red balls = $C(3, 3)$

Probability $= \dfrac{C(3,3)}{C(12,3)} = \dfrac{1}{220}$

8b. Favorable outcomes = combinations of choosing 3 balls from 5 pink balls = $C(5, 3)$

Probability $= \dfrac{C(5,3)}{C(12,3)} = \dfrac{10}{220} = \dfrac{1}{22}$

8c. Favorable outcomes = combinations of choosing 3 balls from 3 red and 5 pink balls = $C(8, 3)$

Probability $= \dfrac{C(8,3)}{C(12,3)} = \dfrac{56}{220} = \dfrac{14}{55}$

8d. Favorable outcomes = 3 ways to choose a red ball × 5 ways to choose a pink ball × 4 ways to choose a yellow ball $= 3 \times 5 \times 4$

Probability $= \dfrac{3 \cdot 5 \cdot 4}{C(12,3)} = \dfrac{60}{220} = \dfrac{3}{11}$

9a. Total possible outcomes = $C(52, 2)$

Favorable outcomes = combinations of choosing 2 cards from 13 clubs = $C(13, 2)$

Probability $= \dfrac{C(13,2)}{C(52,2)} = \dfrac{78}{1326} = \dfrac{1}{17}$

9b. Favorable outcomes = combinations of choosing 2 cards from 39 non-clubs = $C(39, 2)$

Probability $= \dfrac{C(39,2)}{C(52,2)} = \dfrac{741}{1326} = \dfrac{19}{34}$

LESSON 155

1. $P = 3/6 = 1/2$

2. $P = 5/20 = 1/4$

3. H1, H2, H3, H4, H5, H6, T1, T2, T3, T4, T5, T6

4. HHH, HHT, HTH, HTT, THH, THT, TTH, TTT

5. 25

6. 20

7. 10

8. 8

9. 4/25

10. 9/64

11. 1/10

12. 3/28

13. 1/12

14. 5/12

15. 5/6

16. 11/26

17. 24 ways

18. 12 ways

19. 10 teams

20. 1/30

21. 3/28

LESSON 158

1. $x = 3$
2. $x = -2$
3. $x = 7/2$
4. $x = 2/3$
5. $x = 2, x = 8$
6. $x = 5/3, x = 3$
7. $x = 0, x = 4/3$
8. $x = 5, x = 9$
9. $x > 7$
10. $x \leq 12/7$
11. $x \leq 9/4$
12. $x > 3$
13. $5 < x \leq 6$
14. $x \geq 5$
15. $-1 < x < 5$
16. $-1 \leq x \leq 1$
17. 7, 9, 11
18. $22
19. 6.5 cm
20. 5 dimes, 4 quarters
21. 2.5 hours
22. 3 hours
23. 1 liter
24. 4 gallons
25. $6.80 per pound

LESSON 159

1.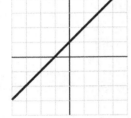
2.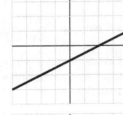
3.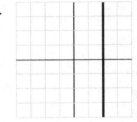
4.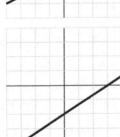
5.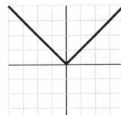
6.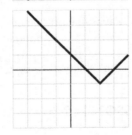

7. Perpendicular
8. Neither
9. Perpendicular
10. Parallel
11.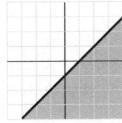
12.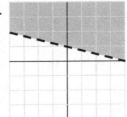

13. $y = -2x + 6$
    $2x + y = 6$
14. $y = \frac{3}{4}x + 2$
    $3x - 4y = -8$
15. $y = -4x + 3$
    $4x + y = 3$
16. $y = 5x - 9$
    $5x - y = 9$
17. $y = 38x + 55$
18. $y = -12x + 350$
19. $5x + 10y = 60$
20. $2x + 5y = 100$
21. $8x + 5y = 1800$

LESSON 160

1. Solution: (1, 1)
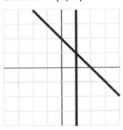
2. Solution: (−3, 2)
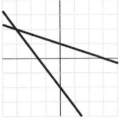

3. (0, 3)
4. (−3, 2)
5. Infinite
6. (3, 3)
7. None
8. (5, 5)

9.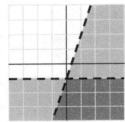
10.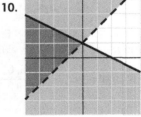

11. 58
12. 5 adults, 5 children
13. 9 4-seat tables
    5 8-seat tables
14. First bus: 2 hours
    Second bus: 3 hours
15. Plane: 330 mph
    Wind: 10 mph
16. Train 1: 150 mph
    Train 2: 130 mph
17. Solution A: 6 milliliters
    Solution B: 3 milliliters
18. Coffee A: 2 pounds
    Coffee B: 6 pounds

LESSON 161

1. D: {−1, 1, 2, 4}
    R: {−1, 0, 1, 2}
    Not a function
2. D: $x > -1$
    R: $0 \leq y < 2$
    Function
3. D: $x \geq 1$
    R: $y \leq 3$
    Not a function
4. D: $0 \leq x \leq 4$
    R: $-1 \leq y \leq 3$
    Function
5. $f(-3) = 5$
    $f(0) = 2$
    $f(3) = 1$
6. $g(-3) = 0$
    $g(0) = -9$
    $g(3) = 0$

7. Linear; $y = -x + 5$ **8.** Quadratic

9. Exponential   **10.** Linear; $y = 2x + 3$

11. 3/2   **12.** 1/2

13. $-2/3$ **14.** $-3/4$

15. $f^{-1}(x) = x - 2$ **16.** $g^{-1}(x) = -\dfrac{1}{2}x + \dfrac{3}{2}$

17. $y = -2x$
    $y = -6$

18. $xy = 12$
    $y = 4$

19. 2,720 meters   **20.** 20 minutes

21. Arithmetic sequence
   $a_n = 5n - 1$
   $a_1 = 4, a_n = a_{n-1} + 5$

22. Geometric sequence
   $a_n = 3(2)^{n-1}$
   $a_1 = 3, a_n = 2a_{n-1}$

23. Geometric sequence
   $a_n = 128(0.5)^{n-1}$
   $a_1 = 128, a_n = 0.5a_{n-1}$

24. Arithmetic sequence
   $a_n = -3n + 14$
   $a_1 = 11, a_n = a_{n-1} - 3$

25. $5,700   **26.** $52,000

27. 8 feet   **28.** $8,192

LESSON 162

1. 5   **2.** 0.2   **3.** -3 **4.** 10

5. $2\sqrt{7}$ **6.** $3\sqrt[3]{2}$ **7.** $x\sqrt{x}$ **8.** $4xy^2$

9. $\dfrac{3\sqrt{2}}{7}$ **10.** $\dfrac{2\sqrt[3]{6}}{5}$ **11.** $\dfrac{x\sqrt{x}}{y^2}$ **12.** $\dfrac{x\sqrt[3]{x}}{yz}$

13. $7\sqrt{2}$ **14.** $4y\sqrt{6x}$ **15.** 4   **16.** $x\sqrt{3}$

17. $2\sqrt{2}$ **18.** $\dfrac{\sqrt{5}}{2}$

19. $x = 4$ **20.** No solution

21. $x = 3$ **22.** $x = 5$

23. $x = -2$ **24.** $x = 2/3$

25. Side length = 6 cm
   Diagonal = 6√2 cm

26. 2√14 inches

27. 9 + 12 + 15 = 36 cm   **28.** 7√3 feet

29. AD = 2 and DC = 1, so AC = √5.
AB:AC = 2:1, so AB = 2√5.
AB = 2√5 and AC = √5, so BC = 5.
The perimeter is 2√5 + √5 + 5 = 5 + 3√5 cm.

30. AB = 5 and BC = 8, so AC = √89.
AC = √89 and CG = BF = 6, so AG = 5√5.
The diagonal of the rectangular prism is 5√5 inches.

LESSON 163

1. 1/2   **2.** 32   **3.** $12x$ **4.** $3y^6/x^2$

5. $25x^6$ **6.** $8/y^9$ **7.** $24x^4$ **8.** $5x^7$

9. 2   **10.** $8y^6/x^6$ **11.** $-8x$ **12.** $3x^3y^2$

13. 4.8×10^{10} **14.** 3×10^4

15. 2.5×10^4 **16.** 3×10^{-6}

17. 2   **18.** 1/2   **19.** 16   **20.** 1/9

21. 7   **22.** $x^{5/6}$ **23.** 2   **24.** $4x^{2/3}$

25. $y = 3000(1.04)^x$ About $ 4,105.71

26. $y = 20(2)^x$ 2,560 bacteria

27. $y = 23000(0.9)^x$ About $8,019.60

28. $y = 40000(0.95)^x$ About 30,951

29. $y = 500(1.15)^x$ About 2,023 bears

LESSON 164

1. $3x + 1$ **2.** $-x^2 + 2x + 8$

3. $-4x^4 + 8x^3 - 4x^2$ **4.** $x^2 + x - 20$

5. $x^2 - 6x + 9$ **6.** $x^2 - 1$

7. $5x^2 + 19x - 4$ **8.** $2x^3 - 5x^2 - 13x + 4$

9. $3x^3$ **10.** $4x^2 - 2$

11. $x + 2$ **12.** $x + 5 + \dfrac{10}{x - 5}$

13. $x(x + 7)$ **14.** $5x^2y(x + y)$

15. $(x - 2)(x^2 + 1)$ **16.** $(2x - 3)(x^2 + 2)$

17. $(x + 2)(x - 3)$ **18.** $(x - 2)^2$

19. $(x + 2)(x + 7)$ **20.** $(x + 1)(2x + 5)$

21. $(3x + 7)(3x - 7)$ **22.** $(3x - 4)(2x + 3)$

23. $x(3x - 1)^2$ **24.** $2(x + 4)(x + 1)(x - 1)$

25. $x^2 + 5x + 6$ **26.** $4x^2 + 12x + 9$

27. $16x^2 - 25$ **28.** $27x^3 + 1$

29. $x + 6$ **30.** $x + 7 + \dfrac{12}{2x - 3}$

31. $(x - 3)(x - 4)$ **32.** $(3x - 1)(x + 2)$

33. $3(x + 1)(2x - 3)$ **34.** $4(x - 1)(2x + 5)$

35. $2x(x + 4)(x - 4)$ **36.** $(x - 3)(x + 2)(x - 2)$

LESSON 165

1. $x = 8, x = 6$
2. $x = 1, x = -2$
3. $x = -2, x = -4$
4. $x = 5, x = -1/2$
5. $x = -1 \pm \sqrt{5}$
6. $x = 2 \pm 2\sqrt{3}$
7. $x = (-1 \pm \sqrt{13})/2$
8. $x = 1/3, x = -3$
9. $x = 2, x = -1$
10. $x = -3, x = 7$
11. $x = -4 \pm 2\sqrt{7}$
12. $x = 6, x = 1$
13. $x = -1$
14. No solution
15. $x = 3/2, x = 1/2$
16. $x = 0, x = 2, x = -3$
17. 8 and 12
18. 5 and 8
19. Legs = 6 ft
    Area = 18 ft^2
20. Legs = 4 in
    Hypotenuse = 4√2 in
    Perimeter = 8 + 4√2 in
21. 8 cm, 15 cm, 17 cm
22. Width = 4 in
    Length = 15 in
    Perimeter = 38 in
23. $x = 2 \pm \sqrt{10}$
24. $x = 4, x = -4$
25. $x = (7 \pm \sqrt{21})/2$
26. $x = 3 \pm \sqrt{11}$
27. $x = 5, x = -3$
28. $x = 0, x = -3/2$
29. $x = (-1 \pm \sqrt{17})/4$
30. No solution

LESSON 166

1.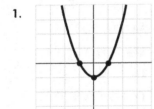
2.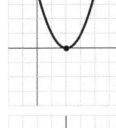
3.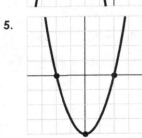
4.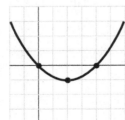
5.
6.

7.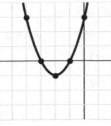
8.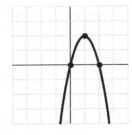
9.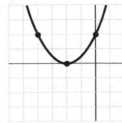

10. Vertex: (1, 3)
    y-intercept: 4
    x-intercept(s): none
11. Vertex: (1, –8)
    y-intercept: –6
    x-intercept(s): –1, 3
12. Vertex: (2, 0)
    y-intercept: 4
    x-intercept(s): 2
13. Vertex: (3, 4)
    y-intercept: –5
    x-intercept(s): 1, 5
14. $y = x^2 - 6x + 10$
15. $y = 2x^2 - 8x + 6$
16. $y = (x + 2)^2 + 3$
17. $y = 2(x - 1)^2$
18. $y = -x^2 + 6$
19. $y = -3x^2$
20. a. After 1 second
    b. 64 feet
    c. After 3 seconds
    d. After 2 seconds
21. a. After 2 seconds
    b. 64 feet
    c. 4 seconds
    d. After 1 second and
       after 3 seconds
22. a. After 3 seconds
    b. After 2 seconds

LESSON 167

1. $\dfrac{x^2}{5}; x \neq 0$
2. $\dfrac{1}{x - 2}; x \neq 0, 2$
3. $\dfrac{1}{x + 4}; x \neq -4, 5$
4. $-\dfrac{3}{x}; x \neq 0, 1, -8$
5. $3(x + 2); x \neq 0, -2$
6. $4x - 5; x \neq -5, -2$
7. $x + 1; x \neq -2, -1, 2$
8. $\dfrac{x - 8}{x}; x \neq 0, -\dfrac{5}{2}, -2$
9. $x + 1; x \neq -1$
10. $\dfrac{x}{x^2 + 9}; x \neq -3, 3$
11. $\dfrac{6}{x(x + 6)}; x \neq 0, -6$
12. $\dfrac{2x}{x - 4}; x \neq 4, -2$
13. $x = 7$
14. $x = 2, x = -2$

15. $x = 7/10$

16. $x = 1$

17. $x = 0, x = 14$

18. $x = 6$

19. 2 hours

20. 12 minutes

21. 3 hours

22. 75 minutes

23. Brian: 6 hours
Dan: 12 hours

LESSON 168

1. Mean = 5.2   Median = 4   Mode(s) = 4

2. Mean = 7   Median = 7.5   Mode(s) = 8

3. Mean = 6   Range = 7   S. deviation = 2.3

4. Mean = 7   Range = 4   S. deviation = 1.2

5. 3, 4, 5.5, 8, 10; IQR = 4

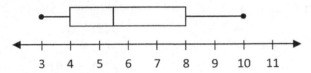

6. 5, 6, 7, 8, 9; IQR = 2

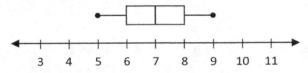

7. The distribution is skewed right, so the median and interquartile range are better.

8. The distribution is symmetric, so the mean and standard deviation are better.

The first distribution appears to have the greater standard deviation because it is spread out more.

9. Median = 42
Range = 46

10. 20 customers

11. 6/20 = 30%

12. 5/20 = 25%

13. 20 members

14. 6 members

15. 8/20 = 40%

16. Positive correlation
About $y = x + 1$

17. Positive correlation
About $y = 2x - 4$

18. Negative correlation
About $y = -x + 6$

19.

	Burger	Wrap	Total
Soda	51	45	96
Water	21	33	54
Total	72	78	150

20.

	Burger	Wrap	Total
Soda	0.34	0.3	0.64
Water	0.14	0.22	0.36
Total	0.48	0.52	1.0

21.

	Burger	Wrap	Total
Soda	0.53	0.47	1.0
Water	0.39	0.61	1.0
Total	0.48	0.52	1.0

22.

	Burger	Wrap	Total
Soda	0.71	0.58	0.64
Water	0.29	0.42	0.36
Total	1.0	1.0	1.0

LESSON 169

1. 1/4   **2.** 1/4   **3.** 125   **4.** 60

5. 75   **6.** 36   **7.** 1/6   **8.** 1/32

9. 4/25   **10.** 4/9   **11.** 2/15   **12.** 5/12

13. 1/6   **14.** 5/36   **15.** 2/3   **16.** 10/13

17. 120   **18.** 60   **19.** 10   **20.** 2/5

21. 2/33

LESSON 170

1. $x = -3/4$ **2.** $x = 11$

3. $x = 1$ **4.** $x = 13$

5. $x = 7/3$ **6.** Infinitely many solutions

7. No solution   **8.** $x = -7$

9. $x = -9$ **10.** $x = -50$

11. $x = 2/5$ **12.** $x = -1$

13. $x = -4, x = 4$ **14.** $x = -9, x = 5$

15. $x = -1/3, x = 3$ **16.** $x = -1, x = 2$

17. 4 hours   **18.** 2 liters

LESSON 171

1. $x < -5$ **2.** $x < 4$

3. $x \leq -1/2$ **4.** $x \leq -3$

5. $x < -1$ **6.** $x \geq 5/3$

7. $x < 3/5$ **8.** $x > -7$

9. $x \geq 6$ **10.** $x \geq -2$

11. $x > 2$ **12.** $x \leq 2$

13. $x < -1$ **14.** $x \geq 3$

15. $3 < x \leq 9$ **16.** $x < 3$

17. $\dfrac{1}{4} < x < \dfrac{5}{4}$ **18.** $x \leq \dfrac{3}{2}$ or $x \geq \dfrac{7}{2}$

LESSON 172

1. $(-1, -5)$ **2.** $(2, 1)$ **3.** None   **4.** $(-4, 0)$

5. $(7, -3)$ **6.** Infinite   **7.** $(4, 7)$ **8.** $(-4, 2)$

9. Infinite   **10.** $(-2, 6)$ **11.** $(4, 4)$ **12.** None

13. $(3, -5)$ **14.** $(2, -3)$

15. 5 dimes, 6 nickels

16. 15 8-seat tables
5 12-seat tables

LESSON 173

1. $x = 1$ **2.** $x = 4$

3. $x = 9$ **4.** No solution

5. $x = 51$ **6.** $x = 21$

7. $x = 13$ **8.** $x = 3$

9. No solution   **10.** $x = -2$

11. $x = 4$ **12.** $x = 2$

13. $x = 3$ **14.** $x = 1$

15. $x = -8$ **16.** $x = 27$

17. $x = 6$ **18.** $x = 2$

19. 15 ft   **20.** $2\sqrt{13}$

LESSON 174

1. $x = 3 \pm 2\sqrt{5}$ **2.** $x = -2, x = -5$

3. $x = -3, x = -5$ **4.** $x = -2/3, x = 4$

5. $x = -1 \pm \sqrt{2}$ **6.** $x = 3 \pm 2\sqrt{3}$

7. $x = \left(1 \pm \sqrt{5}\right)/2$ **8.** $x = 1, x = 2/5$

9. $x = 4 \pm 2\sqrt{3}$ **10.** $x = -2 \pm \sqrt{7}$

11. $x = 4, x = 2$ **12.** $x = \left(7 \pm \sqrt{13}\right)/2$

13. $x = \left(5 \pm \sqrt{13}\right)/2$ **14.** $x = 5$

15. No solution   **16.** $x = 0, x = -4, x = 4$

17. 3 and 13   **18.** 5 cm and 14 cm

LESSON 175

1. $x = 1$ **2.** $x = 6, x = -6$

3. No solution   **4.** $x = 15$

5. $x = 1$ **6.** $x = 0$

7. No solution   **8.** $x = -1$

9. No solution   **10.** $x = 2 \pm 2\sqrt{3}$

11. $x = 5/2$ **12.** $x = 4, x = -3$

13. 2 hours   **14.** 3 1/3 hours

15. Pipe A: 5 hours
Pipe B: 20 hours

LESSON 180

1. Lesson 4
$5x - 3 = 7$
$5x = 10$
$x = 2$

2. Lessons 50 and 71
$f(3) = 8$
$f(0) = 1$
$f(3) - f(0) = 7$

3. Lesson 15
$m = \dfrac{1-4}{-3-2} = \dfrac{3}{5}$

4. Lesson 65
$\sqrt{36x^2} = 6x$

5. Lessons 80 and 81
$x^2 - 9 + x^2 - 6x + 9$
$= 2x^2 - 6x$

6. Lesson 19
The answer is **D**.

7. Lesson 6
$4x + 1 = -9$ or
$4x + 1 = 9$
$4x = -10$ or $4x = 8$
$x = -\dfrac{5}{2}$ or $x = 2$
$\left(-\dfrac{5}{2}\right) \times 2 = -5$

8. Lesson 23
Given $m = -1/3$
Perpendicular $m = 3$
$y = mx + b; (1, 5)$
$5 = 3(1) + b$
$b = 2$
$y = 3x + 2$

9. Lessons 19 and 33

A system has no solution when the lines are parallel. Parallel lines have the same slope.

First line $m = k/3$ $\rightarrow$ $k/3 = -5$
Second line $m = -5$ $k = -15$

So, $k = -15$ makes the system have no solution.

10. Lesson 74

$x^{-5}y^{-4} \cdot 2^3 x^6 y^3 = 8xy^{-1} = \dfrac{8x}{y}$

11. Lesson 121

The vertex is at (1, 2):

$y = a(x - 1)^2 + 2$

Use (0, 1) to find a:

$1 = a(0 - 1)^2 + 2$

$1 = a + 2$

$a = -1$

Equation:

$y = -(x - 1)^2 + 2$

12. Lesson 40

$-11 \le 5 - 2x \le 11$

$-16 \le -2x \le 6$

$-3 \le x \le 8$

13. Lessons 50 and 111

$a^2 - 8 = 1$

$a^2 = 9$

$a = 3, a = -3$

14. Lesson 101

$4x^2(x + 2) - (x + 2)$

$= (x + 2)(4x^2 - 1)$

$= (x + 2)(2x + 1)(2x - 1)$

15. Lesson 111

$x^2 - 2x = 2$

$x^2 - 2x + 1 = 2 + 1$

$(x - 1)^2 = 3$

$x - 1 = \pm\sqrt{3}$

$x = 1 \pm \sqrt{3}$

The sum is 2.

16. Lesson 76

$3 + 4 + 3 = 10$

17. Lesson 22

Slope = −1

y-intercept = −2

$y = -x - 2$

18. Lesson 32

eq1 × 2 + eq2

$5x = 15$

$x = 3$

$2(3) + y = 5$

$y = -1$

Solution: (3, −1)

19. Lesson 68

$4\sqrt{x + 1} = 8$

$\sqrt{x + 1} = 2$

Square both sides.

$x + 1 = 4$

$x = 3$

20. Lessons 95, 99, and 125

$\dfrac{(x - 1)^2}{(x - 1)(x + 3)}$

$= \dfrac{x - 1}{x + 3}$

21. Lessons 118 and 119

Intercept form:

$y = (x - 2)(x + 5)$

x-intercepts: 2, −5

Distance = 2 − (−5) = 7

22. Lesson 20

The answer is **A**.

23. Lesson 128

Excluded: $x \ne -2, 3$; LCD $= 2(x + 2)(x - 3)$

Multiply both sides by the LCD, then solve for x.

$2(x - 3) + 4(x + 2) = (x + 2)(x - 3)$

$x^2 - 7x - 8 = 0$

$(x + 1)(x - 8) = 0$

$x = -1, x = 8$

24. Lesson 56

Use $y = kx$.

$10 = 8k$, so $k = 5/4$.

$y = (5/4)12 = 15$

15 feet

25. Lesson 9

x = number of nickels

$x + 3$ = number of dimes

$0.1(x + 3) + 0.05x = 1.05$

Solve for x, and $x = 5$.

5 nickels and 8 dimes

26. Lesson 130

x = Eli's time alone

$\dfrac{1}{10} + \dfrac{1}{x} = \dfrac{1}{6}$

$3x + 30 = 5x$

$x = 15$

15 hours

29. Lesson 10

t = time to meet

$60t + 65t = 250$

Solve for t, and $t = 2$.

2 hours

31. Lesson 51

The answer is **C**.

C is exponential.

33. Lesson 11

x = liters of 25% solution

$0.25x + 0.4(4) = 0.3(x + 4)$

Solve for x, and $x = 8$.

8 liters of 25% solution

35. Lesson 58

Arithmetic sequence

$a_1 = 5, d = 7$

$a_n = 7n - 2$

$a_{15} = 7(15) - 2 = 103$

37. Lessons 69 and 113

$8^2 + x^2 = 17^2; x = 15$

The other leg is 15 cm.

Perimeter = 8 + 15 + 17

= 40 cm

39. Lesson 144

64/77 = 0.83116...

About 83% of the teens

40. Lesson 154

Total possible outcomes = $P(6, 6)$

Favorable outcomes = permutations of 5 remaining books after math is placed in the first position = $P(5, 5)$

Probability $= \dfrac{P(5, 5)}{P(6, 6)} = \dfrac{5!}{6!} = \dfrac{1}{6}$

27. Lessons 22 and 41

$y > 2x + 1$

28. Lesson 26

Rate of change = −9 − 11

Initial value = 300

$y = -20x + 300$

30. Lesson 34

x = # of 4-seat tables

y = # of 6-seat tables

$x + y = 20, 4x + 6y = 90$

$x = 15, y = 5$

15 4-seat tables

5 6-seat tables

32. Lesson 113

x = width

$10 - x$ = height

$x(10 - x) = 24$

$x = 4, x = 6$

4 inches by 6 inches

34. Lesson 149

3 independent events

$P = 1/2 \times 1/2 \times 1/2$

The probability is 1/8.

36. Lesson 123

$h(t) = -16(t + 1)(t - 4)$

$h = 0$ at $t = -1$ and $t = 4$

4 seconds

38. Lesson 78

Exponential growth

$y = 10(2)^x$

3 hours = 9 x 20 minutes

When $x = 9$, $y = 5120$.

5,120 bacteria

Made in the USA
Coppell, TX
06 November 2023

23878513R00057